FACE TO FACE

BIBLICAL REFLECTIONS ON
THE FOUNTAIN OF TEARS

Geoff Barnard

Abbreviations:

NIV = New International Version
KJV = King James Version
NKJV = New King James Version
RSV = Revised Standard Version
NRSV = New Revised Standard Version
YLT = Young's Literal Translation
NASV = New American Standard Version

ISBN 978-965-7542-46-0

This book can be ordered by contacting:

Author's e-mail: gjrb2@aol.com

or   ♪

Website: www.lulu.com

A Tsur Tsina Publication

*Now we see but a poor reflection as in a mirror,
then we shall see face to face.*

*Now I know in part; then I shall know fully,
even as I am fully known.*

1 Corinthians 13:12

The Hall of Remembrance

Yad Vashem, Jerusalem

This Book is Dedicated to the Unknown

CONTENTS

A Personal Note from the Author

PREPARING THE WAY

My Father, Philip Barnard, was born into an English Jewish family in 1891. By the time I was born in 1947 and, particularly after his mother had died when I was two years old, he had ceased attending synagogue, even on the high holy days in the Jewish calendar, *Rosh Hashanah* and *Yom Kippur*. My mother was not Jewish so I did not receive any Jewish education and never went to synagogue. I did not attend church either, apart from the assemblies at my Grammar School during the early 1960s.

Geoff and Philip on a boating lake around 1954

Geoff and Philip around 1962

Many of my friends at school, however, were active Christians and when Billy Graham came to town in 1966, they encouraged me to go with them. During that month long crusade in June, I went five times.

On June 29th, I went for the final time and it was then that I felt God speaking to me personally. I decided to "get up out of my seat" and make a public commitment of my belief in God. I started going to Church and before long, my commitment to God had become a commitment to Jesus.

I was baptized on the 26th February 1967. My Dad who was now nearly 76 years old would not come to my baptism although he did come several times to my church. He always wore his old trilby hat inside the church. He never forgot that he was, after all, a Jew by birth. My father died in 1973 when I was 25.

My specialty at school was science and I did reasonably well in my A levels although not nearly well enough to go to Cambridge and become a vet, which had been my ambition. I had to let go of my dream. In fact, in 1967, I decided not to go to University at all but to take a job as a Junior Technician at the Institute for Child Health in the centre of London. It was not my first choice. Who wants to commute into the centre of London every day?

However, little did I realise at the time that this job was the beginning of the road that was eventually to lead to Israel. The head of the department, Professor Otto Wolff and many of his staff were Jewish and several research scientists were Israelis. I had only been there for two months when the six-day war broke out in June 1967. During this period, the tea breaks were amazing when English and Israeli Jews were discussing the significance of what was taking place.

I began to take a serious interest in the nation of Israel and decided that one day I would like to visit. I had to wait for another 11 years. By this time I was working for the Medical School of King's College Hospital in South London.

Professor Otto Wolff   **Professor Bill Collins**

Although I had no intention of becoming a researcher, my dear Professor, Bill Collins, obviously saw that capability in me. I owe such a lot to this man. I had already obtained a degree through part-time study and now I was registered for a PhD in biochemistry.

Bill and Geoff with the Queen Mother [1]

Bill had already established a relationship with a department at the Weizmann Institute of Science in Rehovot, Israel as he had spent three months there in 1973 with his family on sabbatical leave. I well remember the day we were on the train together and he said to me *"Geoff would you like to go to Israel?"*

Obviously, I wanted to, and Bill was giving me the opportunity to continue the relationship that he had already established. My bags were packed and, in March 1978, I spent three weeks in Israel working with Dr. Fortune Kohen in the Department of Hormone Research. I thought it would be my only trip. I was wrong.

Dr. Fortune Kohen   The Weizmann Institute of Science

---

1 This event took place in 1979 when the Queen Mother came to open the new Rayne Institute. From left to right: Pat Collins (Bill's wife), Bill, Unknown (in the doorway), the Queen Mother and Geoff.

During that visit, I tried to see as much of the country as I could as well as doing justice to my work. On the final weekend of my trip, I decided to go to Haifa. A friend from my church had recommended that I go and spend Friday night and Saturday at a Christian hostel in that northern city. I found my way to HaGeffen Street in time for the beginning of the Sabbath.

In 1978, there were not so many congregations in Israel. Many believers would travel in from the north of the country to come to the hostel for worship and teaching. I was a 30 year old fairly conservative academic scientist. Little did I realise that this visit to Haifa was going to change the course of my life for I was to meet a 23-year old Canadian kibbutznik, Rick Wienecke.

Rick 1st April 1978

All through Saturday 1st April 1978, I sat and listened to Rick's story. He told me that he had come from Vancouver, Canada in search of God. This was after he had read the novel *Exodus* written by Leon Uris which convinced that if God existed, he must have something to do with the Jewish people. For the first time, he came to understand that it was out of the ashes of the Holocaust that the nation of Israel was re-established in 1948. Eventually, he decided to come and see Israel for himself and, shortly after his arrival in 1977, he gave his life to Jesus. I sat listening to him with rapt attention. I was so inspired by his story.

When the buses began running again late on Saturday afternoon, I remember walking away from the hostel overcome with emotion. I determined that if ever I had a second chance to come to Israel, I would take the first opportunity to go again to Haifa and meet up with Rick.

There was no way I could keep in touch with him, but my second opportunity duly came in January 1979. This time it was a two-week stint at the Weizmann Institute. I couldn't wait for the weekend. On Friday 13th January 1979, I took the bus to Haifa, got settled into the hostel and waited … and waited ... and waited. Rick didn't show up! I was devastated. I asked around *"Does anyone know Rick Wienecke?"* Of course, nearly everyone did. *"So why isn't he here?"*

Rick had moved back to the kibbutz Ramat Hakovesh, where he would spend the next seven years. He had started attending another congregation that met in Herzliya. *"How can I get there?"* I asked.

I made a new friend in Tommy and he told me that he could take me to the congregation house when the buses started again. I could not wait. Together, we went down south and we walked to the congregation house. The door opened and I saw Rick on the other side of the room. I rushed over to him and threw my arms around him. I cried out *"Oh Rick, I found you; I have so wanted to see you again".*

Rick turned to his friends and said quietly, *"Who is this guy?"* That meeting in 1978 had made a lasting impression on me. Rick could not remember it at all!

Rick and Tommy 14th January 1979

Anyway, we became the closest of friends and every time I had the chance to work at the Weizmann, we would meet. I got to know Dafna who became his wife; I also had the privilege of watching those wonderful gifts of sculpting emerge.

In 2001, Rick was staying with us when we were living in Dorset in the south of England. Rick was attending a conference in Southampton called *"Payback".* It was during this time that the Lord commissioned Rick to begin the work that was going to become the Fountain of Tears. 2001 was also to be a momentous year for me.

On the 28th February, which happens to be Caryl's birthday, I met the man who was to be my last Professor in the UK. He suggested that we write a grant application together so that I could work with him. Professor Ian McConnell was the Professor of Veterinary Science at the University of Cambridge. I joined his department in April 2002, 36 years after I had given up any hope to get to this very place in 1966 at the age of 18. God never forgets.

Professor Ian McConnell

While I was at Cambridge, I still had the opportunity to travel to Israel. In June 2005, Caryl and I went on a week's holiday to *"touch base"* with our best friends in Israel. Of course, Rick and Dafna were top of the list. Little did we realize what God had in store for us. We decided to meet Rick and Dafna in Arad where they were signing the documents for their new house on the edge of the Negev desert. The real estate agent who found them their house mentioned to us that there was a house for sale across the street and would we be interested.

We decided to look and Caryl immediately felt that we could live here and we put in an offer. Nevertheless, we had to leave the country virtually the next day but the house was soon to be ours. Because the Lord had given us this house in Israel, we began the process of making "Aliyah" to become Israeli citizens. I could do it because of my father being Jewish.

My time in Cambridge came to an end in 2009 and it was during that year that Caryl and I got our Israeli citizenship. We now live here in Arad because of that friendship which began 39 years ago. I believe that one of the reasons that the Lord has brought us here is to support Rick and Dafna and the work of the Fountain of Tears. This book is one result of that partnership and it is my prayer that it will contribute a biblical foundation for the work.

As well as the countless millions of unknown Holocaust victims, this book is dedicated to the Messiah, who was, who is and who is to come. He has brought us also to the edge of the desert to contribute to that voice that is crying in the wilderness, *"Prepare the way for the Lord".*

Geoff Barnard
April 2017

PROLOGUE

Reasons to Write this Book

The Fountain of Tears

I have known Rick Wienecke, the artist who created the Fountain of Tears, for over 39 years. The fact that the Lord would bring us together is clear evidence that:

Isaiah 55:8-9 (RSV) *For my thoughts are not your thoughts, neither are your ways my ways, says the LORD. For as the heavens are higher than the earth, so are my ways higher than your ways and my thoughts than your thoughts.*

The Artist at Work

Rick often tells me that he is not a theologian. I have sometime disputed this but now I see that this is true. He is an artist; I am an academic. With hindsight, you can see something of the wisdom of God in choosing Rick to be THE artist of the Fountain of Tears.

When Rick came to understand that the Lord was asking him to create a memorial to the six million who perished in the Holocaust and that this memorial would also include the suffering of Jesus in his crucifixion, he began to argue.

The first thing that Rick said to the Lord was *"You cannot do this here in Israel"*. Rick knew perfectly well the controversy that this work might cause. He was concerned that he would lose everything that the Lord had given him over many years. The problem for Rick was that the Lord was not listening to his argument.

But the commission would not go away. Rick often tells his story that he had to find a better argument. I also love to tell this story to the many groups that come to see the Fountain. The "better" argument was this. Rick told the Lord:

*"I am not Jewish, I am Canadian. My ancestry is Canadian. There is no connection between what was happening in Canada and what was taking place in Europe during the Holocaust. I do not have any resource to draw on. **I have no memory of this.**"*

Rick believed this to be a really good argument and that the Lord would change his mind and find someone else. But the fact is this; when Rick said to the Lord *"I have no memory of this"*, immediately he felt the Lord say to him three words. The Lord said to Rick:

"But I do"

When you think about it you realize that the Lord knows every name of every person who died in the Holocaust. The Psalmist says:

Psalm 147:2-5 (NKJV) *The LORD builds up Jerusalem; He gathers together the outcasts of Israel. He heals the brokenhearted and binds up their wounds. He counts the number of the stars; He calls them all by name. Great is our Lord, and mighty in power; His understanding is infinite.*

If the Lord knows the names of every star, how much more does he know the names of every man, women and child that perished in the Holocaust? I believe these names are engraved on his heart. He never forgets.

He has numbered the stars and calls them each by name

Isaiah 49:14-16 (NIV) *But Zion said, "The LORD has forsaken me, the Lord has forgotten me." "Can a mother forget the baby at her breast and have no compassion on the child she has borne? Though she may forget, I will not forget you! See, I have engraved you on the palms of my hands ... ".*

The communication of the Fountain of Tears is the communication of a Father's heart to his children. His love communicated through art touches the heart. Because the communication through the Fountain is from him, it is easy to understand why he chose this non-Jewish Canadian kibbutznik. Rick is not a theologian. He does not have a theological agenda.

The Lord is free to speak, for his thoughts are not our thoughts. And the fact is the Lord speaks to everyone who has an open heart. It has been a great privilege to see this at the Fountain of Tears to Jew and Christian alike. Often when we speak at the Fountain and perhaps show a brief DVD describing each piece and panel, people are stunned. Many times there are tears and people do not know what to say. It is because the communication of the Father's heart has touched their hearts. And we are encouraged to speak to the heart of Jerusalem.

Isaiah 40:1-2 (NIV) *Comfort, comfort my people, says your God. Speak tenderly to Jerusalem, and proclaim to her that her hard service has been completed, that her sin has been paid for, that she has received from the LORD's hand double for all her sins.*

The literal meaning of *"speak tenderly to Jerusalem"* is *"speak to the heart of Jerusalem"*. The question for us, therefore, is how do we speak to hearts and not to ears? I am sure there are many ways but communication through art definitely speaks to the heart. I see it all the time. This communication avoids intellectual objection, or at least it should. Perhaps this is why the Lord has brought an academic alongside the artist. The fact is that there are sometimes theological objections that need to be addressed.

The Artist and the Academic

Addressing Christian Misunderstanding

1. Replacement Theology

The evangelical Christian world is much divided when it comes to the Jewish people and the Nation of Israel. Even though evangelicals believe that the Bible is the word of God and essential truth, many hold to the idea that all the blessings and promises given by God to the people of Israel are now transferred exclusively to the church.

This idea is given the technical name, supersessionism or, more commonly replacement theology. Furthermore, replacement theology holds to the belief that the Christian Church has replaced Israel as God's chosen people and that the Mosaic covenant is now obsolete and replaced by the New Covenant. The Fountain of Tears challenges this belief.

God is faithful and he will fulfil every promise that he has ever made to the people of Israel. God has not forsaken his people and with the Apostle Paul we state categorically:

Romans 11:1 (NIV) *I ask then: Did God reject his people? By no means!*

Throughout the pages of this book we will amplify this truth. We will also look at the establishment of the New Covenant which is sealed in Jesus' blood and we will remember the words of the prophet Jeremiah:

Jeremiah 31:33-34 (RSV) *But this is the covenant which I will make with the house of Israel after those days, says the LORD: I will put my law within them, and I will write it upon their hearts; and I will be their God, and they shall be my people. And no longer shall each man teach his neighbor and each his brother, saying, 'Know the LORD,' for they shall all know me, from the least of them to the greatest, says the LORD; for I will forgive their iniquity, and I will remember their sin no more."*

2. A History of Christian anti-Semitism

Replacement theology led the Christian church to become the enemy of the Jewish people throughout history. Over many centuries, Jewish people found more shelter in Islamic countries than ever they did in Christian Europe. The people who perhaps are the most indebted to the Jewish people became alienated and feared. When we consider the Crusades, the Expulsions, the Inquisitions, the Pogroms, we see that even if millions of Jewish people died in the Holocaust, millions more died under the shadow of the cross held by the Institutional Church. Christians need to know their history and the Fountain of Tears opens a window of understanding into this tragic past.

Although true Christian believers might want to dispute these difficult truths, the Jewish people have a long collective memory.

3. The Significance of the Holocaust

Perhaps more than anything else, the Fountain of Tears enables Christians to appreciate the ongoing significance of the Holocaust in the life of the nation of Israel. Jewish people see the Shoah which took place in the 1930's and 1940's, and which culminated in the murder of 6 million by the Nazis, as the climax of nearly 2000 years of Christian anti-Semitism. How could it be that a highly cultured and developed, mainly Lutheran Protestant country such as Germany allowed this evil to overtake them? How could it be that the largely Christian Western nations stood by and did nothing?

It is really no surprise that:

Romans 11:28 (NIV) *As far as the gospel is concerned; they are enemies on your account.*

Even as I write this, I see these words in another light. The Jewish people have become enemies of the Christian Gospel and we are accountable. As believers, we need to recognize that we are indebted to the Jewish people. We need to consider the impact of Christian history on the life of the Jewish people, face to face.

The Fountain of Tears reassures us that the Apostle Paul does not leave us stranded with the above words for he says in these verses:

Romans 11:28-29 (NIV) *As far as the gospel is concerned, they are enemies on your account; but as far as election is concerned, they are loved on account of the patriarchs, for God's gifts and his call are irrevocable.*

Holocaust

The word "Holocaust" is very ancient. It is derived from the Greek *holókaustós* [ὀλόκαυστος] and literally means: hólos, *"whole"* and kaustós, *"burnt"*. It was used in pagan Greek ritual and described an offering that was totally consumed by fire.

The Septuagint (the Greek translation of the Hebrew Bible) which was completed in the second century BCE, consistently translated the Hebrew word olah [עוֹלָה] with a derivative of the Greek word *holókaustós,* namely, *holokautōma* [ὀλοκαύτωμα]. The Hebrew word olah literally means *"that which is offered up";* it signifies a burnt offering offered whole to the Lord.

An interesting example is in Psalm 40:6

Psalm 40:6 (KJV) *Sacrifice and offering thou didst not desire; mine ears hast thou opened:* **burnt offering** *and sin offering hast thou not required.*

Psalm 39:7 (Septuagint equivalent verse) θυσίαν καὶ προσφορὰν οὐκ ἠθέλησας ὠτία δὲ κατηρτίσω μοι **ὀλοκαύτωμα** καὶ περὶ ἁμαρτίας οὐκ ᾔτησας

The word also appears in Latin as *holocaustum* and was used in the Middle Ages to describe animal sacrifices in the Bible.

For example, Numbers 28:19 in the Latin Vulgate:

> offeretisque incensum **holocaustum** Domino vitulos de armento duos
> arietem unum agnos anniculos inmaculatos septem

This verse in the NIV is translated: *But you shall offer an offering made by fire, a burnt offering to the Lord: two young bulls, one ram, and seven male lambs a year old; they shall be without blemish to the best of your knowledge.*

Throughout history, the word has been used in the general sense for great destruction resulting in the extensive loss of life, especially by fire. It is important to note, however, that the word became connected to the murder of the six million in more recent times. It is only from the 1960's that the word was used by scholars and popular writers to specifically refer to the Nazi Genocide. Remarkably, it was the television mini-series (1978) which was entitled *"Holocaust"* that brought this word and its association with the Jewish people into more common usage.

The biblical word "Shoah" [שׁוֹאָה] meaning calamity, desolation or destruction is the preferred word in Israel to describe the Nazi genocide during the Second World War. Perhaps it is preferred mainly because of the ancient pagan association of the word *Holocaust*. Perhaps there are other reasons.

The word Shoah appears in Psalm 35:8

Psalm 35:8 (KJV) *Let destruction* [שׁוֹאָה] *come upon him at unawares; and let his net that he hath hid catch himself: into that very destruction* [בְּשׁוֹאָה literally "into destruction"].

Also and very significantly,

Isaiah 47:11 (KJV) *Therefore shall evil come upon thee; thou shalt not know from whence it riseth: and mischief shall fall upon thee; thou shalt not be able to put it off: and desolation* [שׁוֹאָה] *shall come upon thee suddenly, which thou shalt not know.*

Addressing Jewish Concerns

A second reason to write this book is to consider and sympathize with Jewish understanding and misconception.

1. The Two Greatest Tragedies in our History

Rick often tells the story of the Jewish business woman who works for the local council in Arad. She had heard about the Fountain of Tears and decided to come and see for herself. As she walked through the entrance, the first person she sees is Jesus. Then she focuses on the Holocaust. At that point, Rick and Dafna thought she was having a fit. The lady began to hit at her chest and her mouth. She cried out *"I can't breathe".*

Rick and Dafna rushed over to her and asked her what was wrong. She said to them:

> *"You have taken the two greatest tragedies in our history and you have put them at the same table"*

The Jewish people, perhaps the Nation as a whole, sees the crucifixion of Jesus as the greatest tragedy in their history. Why is this? It is because of the accusation that the Jewish people are the *"Christ Killers".* This accusation has haunted them throughout the centuries. As mentioned previously, millions of Jewish people have perished under the shadow of the cross.

The book attempts to address some of these issues and concerns. My heart-felt prayer is that the following chapters will facilitate even greater dialogue between Christian and Jewish theologians.

2. Jewish Replacement Theology

One of the main messages of the Fountain of Tears is the significance of the Land of Israel for the Jewish people. God is bringing his people back from the four quarters of the earth. It is this author's total conviction and belief that Israel is the only safe place for Jewish people world-wide.

In these turbulent times, the specter of anti-Semitism is raising its ugly head once more right across the world. This is exacerbated by the persistent hatred by radical Islam against what they describe as "The Occupation". The existence of the State of Israel is anathema to radical Islam. Unfortunately, the western media is sympathetic to this warped idea. However, because of perceived hostility and western affluence, many Jewish people see the Diaspora as their home. **This is Jewish replacement theology.**

The Promised Land?

For example, many millions of Jewish people in the USA are too comfortable. The USA is their promised land. But times are changing; the Jewish people will have to leave their comfort. Israel is their home, as the Fountain of Tears and this book make perfectly clear.

3. The Person of Jesus

The Fountain of Tears gives Jewish people an opportunity to reconsider the person of Jesus. For some it is a real shock to realize that Jesus was and is a Jew. Many have considered him just the Christian God. The Fountain of Tears and, I hope, this book will challenge their fears. He is and will always be the King of the Jews. As the angel Gabriel said to Mary (Miriam) his mother:

Luke 1:32-33 (KJV) *He will be great and will be called the Son of the Highest, and the Lord God will give Him the throne of His father David. And He will reign over the House of Jacob **forever, and of His kingdom there will be no end**.*

This is in accord with the Prophet Isaiah:

Isaiah 9:7 (NIV*) He will reign on David's throne and over his kingdom, establishing and upholding it with justice and righteousness **from that time on and forever.** The zeal of the LORD Almighty will accomplish this.*

The person of Jesus has been misrepresented to Jewish people by many Christians of all persuasions throughout the centuries. The Jewish people have been estranged from the one who gave his life for them. My prayer is that through these pages, he may once again be known.

1 Corinthians 13:12 (NIV) *Now we see but a poor reflection as in a mirror; then we shall see face to face. Now I know in part; then I shall know fully, even as I am fully known.*

We now turn to a very important introductory chapter before we look at each piece and each panel of the Fountain in detail. We will consider the identity of the Servant in the Book of Isaiah. This controversial issue that divides Christian and Jewish scholarship, perhaps more than any other, is crucial in helping us to understand the message of the Fountain of Tears.

Face to Face

Chapter One

The Identity of the Servant in Isaiah

The issue regarding the identity of *"the servant"*, particularly in the book of Isaiah, remains one of the most controversial and divisive subjects in the theological debate between Jews and Christians. The majority evangelical Christian position is clear; Jesus is the suffering servant. However, Jewish theologians understand that the servant spoken of from Isaiah chapter 40 onwards is collectively the nation of Israel.[1] There is obviously justification for this position as seen in Isaiah chapter 41.

Isaiah 41:8-9 (RSV) *But you, Israel, my servant, Jacob, whom I have chosen, the offspring of Abraham, my friend; you whom I took from the ends of the earth, and called from its farthest corners, saying to you, "You are my servant, I have chosen you and not cast you off".*[2]

This passage seems to be explicit. Israel is clearly described as a servant (even *"my"* servant). However, the context of this declaration needs to be looked at carefully. The passage is prophetic and describes a time when God has taken his people from the ends of the earth, even from its farthest corners. This cannot describe the situation of the people of Israel at the time of Isaiah, after the return from Babylon, or even at the time of Jesus. The greatest diaspora of Israel was still to take place following the destruction of the Temple in 70 CE. It is only in the modern era that God has begun to bring back his people from the farthest corners of the earth as he promised he would. We read about this in many places in the Jewish Scriptures.[3]

Deuteronomy 30:4-5 (RSV) *If your outcasts are in the uttermost parts of heaven, from there the LORD your God will gather you, and from there he will fetch you; and the LORD your God will bring you into the land which your fathers possessed, that you may possess it; and he will make you more prosperous and numerous than your fathers.*

Isaiah 11:12 (NIV) *He will raise a banner for the nations and gather the exiles of Israel; he will assemble the scattered people of Judah from the four quarters of the earth.*

---

[1] The servant is clearly the nation of Israel in **the majority** of the occurrences in Isaiah chapters 40 through 55. There are, however, several instances where the identity of the servant is more enigmatic and, in some cases, cannot be Israel. These occur in what scholars often refer to as the "servant songs and poems." These are to be found in Isaiah 42:1-8; Isaiah 49:1-7; Isaiah 50:4-11; Isaiah 52:13-53:12.

[2] See also Isaiah 42:18-19; 43:10; 44:1,2, 21, 26; 45:4; 48:20; 49:3.

[3] The Jewish Scriptures are often called the Tanach or Tanakh. This is an acronym for the Torah (the five books of Moses), the Nevi'im (the prophets) and the Ketuvim (the writings).

A Banner for the Nations

Jeremiah 31:8 (NIV) *See, I will bring them from the land of the north and gather them from the ends of the earth.*

Nehemiah 1:8-9 (NIV) *"Remember the instruction you gave your servant Moses, saying, 'If you are unfaithful, I will scatter you among the nations, but if you return to me and obey my commands, then even if your exiled people are at the farthest horizon, I will gather them from there and bring them to the place I have chosen as a dwelling for my Name.' "*

None of these passages were exhaustively fulfilled by the return of the exiles from Babylon. However, we have lived to see these words fulfilled in our day and this process will continue in the days to come. God is stressing in his word through the prophet (Isaiah 41:9) that he has not rejected his people but they remain chosen for a purpose. They are and will be *"his"* servant. We hear the words of the Apostle Paul ringing an endorsement.

Romans 11:1-2 (RSV) *I ask, then, has God rejected his people? By no means! I myself am an Israelite, a descendant of Abraham, a member of the tribe of Benjamin. God has not rejected his people whom he foreknew.*

God has not Rejected His People

The passage in Isaiah 41 must be in the mind of Paul. This word is written to the descendants of Abraham through Jacob and the Apostle describes himself in exactly these terms. However, we need to note that there is something of a paradox in Romans 11. Paul asks, *"Did God reject his people?"* and the immediate answer is an emphatic No! However, in the New International Version (NIV) and many other English translations, Paul seems to suggest the following a little later in this chapter in Romans:

Romans 11:15 (NIV) *For if their rejection is the reconciliation of the world, what will their acceptance be but life from the dead?*

This does not make any sense. If God has not rejected his people Israel, how can their rejection be the reconciliation of the world? We need, therefore, to consider the Greek text of these verses in Romans chapter 11 in order to understand this conundrum.

The Greek word translated *"rejected"* in Romans 11:1 and 2 is ἀπώσατο transliterated *"aposato"*. The only other use of this word (in the same form) in the New Testament is in Stephen's sermon recorded in Acts chapter 7.

Acts 7:27 (NIV) *But the man who was ill-treating the other pushed Moses aside and said, 'Who made you ruler and judge over us?'*

In this verse, the Greek verb ἀπώσατο is translated as *"pushed ... aside"*. The correct sense of this word may be reflected in the King James Version (KJV) translation in Romans chapter 11.

Romans 11:1-2 (KJV) *I say then, hath God **cast away** his people? God forbid for I also am an Israelite, of the seed of Abraham, of the tribe of Benjamin. God hath not **cast away** his people which he foreknew.*[4]

On the other hand, the word translated *"rejection"* in Romans 11:15 (NIV) is ἀποβολὴ which is transliterated *"apobole"*. The only other use of this word in this form is in the book of Acts.

Acts 27:22 (KJV) *And now I exhort you to be of good cheer: for there shall be no loss* [ἀποβολη] *of any man's life among you, but of the ship.*

A better translation of the Greek word *"ἀποβολὴ"* is *"loss"*.

The word translated *"acceptance"* in Romans 11:15 (NIV) is πρόσλημψις which is transliterated *"proslempsis"*. This is the only use of the word in this particular form in the New Testament. However, related words are used in Romans 14:1, 15:7 and Philippians 4:15. Accordingly the sense on this word is *"a receiving"* or *"reception"*. This is reflected in the KJV translation.

Romans 11:15 (KJV) *For if the casting away of them be the reconciling of the world, what shall the receiving of them be, but life from the dead?*

---

[4] However, it is this writer's opinion that "pushed aside" would be better.

Life from the Dead

An even better translation of Romans 11:15 would be this:

Romans 11:15 (GB) *For if their loss is the reconciliation of the world, what will their reception be but life from the dead?*

This now makes perfect sense as Paul is looking into the far distant future and sees a time when the nation *as a whole* will no longer be lost but is found (i.e. received). I can't help thinking of the story of the Prodigal Son.[5]

Luke 15:24 (NIV) *For this son of mine was dead and is alive again; he was lost and is found.' So they began to celebrate.*

The Prodigal Son [6]

[5] See Kenneth E. Bailey (2011) Jacob and the Prodigal: How Jesus Retold Israel's Story. IVP Academic.
[6] The Prodigal Son - Sculpture by Rick Wienecke — visit www.castingseeds.com

Israel's restoration and revival is just that, it will be life from the dead! In addition, this sets the passage in Isaiah 41:8-9 into its correct prophetic context. In the distant future in relationship to the time of Isaiah and the time of Paul, God reassures the people that they have not been rejected or pushed aside, but remain his chosen people.

Seen in this prophetic context, the next words of Isaiah 41 also make perfect sense.

Isaiah 41:10-14 (RSV) *Fear not, for I am with you, be not dismayed, for I am your God; I will strengthen you, I will help you, I will uphold you with my victorious right hand. Behold, all who are incensed against you shall be put to shame and confounded; those who strive against you shall be as nothing and shall perish. You shall seek those who contend with you, but you shall not find them; those who war against you shall be as nothing at all. For I, the LORD your God, hold your right hand; it is I who say to you, "Fear not, I will help you." Fear not, you worm Jacob, you men of Israel! I will help you, says the LORD; your Redeemer is the Holy One of Israel.*

We still await the complete fulfillment of these words as there has never yet been a time in history when the enemies of Israel could not be found. Isaiah 41 is describing the distant future when God has brought his chosen people back to the land from the four quarters of the earth. This is beginning to happen in our day.

The Servant as an Individual in the Book of Isaiah

Several characters are described as servants in the first part of the book of Isaiah, namely, Isaiah himself, Eliakim and King David.

Isaiah as Servant

Isaiah 20:3 (NIV) *Then the LORD said, "Just as my servant Isaiah has gone stripped and barefoot for three years, as a sign and portent against Egypt and Cush*

Eliakim as Servant

Isaiah 22:20-22 (RSV) *In that day I will call my servant Eliakim the son of Hilkiah, and I will clothe him with your robe, and will bind your girdle on him, and will commit your authority to his hand; and he shall be a father to the inhabitants of Jerusalem and to the house of Judah. And I will place on his shoulder the key of the house of David; he shall open, and none shall shut; and he shall shut, and none shall open.[7]*

The Key of David

David as Servant

Isaiah 37:35 (NIV) *I will defend this city and save it, for my sake and for the sake of David my servant.*

Accordingly, it is consistent to recognize that the term *"servant"* can be applied to the nation as a whole as well as to individuals within it. This becomes important when we consider the identity of the servant in other passages in Isaiah, some of which have been described as *"servant songs"*. We need to look at each of these passages in turn and in some detail.

---

[7] Compare the NT words that are written about Jesus in Revelation 3:7 "...who holds the key of David. What he opens no one can shut, and what he shuts no one can open." These are extremely significant words. Eliakim, the archetypal servant is dressed in robe and sash. Jesus' appearance as described in Revelation 1:13 "... someone "like a son of man," dressed in a robe ...with a golden sash around his chest." Eliakim's name means 'my God will raise up' or 'my God, he shall arise' or even 'raised up by God'. Eliakim clearly prefigures the risen exalted Jesus who holds the keys of Death and Hades (Revelation 1:18). One day **all** the keys will be put in **all** the locks. On that day, Jesus will be the true and eternal Father to those who live in Jerusalem and to the house of Judah.

The Structure of the Book of Isaiah

The Isaiah Scroll found at Qumran [8]

The book of Isaiah has a remarkable structure. It has 66 chapters which can be divided into 39 and 27. This reflects the Bible as a whole. The first part of Isaiah (chapters 1 to 39) contains a great deal of historical detail and the book opens as follows:

Isaiah 1:1 (NIV) *The vision concerning Judah and Jerusalem that Isaiah son of Amoz saw during the reigns of Uzziah, Jotham, Ahaz and Hezekiah, kings of Judah.*

The second part of Isaiah (from chapter 40) looks well beyond the reign of these kings. In fact, they are no longer mentioned. The only historical king that is described in these later chapters is Cyrus, king of Persia who allowed the exiles who had been taken into Babylon to return to Jerusalem if they so wished. [9]

Isaiah 45:13 (NIV) *I will raise up Cyrus in my righteousness: I will make all his ways straight. He will rebuild my city and set my exiles free, but not for a price or reward, says the LORD Almighty.*

---

[8] The Isaiah Scroll or 1QIsa (also called the Great Isaiah Scroll) was found in a cave near the Dead Sea (Qumran Cave 1) with six other scrolls by Bedouin shepherds in 1947. It is the most complete scroll out of the 220 found, being complete from beginning to end. It is the oldest complete copy of the Book of Isaiah known, dating from before 100 BCE [from http://en.wikipedia.org/wiki/Isaiah_scroll].
[9] 2 Chronicles 36: 22-23; Ezra 1:1-3

Cyrus the Great

He is also called the Lord's anointed (Isaiah 45:1) and there is a reason for this.

Isaiah 45:4 (NIV) *For the sake of Jacob my servant, of Israel my chosen, I summon you by name and bestow on you a title of honor, though you do not acknowledge me.*

The only other person who is also described as king in these later chapters in the book of Isaiah is God himself. For example:

Isaiah 44:6-7 (RSV) *Thus says the LORD, the King of Israel and his Redeemer, the LORD of hosts: "I am the first and I am the last; besides me there is no god. Who is like me? Let him proclaim it, let him declare and set it forth before me. Who has announced from of old the things to come? Let them tell us what is yet to be.*

These verses might summarize the structure of the book of Isaiah. The second part of Isaiah (from chapter 40 onwards) describes what was and is to come. It is describing events that are prefigured in the return from Babylon but which speak of greater fulfillment in the distant future.

It would be a profound mistake, however, to suggest that the first 39 chapters of Isaiah are not prophetic. Firstly, they are the words of God spoken through the prophet. Secondly, there are many passages (e.g. Isaiah 2:1-5; 4:2-6; 9:7; 11:1-16; 12:1-6; 14:1-2; 19:19-25; 24:1-23; 25:6-9; 26:19; 27:6; 29:22-24; 34:8; 35:1-10) which clearly refer to a more distant future for their complete fulfillment. We will have occasion to refer to some of these passages in our discussion.

The Structure of the Servant Songs

Within Christian scholarship, the *"servant songs"* were first identified as separate songs or poems by the German Lutheran theologian Bernhard Duhm in his commentary on the Book of Isaiah.[10] It is important for us to note, however, that this theologian also separated the Book of Isaiah into three parts: (1) Isaiah (chapters 1 through 39); (2) Deutero-Isaiah (chapters 40 through 55); and (3) Trito-Isaiah (chapters 56 through 66). Although the servant songs are to be found in what he and others considered Deutero-Isaiah, Duhm, nevertheless, still argued that the servant songs were separate compositions.

Although the majority of evangelical scholarship might reject the division of Isaiah into two or three separate works, the concept of the servant songs has remained and gained wide acceptance in both Jewish and Christian theology.

Bernhard Lauardus Duhm (1847–1928)

It is now generally accepted that there are four separate songs.[11]

---

[10] D. Bernhard Duhm (1902) Das Buch Jesaia: Übersetzt und Erklärt Göttingen: Vandenhoeck and Ruprecht,
[11] Some scholars regard Isaiah 61:1-3 as a fifth servant song even though the word *"servant"* is not used.

The First Servant Song

The first servant song is to be found in Isaiah 42:1-4

Isaiah 42:1-4 (NIV) *Here is my servant, whom I uphold, my chosen one in whom I delight; I will put my Spirit on him and he will bring justice to the nations. He will not shout or cry out, or raise his voice in the streets. A bruised reed he will not break, and a smoldering wick he will not snuff out. In faithfulness he will bring forth justice; he will not falter or be discouraged till he establishes justice on earth. In his law the islands will put their hope.*[12]

A Bruised Reed He will not Break

Thus far, we have seen clearly that the nation of Israel is described as a servant (Isaiah 41:8-9) and although it is possible to speak of the people of Israel in the singular, the simplest interpretation of the above passage is to consider that the words are speaking of an individual. Thus, the words can also be applied to Jesus because of the testimony we read in the Gospels.

For example, in the Gospel of Matthew we read:

Matthew 3:16-17 (RSV) *When Jesus was baptized, he went up immediately from the water, and behold, the heavens were opened and he saw the Spirit of God descending like a dove, and alighting on him; and lo, a voice from heaven, saying, "This is my beloved Son, with whom I am well pleased."*

---

[12] More literally: In his Torah, the Islands will put their hope.

This is My Beloved Son

Matthew 12:17-21 (NIV) *This was to fulfill what was spoken through the prophet Isaiah: "Here is my servant whom I have chosen, the one I love, in whom I delight; I will put my Spirit on him, and he will proclaim justice to the nations. He will not quarrel or cry out; no-one will hear his voice in the streets. A bruised reed he will not break, and a smoldering wick he will not snuff out, till he leads justice to victory. In his name the nations will put their hope."*

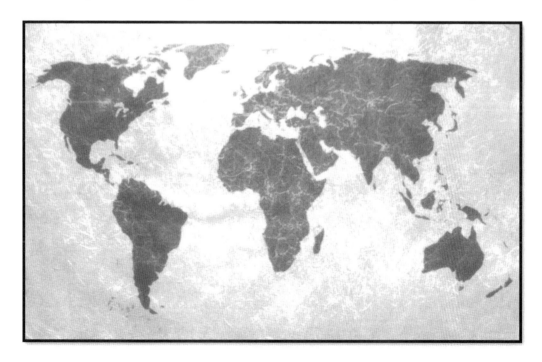

In his Name the Nations will put their Hope

The islands of Isaiah become the nations of Matthew.[13] In particular, the servant is committed to bringing justice to the ends of the earth. This remains the calling of the nation of Israel as a whole and the gifts and calling of God are, in the words of the Apostle Paul, irrevocable (Romans 11:29).

Isaiah 43:10-11 (RSV) *"You are my witnesses," says the LORD, "and my servant whom I have chosen, that you may know and believe me and understand that I am He. Before me no god was formed, nor shall there be any after me. I, I am the LORD, and besides me there is no savior".*

Isaiah 44:1-2 (RSV) *But now hear, O Jacob my servant, Israel whom I have chosen! Thus says the LORD who made you, who formed you from the womb and will help you: Fear not, O Jacob my servant, Jeshurun whom I have chosen.*

Isaiah 44:21 (RSV) *Remember these things, O Jacob, and Israel, for you are my servant; I formed you, you are my servant; O Israel, you will not be forgotten by me.*

These are some of the verses in these chapters in the book of Isaiah that clearly state that the nation of Israel is a (even *"my"*) servant.

The Second Servant Song

The second servant song is to be found in Isaiah chapter 49.

Isaiah 49:1-3 (RSV) *Listen to me, O coastlands, and hearken, you peoples from afar. The LORD called me from the womb, from the body of my mother he named my name. He made my mouth like a sharp sword, in the shadow of his hand he hid me; he made me a polished arrow, in his quiver he hid me away. And he said to me, "You are my servant, Israel, in whom I will be glorified."* [14]

---

[13] The other significant change in the New Testament passage is *from "his Torah"* (Isaiah 42:4) to "his Name" (Matthew 12:21). Matthew's *"name"* in contrast to the Masoretic Text's "Torah" is due the Septuagint translation which has *"onoma"* (name) in the place of Torah. One might conclude from these changes that the Gentile Nations are not obligated to keep the Torah but to trust in the Name of the Lord. This idea resonates with John 1:17 For the law was given through Moses; grace and truth came through Jesus Christ. Jewish scholarship also agrees that the Gentiles are not obligated to keep Torah in its entirety. This also accords with the decisions taken by the Council of Jerusalem (Acts 15).

[14] In this passage, the name of the Servant becomes now more prominent (see previous footnote). In addition, the mouth of the Servant is likened to a sharp sword. This prefigures the description of the risen exalted Jesus in Revelation 1:16 ... out of his mouth came a sharp double-edged sword.

Isaiah 49:4-6 (RSV) *But I said, "I have labored in vain, I have spent my strength for nothing and vanity; yet surely my right is with the LORD, and my recompense with my God." And now the LORD says, who formed me from the womb to be his servant, to bring Jacob back to him, and that Israel might be gathered to him, for I am honored in the eyes of the LORD, and my God has become my strength, he says: "It is too light a thing that you should be my servant to raise up the tribes of Jacob and to restore the preserved of Israel; I will give you as a light to the nations, that my salvation may reach to the end of the earth."*

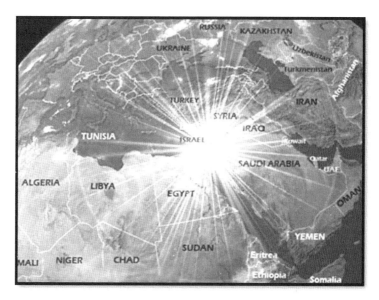

A Light to the Gentiles

There are two elements to the calling of the servant expressed in these verses. The first and smaller element is the restoration of the nation, which may be seen in both physical and spiritual terms. The second and more extensive element is to be a light to the Gentiles and to bring the knowledge of God's salvation to the ends of the earth. Those involved in the fulfillment of the first element may not necessarily be the same as those who fulfil the second element. Thus, as with the first servant song, I believe that it is legitimate to see the servant as both the nation as a whole and specific individuals within it.

In these verses, God says again that Israel is his servant and he is going to display his splendor within the nation. However, the response is somewhat muted. *"I have labored to no purpose; I have spent my strength in vain and for nothing."* This sense of disappointment on behalf of the nation as a whole is most poignantly expressed in words that we read a little later in chapter 49.

Isaiah 49:14-19 (NIV) *But Zion said, "The LORD has forsaken me, the Lord has forgotten me." "Can a mother forget the baby at her breast and have no compassion on the child she has borne? Though she may forget, I will not forget you! See, I have engraved you on the palms of my hands; your walls are ever before me. Your sons hasten back, and those who laid you waste depart from you. Lift up your eyes and look around; all your sons gather and come to you. As surely as I live," declares the LORD, "you will wear them all as ornaments; you will put them on, like a bride." Though you were ruined and made desolate and your land laid waste, now you will be too small for your people, and those who devoured you will be far away.*

"See, I have Engraved you on the Palms of my Hands"

Thus, the Lord contrasts Israel's disappointment with his determination to restore the nation in the future. God is yet going to display his splendor in Israel.[15] Nevertheless, the calling of the servant in the meantime **is** to be a light to the Gentiles and to bring the knowledge of God's salvation plan to the ends of the earth. If the nation as a whole believes that it has labored for no purpose, there has to be a subset (remnant) within the nation that begins to achieve this. This is both the calling of an individual and his followers. Without question, this has been fulfilled in the life of Jesus and the earliest disciples, all of whom were members of the house of Israel.

Luke 2:28-32 (RSV) *He took him up in his arms and blessed God and said, "Lord, now lettest thou thy servant depart in peace, according to thy word; for mine eyes have seen thy salvation which thou hast prepared in the presence of all peoples, a light for revelation to the Gentiles, and for glory to thy people Israel."*

---

[15] Isaiah 35:1-2; Isaiah 61:3; Nahum 2:2

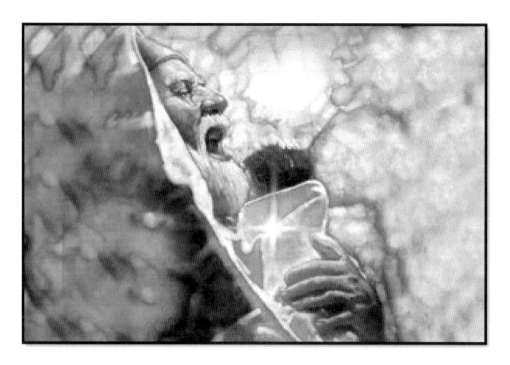

Simeon and the Child Jesus [16]

Acts 13:46-47 (RSV) *And Paul and Barnabas spoke out boldly, saying, "It was necessary that the word of God should be spoken first to you. Since you thrust it from you, and judge yourselves unworthy of eternal life, behold, we turn to the Gentiles. For so the Lord has commanded us, saying, 'I have set you to be a light for the Gentiles, that you may bring salvation to the uttermost parts of the earth.'"*

Paul and Barnabas speak somewhat harshly to their Jewish audience, but so does the Lord in Isaiah chapter 42 after the first servant song. For the sake of clarity, let's look again at two of these verses.

Isaiah 42:1 and 4 (NIV) *"Here is my servant, whom I uphold, my chosen one in whom I delight … **he will not falter or be discouraged** till he establishes justice on earth. In his law the islands will put their hope."*

---

[16] This painting is entitled "Simeon's Moment" by Ron DiCianni. This wonderful work of art shows the aged Simeon holding the baby in his arms against a backdrop of the Nations of the World. It can be seen and full color and copies can be purchased at the following website: http://www.tapestryproductions.com/products/artist/rondicianni/simeonsmoment.php

He will bring forth Justice

I submit that the establishment of justice on earth is part of the greater calling of the servant (i.e. to be a light to the Gentiles). Unlike the disappointment expressed in the second servant song, **this servant is not discouraged and he doesn't falter.** So what do we make of these words that we read a little later in chapter 42? Are they part of the servant songs or not?

Isaiah 42:18-20 (NIV) *Hear, you deaf; look, you blind, and see! Who is blind but my servant, and deaf like the messenger I send? Who is blind like the one committed to me, blind like the servant of the LORD? You have seen many things, but have paid no attention; your ears are open, but you hear nothing.*

This passage, perhaps more than any other, provides evidence that the identity of the servant in Isaiah <u>has</u> to be **both** nation and individual(s).[17] In the nation as a whole, there are eyes that cannot see and ears that cannot hear. Surely this is one of the greatest mysteries in Scripture and this theme resonates throughout the entire Bible. For example, Moses castigates his people:

Deuteronomy 29:2-4 (RSV) *And Moses summoned all Israel and said to them: "You have seen all that the LORD did before your eyes in the land of Egypt, to Pharaoh and to all his servants and to all his land, the great trials which your eyes saw, the signs, and those great wonders; but to this day the LORD has not given you a mind to understand, or eyes to see, or ears to hear.*

---

[17] It is very important to remember that Isaiah was commissioned to announce to Israel their seeing but not perceiving and hearing and not understanding (Isaiah 6:9-10) before they went into exile. It is very hopeful to know that Israel is not disqualified from being YHWH's servant due to blindness and deafness and imprisonment. The highest calling is on them in their broken state.

What Moses is actually saying is that God has not given his people a mind, eyes or ears that can respond to everything that he has done for them. This is all the more remarkable when we read the words of a proverb:

Proverb 20:12 (NIV) *Ears that hear and eyes that see - the LORD has made them both.*

Eyes that See

If the Lord is the one who makes eyes that see and ears that hear, why did he not give these to his own people? The call of the prophet Isaiah has terrible consequences for the nation:

Isaiah 6:8-10 (NIV) *Then I heard the voice of the Lord saying, "Whom shall I send? And who will go for us?" And I said, "Here am I. Send me!" He said, "Go and tell this people: "'Be ever hearing, but never understanding; be ever seeing, but never perceiving.' Make the heart of this people calloused; make their ears dull and close their eyes. Otherwise they might see with their eyes, hear with their ears, understand with their hearts, and turn and be healed."*

These words are alluded to by Jesus and also by the Apostle Paul.

Matthew 13:14-15 (NIV) *In them is fulfilled the prophecy of Isaiah: "'You will be ever hearing but never understanding; you will be ever seeing but never perceiving. For this people's heart has become calloused; they hardly hear with their ears, and they have closed their eyes. Otherwise they might see with their eyes, hear with their ears, understand with their hearts and turn, and I would heal them.* [18]

---

[18] This is a remarkable passage and it would be easy to conclude that it is permanent condition. This, however, would be a profound mistake. A day will come when eyes will be opened and ears will hear (see Isaiah 35:3-5). Healing will follow and a national calling will be fulfilled.

Romans 11:7-8 (NIV) *What then? What Israel sought so earnestly it did not obtain, but the elect did. The others were hardened, as it is written: "God gave them a spirit of stupor, eyes so that they could not see and ears so that they could not hear, to this very day."*

For some reason, only known to the Lord, he did not provide the appropriate sensory conditions so that the nation as a whole could respond to his love and grace. However, there is a remnant and there is also an individual who can both hear and see.

Isaiah 11:1-4 (NIV) *A shoot will come up from the stump of Jesse; from his roots a branch will bear fruit. The Spirit of the LORD will rest on him[19] - the Spirit of wisdom and of understanding, the Spirit of counsel and of power, the Spirit of knowledge and of the fear of the LORD - and he will delight in the fear of the LORD. He will not judge by what **he sees** with his eyes, or decide by what **he hears** with his ears; but with righteousness he will judge the needy, with justice he will give decisions for the poor of the earth. He will strike the earth with the rod of his mouth; with the breath of his lips he will slay the wicked.*

A Shoot from the Stump of Jesse

---

[19] This is totally consistent with the first servant song in Isaiah 42.

Because of the resonance of the themes contained within this passage and the first servant song in Isaiah chapter 42, we may conclude that there has to be an individual who will bring the knowledge of salvation to the ends of the earth. In this somewhat cryptic passage, he is also described as a fruitful *"branch"*. This **cannot** be the nation of Israel as a whole as he is an individual and a descendant of Jesse, the father of King David. This messianic theme is to be found in other parts of the Tanach.

Jeremiah 33:14-16 (RSV) *Behold, the days are coming, says the LORD, when I will fulfil the promise I made to the house of Israel and the house of Judah. In those days and at that time I will cause a righteous Branch to spring forth for David; and he shall execute justice and righteousness in the land. In those days Judah will be saved and Jerusalem will dwell securely. And this is the name by which it will be called: 'The LORD is our righteousness.'*

The righteous Branch who is also described as *"my servant"* in Zechariah 3:8 (see overleaf) imputes his own righteousness to the people. He becomes the Lord *"**our** righteousness"* and in his days Judah will be saved and Jerusalem will live in safety.

While we await the complete fulfillment of these words, further information about this messianic figure is given in the prophecy of Zechariah.

Zechariah 6:9-13 (RSV) *And the word of the LORD came to me: "Take from the exiles Heldai, Tobijah, and Jedaiah, who have arrived from Babylon; and go the same day to the house of Josiah, the son of Zephaniah. Take from them silver and gold, and make a crown, and set it upon the head of Joshua, the son of Jehozadak, the high priest; and say to him, 'Thus says the LORD of hosts, "Behold, the man whose name is the Branch: for he shall grow up in his place, and he shall build the temple of the LORD. It is he who shall build the temple of the LORD, and shall bear royal honor, and shall sit and rule upon his throne. And there shall be a priest by his throne, and peaceful understanding shall be between them both."'*

The High Priest

In this passage, the Branch is given a name. He is likened to Joshua son of Jehozadak who was the legitimate high priest and who returned with Zerubbabel after the Babylonian captivity.

However, we have a serious problem here! If Joshua is the **legitimate** high priest, he has to be a Levite. He is not from the tribe of Judah. Also, in this passage, the high priest is actually crowned King of Israel. What are we to make of this? Fortunately, Zechariah has already come to our aid.

Zechariah 3:8 (NIV) *"'Listen, O high priest Joshua and your associates seated before you, **who are men symbolic of things to come: I am going to bring my servant**, the branch"* .[20]

Joshua is being used as a visual aid. A day will come when the true branch of the Lord, a descendant of Jesse, of the house of Judah will become the Lord our Righteousness [יהוה צדקנו] transliterated YHWH [21] Zidkenu. The verses that immediately follow the passage in Jeremiah 33:14-16 shown above are in accord with the vision of Zechariah. These verses in Jeremiah are as follows:

Jeremiah 33:17-18 (RSV) *For thus says the LORD: David shall never lack a man to sit on the throne of the house of Israel, and the Levitical priests shall never lack a man in my presence to offer burnt offerings, to burn cereal offerings, and to make sacrifices for ever.*

The Branch who is *"my"* servant is also the Lord, our righteousness, and he will be both king and priest. Remarkably, Joshua the son of Jehozadak is called by a slightly different name in the books of Ezra and Nehemiah.

Ezra 3:2 (RSV) *Then arose Jeshua the son of Jozadak, with his fellow priests, and Zerubbabel the son of Shealtiel with his kinsmen, and they built the altar of the God of Israel, to offer burnt offerings upon it, as it is written in the law of Moses the man of God.*

Nehemiah 12:26 (NIV) *They served in the days of Joiakim son of Jeshua, the son of Jozadak, and in the days of Nehemiah the governor and of Ezra the priest and scribe.*

---

[20] It is worth re-iterating that in his verse we can clearly see that the branch is also my servant. This passage clearly indicates that Joshua the High Priest is THE symbol of another individual who will come in the future. God, who is speaking, is GOING to do this.

[21] The unpronounced name of God also known as the Tetragrammaton

The name Jozadak [יֹוצָדָק] or Jehozadak [יְהֹוצָדָק] consists of two elements, namely, Jo[22] or Jeho[23], which is an abbreviated form of the Tetragrammaton [יְהֹוָה]. The second element is the Hebrew root [צָדַק] which includes the meaning of righteousness. We have noted that the Lord our Righteousness [יְהֹוָה צִדְקֵנוּ] is based on this root [24]. Thus the name Jozadak or Jehozadak could legitimately be translated *YHWH is righteous* or maybe *the righteous God.* As explicitly stated in Ezra and Nehemiah, the son of Jozadak [the righteous God] also has the name *Jeshua* [Yeshua; יֵשׁוּעַ]. The implications of this are very profound.

The Name of the High Priest who is Crowned King

Is it possible that, within these cryptic passages, the name of the one who is to come and who will be *"my"* servant, *"the"* Branch, and both king <u>and</u> high priest is actually "spelled out"? This may be beyond the scope of this study but the point is this: the term *"servant"* used throughout the Tanach and, in particular, the servant songs of Isaiah, is a multi-faceted concept that encompasses the nation, specific individuals and one who is to come and fulfil messianic expectations. An explicit example of this truth is the third servant song found in Isaiah 50:4-10.

The Third Servant Song

Isaiah 50:4-6 (NIV) *The Sovereign LORD has given me an instructed tongue, to know the word that sustains the weary. He wakens me morning by morning, wakens my ear to listen like one being taught. The Sovereign LORD has opened my ears, and I have not been rebellious; I have not drawn back. I offered my back to those who beat me, my cheeks to those who pulled out my beard; I did not hide my face from mocking and spitting.*

---

[22] Other examples include Jonathan, Joseph, Josiah, Jotham etc.
[23] Another example includes Jehoshaphat
[24] Jeremiah 33:16

I offered my back to those who beat me ...[25]

... my cheeks to those who pulled out my beard

---

[25] A scene from Mel Gibson's "The Passion of the Christ".

The third song continues:

Isaiah 50:7-10 (NIV) *Because the Sovereign LORD helps me, I will not be disgraced. Therefore have I set my face like flint, and I know I will not be put to shame. He who vindicates me is near. Who then will bring charges against me? Let us face each other! Who is my accuser? Let him confront me! It is the Sovereign LORD who helps me. Who is he who will condemn me? They will all wear out like a garment; the moths will eat them up.* **Who among you fears the LORD and obeys the word of his servant?** *Let him who walks in the dark, who has no light, trust in the name of the LORD and rely on his God.*

There is a current consensus that this is a servant song even though there is only one mention of the word servant which highlighted in verse 10. The question before us is this: Does this passage describe the nation as a whole or any individual within it? I submit that it cannot mean the nation as a whole although it could possibly mean more than one individual, a remnant of the people of Israel. The reasons for this are actually quite straightforward.

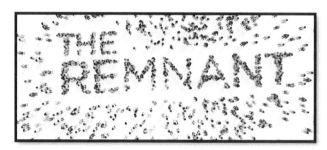

A Remnant will return to the Mighty God [26]

The speaker of these words has an instructed tongue, attentive ears and open eyes. The individual might be the prophet Isaiah himself as he has already been described as *"my"* servant.[27] He speaks presumably to the nation and says to them, *"Who among you fears the LORD and obeys the word of his servant?"*

If this is a correct interpretation, it provides clear evidence that within the nation as a whole, there are individuals that can respond to God and fulfil the calling of the servant as described in this third song. As we have seen, the Bible is consistent that the nation as a whole has neither eyes that see or ears that hear. [28]

---

[26] Isaiah 10:21
[27] Isaiah 20:3
[28] Deuteronomy 29:2-4; Isaiah 6:9-10; Isaiah 42:18-20

Inevitably, the response of the many to the few will be largely negative. The individual is physically abused, mocked and wrongfully accused. This is a consistent pattern for all those who wish to represent the truth. It explains the reality of anti-Semitism and the persecution of believers (Jewish or Christian) throughout the ages. Undeniably, this is also true in the life of Jesus.

Mark 6:2-4 (RSV) *And on the Sabbath he began to teach in the synagogue; and many who heard him were astonished, saying, "Where did this man get all this? What is the wisdom given to him? What mighty works are wrought by his hands! Is not this the carpenter, the son of Mary and brother of James and Joses and Judas and Simon, and are not his sisters here with us?" And they took offense at him. And Jesus said to them, "A prophet is not without honor, except in his own country, and among his own kin, and in his own house."*

A Prophet without Honor

Mark 15:16-20 (RSV) *And the soldiers led him away inside the palace (that is, the praetorium); and they called together the whole battalion. And they clothed him in a purple cloak, and plaiting a crown of thorns they put it on him. And they began to salute him, "Hail, King of the Jews!" And they struck his head with a reed, and spat upon him, and they knelt down in homage to him. And when they had mocked him, they stripped him of the purple cloak, and put his own clothes on him. And they led him out to crucify him.*

Although this servant song can legitimately be applied to Jesus, it does not preclude the fact that this will have been the experience of many other individuals (Jews and Gentiles). Speaking to his first disciples, Jesus marveled at this fact.

Matthew 13:16-17 (NIV) *But blessed are your eyes because they see, and your ears because they hear. For I tell you the truth, many prophets and righteous men longed to see what you see but did not see it, and to hear what you hear but did not hear it.*

"Blessed are your Eyes that See"

Furthermore, the Apostle Peter draws on this servant song in the life of Jesus as an example for others to follow.

1 Peter 2:21-23 (RSV) *For to this you have been called, because Christ also suffered for you, leaving you an example, that you should follow in his steps. He committed no sin; no guile was found on his lips. When he was reviled, he did not revile in return; when he suffered, he did not threaten; but he trusted to him who judges justly.*

Thus, in Peter's understanding, potentially any individual (Jew or Gentile) can fulfil the description of the servant in this third song in the book of Isaiah. We will have occasion to return to this theme and if this is true for the third servant song, how much more could it be true for the fourth which begins at Isaiah 52:13, continuing through to the end of chapter 53.

The Fourth Servant Song

Without doubt, the fourth servant song is the most controversial passage that we have considered thus far. The evangelical consensus is that the suffering servant who is being described is Jesus. The New Testament gives credence to this position.

Matthew 8:17 (NIV) *This was to fulfil what was spoken through the prophet Isaiah: "He took up our infirmities and carried our diseases."*

And the Apostle Peter continues the discourse that we have considered.

1 Peter 2:24-25 (RSV) *He himself bore our sins in his body on the tree, that we might die to sin and live to righteousness. By his wounds you have been healed. For you were straying like sheep, but have now returned to the Shepherd and Guardian of your souls.*

In this last passage, Peter applies both the third and the fourth servant songs to Jesus. However, I wish to emphasize the fact that it does not preclude the possibility of other interpretations. All of the servant songs are multifaceted. For the Christian world to insist that this passage, in particular, can **only** be applied to Jesus and for Jewish scholarship to insist that this can **only** be applied to the nation of Israel does total violence to the beauty and the depth of information that can be understood from these passages of Scripture.

The question before us is why are these very extreme non-biblical positions maintained by the evangelical Christian world and by Jewish scholarship? The evangelical Christian desire to *"read"* Jesus **exclusively** into **some** of these passages leads to theological incoherence. Furthermore, and far more sinister, this Christological imperative actually leads to clear examples of mistranslation of the Hebrew Scriptures. There are many examples of this and we will consider some of them when we look at the fourth servant song in detail. This is totally counterproductive. I re-iterate the servant songs are multi-faceted. They are neither one thing nor the other. The term *"servant"* refers to the nation, to specific individuals within it and to one who will fulfill all messianic expectations.

The response of Jewish scholarship, in particular, while understandable, is likewise flawed. Historically, some (although not all) Jewish theologians considered that the suffering servant of Isaiah is the Messiah.[29] However, almost without exception, modern Jewish scholarship insists that the only interpretation of servant (particularly in the fourth servant song) is the nation of Israel. Why is this? As far as I can tell, there are two obvious reasons.

---

[29] An example is the Rabbi Moses who wrote in the 11th Century a commentary on Genesis: "From the beginning God has made a covenant with the Messiah and told Him, 'My righteous Messiah, those who are entrusted to you, their sins will bring you into a heavy yoke'. And He answered, 'I gladly accept all these agonies in order that not one of Israel should be lost.' Immediately, the Messiah accepted all agonies with love, as it is written: 'He was oppressed and he was afflicted'.

Another example is in the Siphre which is part of the Talmud. "Rabbi Jose the Galilean said, 'Come and learn the merits of the King Messiah and the reward of the Just - from the first man who received but one commandment, a prohibition, and transgressed it. Consider how many deaths were inflicted upon himself, upon his own generation, and upon those who followed them, till the end of all generations. Which attribute is greater, the attribute of goodness, or the attribute of vengeance?'- He answered, 'The attribute of goodness is greater, and the attribute of vengeance is the less.' - 'How much more then, will the King Messiah, who endures affliction and pains for the transgressions (as it is written, 'He was wounded,' etc.), justify all generations. This is the meaning of the word, 'And the LORD made the iniquity of us all to meet upon Him' (Isaiah.53:6)."

1. The Holocaust changed everything for the Jewish people. How is it that the God of Israel allowed six million Jewish people to go to their deaths? There has to be a reason if he is a loving God and not a cruel tyrant. If their deaths (and the deaths of countless millions of Jewish martyrs throughout the centuries) is to bring atonement for sins (their own and perhaps the sins of the Gentile nations) then, maybe, this can explain it. However, this position cannot be supported in the Tanach. There must be other reasons why God allowed the Holocaust.

"My God, My God, Why have you Forsaken Me?" [30]

2. With an increase in modern evangelistic movements such as *"Jews for Jesus"*, there has been a significant backlash in certain Jewish theological circles. For example, *"Messiah Truth"* and *"Outreach Judaism"* with their associated websites [31] provide seminars and other teaching materials to counter missionary arguments. In particular, Christological errors in translation and the ignorance of biblical context of Messianic prophecy are highlighted. There is truth in their concerns. Some zealous evangelists with sincere motives can be totally unfamiliar with the historical context of many of the prophetic passages in the Tanach. In some cases, verses can be lifted out of context and, furthermore, many English translations can be very unhelpful, some being worse than others. Christians need to be aware of this.

---

[30] The Fourth Panel of the Fountain of Tears

[31] http://messiahtruth.yuku.com/; http://www.outreachjudaism.org/

However, the maintenance of these extreme positions, while historically understandable, will never lead to any constructive dialogue. We will remain in our theological trenches and there will be no progress. We need to step out into *"theological no-man's land"* and face each other. I wish to re-iterate once again that the term *"servant"* in the Tanach and in the book of Isaiah, in particular, has multiple meanings. It can mean the nation, specific individuals (a remnant) and, according to at least some classical Jewish scholarship, the Messiah himself.

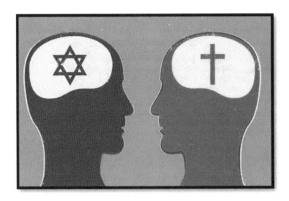

Face to Face

We need to look at the fourth song in some detail. It begins as follows.

Isaiah 52:13-15a (NIV) *See, my servant will act wisely; he will be raised and lifted up and highly exalted. Just as there were many who were appalled at him - his appearance was so disfigured beyond that of any man and his form marred beyond human likeness - so will he sprinkle many nations.*

Who is speaking in these verses? The answer is actually quite simple; God (through the prophet Isaiah) is speaking about his servant. Who is the servant? Is it the nation of Israel or is it an individual? I believe that it is **both.** However, at this moment in history, these words can certainly be applied legitimately to Jesus.

Philippians 2:5-11 (NIV) *Your attitude should be the same as that of Christ Jesus: who, being in very nature God, did not consider equality with God something to be grasped, but made himself nothing, taking the **very nature of a servant**, being made in human likeness. And being found in appearance as a man, he humbled himself and became obedient to death, even death on a cross! Therefore God **exalted** him to the highest place and gave him the name that is above every name, that at the name of Jesus every knee should bow, in heaven and on earth and under the earth, and every tongue confess that Jesus Christ is Lord, to the glory of God the Father.*

Taking the Form of a Servant

It is worth pointing out that there are aspects contained within these verses that are to be emulated by individual believers.[32] We are to make ourselves nothing, taking the very nature of a servant. We hear the words of Jesus:

Matthew 23:11-12 (RSV) *He who is greatest among you shall be your servant; whoever exalts himself will be humbled, and whoever humbles himself will be exalted.*

So do these words in Isaiah 52 describe the nation as a whole? I would maintain that at this time in history they do not. However, I also wish to argue in this chapter and in the chapters following that they **will be** fulfilled in the life of the **entire** nation. My reasoning for this is the prophetic context of these verses which is often overlooked in Christian exegesis.

Isaiah 52:8-12 (NIV) *Listen! Your watchmen lift up their voices; together they shout for joy. When the LORD returns to Zion, they will see it with their own eyes. Burst into songs of joy together, you ruins of Jerusalem, for the LORD has comforted his people, he has redeemed Jerusalem. The LORD will lay bare his holy arm in the sight of all the nations, and all the ends of the earth will see the salvation of our God. Depart, depart, go out from there! Touch no unclean thing! Come out from it and be pure, you who carry the vessels of the LORD. But you will not leave in haste or go in flight; for the LORD will go before you, the God of Israel will be your rear guard.*

---

[32] In other words, your attitude should be the same as that of Christ Jesus (Philippians 2:5)

This sets this passage into a future time when the Lord returns to Zion. They (i.e. the nation as a whole) will see it, they will be comforted and they will have been redeemed. This is also alluded to in the first verses of chapter 40 which sets the scene for the second part of the book of Isaiah.

Isaiah 40:1-5 (RSV) *Comfort, comfort my people, says your God. Speak tenderly to Jerusalem, and cry to her that her warfare is ended, that her iniquity is pardoned, that she has received from the LORD's hand double for all her sins. A voice cries: "In the wilderness prepare the way of the LORD, make straight in the desert a highway for our God. Every valley shall be lifted up, and every mountain and hill be made low; the uneven ground shall become level, and the rough places a plain. And the glory of the LORD shall be revealed, and all flesh shall see it together, for the mouth of the LORD has spoken."*

In the Desert, Prepare the Way for the Lord

All mankind will see the glory of the Lord revealed in the land of Israel. Currently, it is like a desert spiritually and there is a lot of work to be done both by Christian believers and by the nation of Israel. Dialogue would be a good start.

The next verses of this fourth servant song are as follows.

Isaiah 52:15b-53:1 (NIV) *And kings will shut their mouths because of him. For what they were not told, they will see, and what they have not heard, they will understand. Who has believed our message and to whom has the arm of the LORD been revealed?*

This fragment of the song is a perfect illustration of the sometimes very inappropriate way passages of scripture are divided up into chapter and verse. Something is to happen that will stop the world in its tracks. I believe that God through the prophet Ezekiel has something to say about this.

Ezekiel 39:7-8 (RSV) *And my holy name I will make known in the midst of my people Israel; and I will not let my holy name be profaned any more; and the nations shall know that I am the LORD, the Holy One in Israel. Behold, it is coming and it will be brought about, says the Lord GOD. That is the day of which I have spoken.*

When this day dawns, the people of Israel will be exalted in the eyes of the nations. They will fulfill their irrevocable destiny and calling to be a light to the Gentiles. They will be seen as the servant of the Lord. However, there is an issue here that needs further clarification, namely, who is actually saying *"Who has believed our message and to whom has the arm of the LORD been revealed?"* In the context of the preceding verse, we may conclude that it could be the kings of the earth as, for example, Rabbi Tovia Singer maintains:

> *The speakers in this most-debated chapter are the stunned kings of nations who will bear witness to the messianic age and the final vindication of the Jewish people following their long and bitter exile. "Who would have believed our report?" the astonished and contrite world leaders wonder aloud in their dazed bewilderment.* [33]

The next verse to consider in this servant song is:

Isaiah 53:2 (NIV) *He grew up before him like a tender shoot, and like a root out of dry ground. He had no beauty or majesty to attract us to him, nothing in his appearance that we should desire him.*

Now who is speaking? Rabbi Singer maintains that it is still the kings of the earth. It is possible but we certainly cannot be dogmatic about it. However, what is far more significant is to discover who is *"he"* and who is *"him"* in the first part of the sentence? What does it mean when it says *"He grew up before him like a tender shoot and like a root out of dry ground."* ? [34]

---

[33] http://www.outreachjudaism.org/articles/rabbinic-53.html

[34] Apparently, Maimonides (1135-1204) wrote to Rabbi Jacob Alfajumi: "Likewise said Isaiah that He (Messiah) would appear without acknowledging a father or mother: 'He grew up before him as a tender plant and as a root out of a dry ground' etc. (Isaiah 53:2)."

A Root out of Dry Ground

Presumably, the *"him"* mentioned here is God. Would the kings of the earth make such a statement? As far as the *"he"* is concerned, I wish to maintain that it can be **both** an individual and the nation of Israel as a whole.

Historically, as we have already considered, some Jewish exegesis has concluded that this passage is describing the suffering of the Messiah, even Messiah, son of Joseph,[35] in contradistinction to the Messianic King, Messiah, and son of David. The reason for this, among many, may be the allusion in this verse to the Messianic King who is also called the root of Jesse in earlier chapters in the book of Isaiah.

Isaiah 11:1 (RSV) *There shall come forth a shoot from the stump of Jesse, and a branch shall grow out of his roots.*

Isaiah 11:10-12 (RSV) *In that day the root of Jesse shall stand as an ensign to the peoples; him shall the nations seek, and his dwellings shall be glorious. In that day the Lord will extend his hand yet a second time to recover the remnant which is left of his people, from Assyria, from Egypt, from Pathros, from Ethiopia, from Elam, from Shinar, from Hamath, and from the coastlands of the sea. He will raise an ensign for the nations, and will assemble the outcasts of Israel, and gather the dispersed of Judah from the four corners of the earth.*

---

[35] http://en.wikipedia.org/wiki/Messiah_ben_Joseph

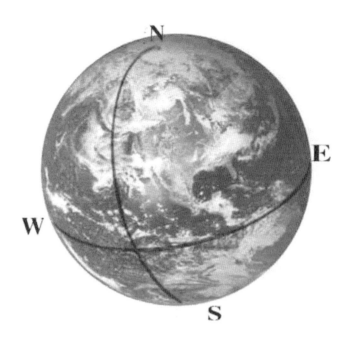

The Four Quarters of the Earth

This is a remarkable passage because it seems to indicate that the Messiah (i.e. the root of Jesse) will be in some sort of relationship with the nations (Gentiles) who will rally to him BEFORE he (i.e. the Messiah) reaches out his hand to gather the exiles of Israel. He is reaching out his hand a second time in the eyes of Isaiah. The first gathering was from Babylon; the second gathering is from the four quarters of the earth.

However, the words[36] will also apply to the nation of Israel.

Isaiah 37:31-32 (RSV) *And the surviving remnant of the house of Judah shall again take root downward, and bear fruit upward; for out of Jerusalem shall go forth a remnant, and out of Mount Zion a band of survivors. The zeal of the LORD of hosts will accomplish this.*

In the *"days to come"*, we will see this fulfilled to the letter.[37]

---

[36] Isaiah 53:2
[37] See also Revelation 7:4-8 and Revelation 14:1

The next verse to consider in this servant song is:

Isaiah 53:3 (NIV) *He was despised and rejected by men, a man of sorrows, and familiar with suffering. Like one from whom men hide their faces he was despised, and we esteemed him not.*

I have absolutely no doubt that this verse can be applied to the nation of Israel **and** to Jesus. The question before us is who is the *"we"* who esteemed him not and who is the *"him"*? There are two legitimate answers.

Despised and Rejected by Men (1)

1. If the speakers of these words are the kings of the nations as is maintained in some modern Jewish theology, then the *"we"* is the Gentile nations and the *"him"* could be interpreted as the nation of Israel. This is a clear description of historic anti-Semitism and I believe it to be a valid interpretation. However, even this does not preclude the legitimacy of the *"him"* being Jesus. The world has been no friend to Jesus and his followers.

John 15:18-19 (RSV) *If the world hates you, know that it has hated me before it hated you. If you were of the world, the world would love its own; but because you are not of the world, but I chose you out of the world, therefore the world hates you.*

Luke 21:16-17 (RSV) *You will be delivered up even by parents and brothers and kinsmen and friends, and some of you they will put to death; you will be hated by all for my name's sake.*

Some have even suggested that the root of anti-Semitism is hatred of Jesus.

2. If the *"he"* is Jesus, then the *"we"* could be interpreted as the nation of Israel. He was despised and rejected and he continues to be so when we consider the nation as a whole.

Despised and Rejected by Men (2)

John 1:11 (NIV) *He came to that which was his own, but his own did not receive him.*

And Paul is explicit:

Romans 11:28-29 (NIV) *As far as the gospel is concerned, they [Israel] are enemies on your account; but as far as election is concerned, they are loved on account of the patriarchs, for God's gifts and his call are irrevocable.*

If we consider that the *"he"* in this verse may be applied to either Jesus or Israel, then the *"we"* is **both** Jews and Gentiles. This is supported by Paul's exegesis in Romans chapter 11.

Romans 11:30-32 (KJV) *For as ye in times past have not believed God, yet have now obtained mercy through their unbelief: Even so have these also now not believed, that through your mercy they also may obtain mercy. For God hath concluded them all in unbelief [Jew and Gentile] that he might have mercy upon all.*

The next verses to consider in this servant song are:

Isaiah 53:4-5 (NIV) *Surely he took up our infirmities and carried our sorrows, yet we considered him stricken by God, smitten by him, and afflicted. But he was pierced for our transgressions, he was crushed for our iniquities; the punishment that brought us peace was upon him, and by his wounds we are healed.*

Rabbi Singer[38] wishes to point out that there is a clear mistranslation in verse five. He suggests that a more accurate translation is *"by his wounds, we WERE healed"*. This is an interesting point because I do not think there is one English translation of the Bible that puts this verse in the past tense.

The Hebrew words so translated are נִרְפָּא־לָנוּ transliterated nirpa-lanu. As far as I can tell, it *could* possibly mean either *"we are healed"* or *"we were healed"*. It is a passive (nifal) form of the verb that is built on the three letter root:

resh [ר] pey [פ] alef [א]

In all its various verbal forms, it carries the meaning of to cure (or to be cured), to heal (or to be healed), to get well or to recover (or to be recovered).

However, the form of the verb in Isaiah 53:5 is, unquestionably, **third person masculine singular** [i.e. he] and can be BOTH present or past [i.e. נִרְפָּא]. The "lanu" is relatively straightforward; it means *"to us"* or *"for us"* or even just "us". In other words, the verse could be translated *"by his wounds, he heals (or he healed) us"*. Again to claim that it is only past **or** present is rather counter-productive.

The next verse to consider in this servant song is:

Isaiah 53:6 (NIV) *We all, like sheep, have gone astray, each of us has turned to his own way; and the LORD has laid on **him** the iniquity of us all.*

---

[38] Rabbi Tovia Singer (1996) In-depth Study Guide to the "Let's Get Biblical!" Tape Series Page 33.

We all like Sheep have gone astray

Can the *"him"* in this verse apply to the nation of Israel? In one way, I think it can. The Jewish people have suffered at the hands of the Gentile nations. Since the fall of Jerusalem beginning in 70 CE, the Jewish people have been persecuted like no other nation. This was graphically described in the book of Deuteronomy.

Deuteronomy 28:62-65 (RSV)   *Whereas you were as the stars of heaven for multitude, you shall be left few in number; because you did not obey the voice of the LORD your God. And as the LORD took delight in doing you good and multiplying you, so the LORD will take delight in bringing ruin upon you and destroying you; and you shall be plucked off the land which you are entering to take possession of it. And the LORD will scatter you among all peoples, from one end of the earth to the other; and there you shall serve other gods, of wood and stone, which neither you nor your fathers have known. And among these nations you shall find no ease, and there shall be no rest for the sole of your foot; but the LORD will give you there a trembling heart, and failing eyes, and a languishing soul.*

However, it matters not who is speaking the words in the fourth servant song. It can be the prophet Isaiah or the kings of the earth. There is no suggestion in the Tanach that the people of Israel would suffer for anything other than their own sin. However, Rabbi Singer [39] wants to persuade us that the Jewish people have suffered because of the iniquity of the nations [40] and that this is the **only** legitimate interpretation of this verse. He gives two passages of scripture to support his position.

---

[39] I wish to stress that I have the greatest respect for Rabbi Tovia Singer. Although we disagree on many fundamental issues, he has taught me a great deal. I am inspired by his passion for the Tanach. Furthermore, his teaching enables a much greater appreciation of the historical context of the prophetic scriptures.

[40] There is a subtle distinction to be made here. There is no doubt that the Jewish people have suffered because of the iniquity of the nations. Anti-Semitism is iniquitous. However, there can be no suggestion that the suffering of the Jewish people provides atonement for the iniquity of the nations.

Firstly, **Ezekiel 36:6-7 (RSV)** *Prophesy concerning the land of Israel, and say to the mountains and hills, to the ravines and valleys, Thus says the Lord GOD: Behold, I speak in my jealous wrath, because you have suffered the reproach of the nations; therefore thus says the Lord GOD: I swear that the nations that are round about you shall themselves suffer reproach.*

With very great respect to Rabbi Singer, nowhere in this Bible passage is there any indication that Israel carries the iniquities of the other nations leading to any healing or atonement. In fact, it is completely the opposite since the Bible makes it abundantly clear that the other nations will be judged on the basis of their response to the nation of Israel

Isaiah 60:12 (NIV) *For the nation or kingdom that will not serve you will perish; it will be utterly ruined.*[41]

Joel 3:1-2 (RSV) *For behold, in those days and at that time, when I restore the fortunes of Judah and Jerusalem, I will gather all the nations and bring them down to the valley of Jehoshaphat, and I will enter into judgment with them there, on account of my people and my heritage Israel, because they have scattered them among the nations, and have divided up my land.*

The other passage that Rabbi Singer chooses to illustrate his position is very significant.

Jeremiah 30:8-13 (RSV) *And it shall come to pass in that day, says the LORD of hosts, that I will break the yoke from off their neck, and I will burst their bonds, and strangers shall no more make servants of them. But they shall serve the LORD their God and David their king, whom I will raise up for them. "Then fear not, O Jacob my servant, says the LORD, nor be dismayed, O Israel; for lo, I will save you from afar, and your offspring from the land of their captivity. Jacob shall return and have quiet and ease, and none shall make him afraid. For I am with you to save you, says the LORD; I will make a full end of all the nations among whom I scattered you, but of you I will not make a full end. I will chasten you in just measure, and I will by no means leave you unpunished. "For thus says the LORD: Your hurt is incurable, and your wound is grievous. There is none to uphold your cause, no medicine for your wound, no healing for you.*

Again in this amazing passage, there is not the slightest indication that Israel carries the iniquities of the nations leading to atonement. In fact, God says that he will destroy the nations that have enslaved the people of Israel. The reason the Rabbi includes this passage is because of the description that Israel is left wounded.

---

[41] It is interesting to note that the Gentile nations are also called to be servants.

The simple fact is Israel **is** wounded. Centuries of persecution by the nations, and the church in particular, culminating in the Holocaust, has profoundly injured them, apparently beyond healing and beyond hope. **But the good Rabbi fails to go on.**

Jeremiah 30:14-17 (RSV) *All your lovers have forgotten you; they care nothing for you; for I have dealt you the blow of an enemy, the punishment of a merciless foe, because your guilt is great, because your sins are flagrant. Why do you cry out over your hurt? Your pain is incurable. Because your guilt is great, because your sins are flagrant, I have done these things to you. Therefore all who devour you shall be devoured, and all your foes, every one of them, shall go into captivity; those who despoil you shall become a spoil, and all who prey on you I will make a prey.* **For I will restore health to you, and your wounds I will heal,** *says the LORD, because they have called you an outcast: 'It is Zion, for whom no one cares'* .

I will heal you [Hebrew: אֶרְפָּאֵךְ]

This is surely one of the greatest promises in the Bible. No-one can heal the open and festering wound of the people of Israel apart from God himself.[42] And he has promised *"I will restore you to health and heal your wounds"*. One day, I hope in the not too distant future, the nation of Israel will cry out לָנוּ־ נִרְפָּא; [he] heals us; [he] has healed us!

---

[42] It is interesting to note that the emphatic pronoun in Hebrew "hoo" (heh, vav, aleph) appears in the key verses describing the servant's sin bearing and redemptive suffering (53:4,5,7,11,12). This is an example of a cryptic identification between the servant and YHWH. In almost most every case in Isaiah 40-55 except Isaiah 41:7 & 42:22, this emphatic pronoun refers to YHWH (Isa 41:4; 42:8; 43:10, 13; 43:25; 45:18, 18; 46:4; 48:12; 51:12; 52:6, 6).

The next verse in the fourth servant song is as follows.

Isaiah 53:7 (NIV) *He was oppressed and afflicted, yet he did not open his mouth; he was led like a lamb to the slaughter, and as a sheep before her shearers is silent, so he did not open his mouth.*

This verse is the experience of Jesus and the experience of those that perished in the Holocaust. It is rather pointless trying to make out that Jesus was actually not always silent and that he spoke some words and indeed cried out several times in a loud voice. Without doubt, this is also true for many entering the gas chambers. However, in both cases, it is appropriate to see both Jesus and the people of Israel as a lamb being led to the slaughter with minimal resistance. [43]

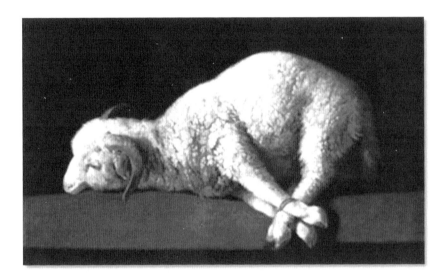

The Sacrifice Lamb

Psalm 44:22 (NIV) *Yet for your sake we face death all day long; we are considered as sheep to be slaughtered.* [44]

Zechariah 13:7 (RSV) *"Awake, O sword, against my shepherd, against the man who stands next to me," says the LORD of hosts. "Strike the shepherd, that the sheep may be scattered; I will turn my hand against the little ones".*

These words are also applied to Jesus and his disciples.[45] Another significant passage is found in the book of Acts.

---

[43] It is important to realise that there are many examples of Jewish resistance during the Second World War.

[44] Quoted by Paul in Romans 8:36

[45] Matthew 26:31; Mark 14:27

Acts 8:32-35 (RSV) *Now the passage of the scripture which he was reading was this: "As a sheep led to the slaughter or a lamb before its shearer is dumb, so he opens not his mouth. In his humiliation justice was denied him. Who can describe his generation? For his life is taken up from the earth." And the eunuch said to Philip, "About whom, pray, does the prophet say this, about himself or about someone else?" Then Philip opened his mouth, and beginning with this scripture he told him the good news of Jesus.*

The next verse in the fourth servant song is as follows.

Isaiah 53:8a (NIV) *By oppression and judgment he was taken away. And who can speak of his descendants?*

The people of Israel have been led away by oppression and judgment but out of the ashes of the Holocaust, the nation has been re-established as God promised.

Out of the Ashes

Isaiah 49:20-22 (RSV) *The children born in the time of your bereavement will yet say in your ears: 'The place is too narrow for me; make room for me to dwell in.' Then you will say in your heart: 'Who has borne me these? I was bereaved and barren, exiled and put away, but who has brought up these? Behold, I was left alone; whence then have these come?'" Thus says the Lord GOD: "Behold, I will lift up my hand to the nations, and raise my signal to the peoples; and they shall bring your sons in their bosom, and your daughters shall be carried on their shoulders.*

Jeremiah 30:20 (NIV) *Their children will be as in days of old, and their community will be established before me; I will punish all who oppress them.*

Can these words apply to Jesus? The prologue of John's Gospel states.

John 1:11-13 (NIV) *He came to that which was his own, but his own did not receive him. Yet to all who received him, to those who believed in his name, he gave the right to become children[46] of God - children born not of natural descent, nor of human decision or a husband's will, but born of God.*

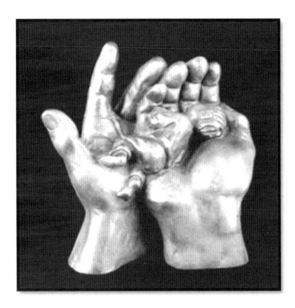

A Child of God [47]

The next verse in the fourth servant song is as follows.

Isaiah 53:8b (NIV) *For he was cut off from the land of the living; for the transgression of my people he was stricken.*

Rabbi Singer has pointed out another mistranslation in the English versions of this passage. He suggests that the last part of verse 8 should read, *"because of the transgression of my people, a plague befell **them**".*[48] The *"them"* <u>has</u> to refer to the people of Israel. An individual is not a *"them".*

---

[46] This text in no way suggests that believers are Jesus' children, but children of the Father through faith in Jesus. In the New Testament there is the distinction between natural children (Jewish people) and adopted children which is what John 1:11-13 is describing. This adoption happens when people believe in his name. This adoption does not distinguish between ethnicities.

[47] The Calling - a sculpture by Rick Wienecke — visit www.castingseeds.com

[48] Rabbi Tovia Singer (1996) In-depth Study Guide to the "Let's Get Biblical!" Tape Series Page 34. The Hebrew here is transliterated "lamo" (Lamed, mem, vav), a poetic form that is said to usually mean **for** or **to** **them** (see Gesenius 102) but literally means **for** or **to** <u>him.</u>

More recently, Rabbi Singer has stated:

> *Therefore, Isaiah 53:8 concludes with their stunning confession, "for the transgressions of my people [the gentile nations] they [the Jews] were stricken." The fact that the servant is spoken of in the third person, plural illustrates beyond doubt that the servant is a nation rather than a single individual.* [49]

With great respect to the Rabbi, what he is suggesting is that the Jewish people have been struck **for** the transgression of Gentiles. This is totally contrary to the teaching of the Tanach.

Accordingly, we need to look again at this complex Hebrew phrase as it is written in the Masoretic text,[50] namely,

מִפֶּשַׁע עַמִּי נֶגַע לָמוֹ

This may be transliterated as "mi-pesha ami nayga lamo".

Firstly, in this version, there is no verb in this particular phrase. Literally, the words mean: from (perhaps out of) transgression [מִפֶּשַׁע], my people [עַמִּי], a plague [נֶגַע], to (perhaps on) them [לָמוֹ]. It is vital to appreciate that the word נֶגַע in this form **is a noun and not a verb**. Here are some examples of its use in the Torah.

Exodus 11:1 (NIV) *Now the LORD said to Moses, "I will bring one more* **plague** [נֶגַע] *on Pharaoh and on Egypt. After that, he will let you go from here, and when he does, he will drive you out completely.*

Leviticus 13:9 (KJV) *When the* **plague** [נֶגַע] *of leprosy is in a man, then he shall be brought unto the priest.*

---

[49] http://www.outreachjudaism.org/articles/rabbinic-53.html

[50] The Masoretic Text (MT) is the authorized Hebrew text of the Jewish Bible. While the Masoretic Text defines the books of the Jewish canon, it also defines the precise letter-text of these biblical books, with their vocalization and accentuation known as the Masorah. The MT is also widely used as the basis for translations of the Old Testament in Protestant Bibles. The MT was primarily copied, edited and distributed by a group of Jews known as the Masoretes between the 7th and 10th centuries CE [taken from http://en.wikipedia.org/wiki/Masoretic_Text].

As mentioned previously, most Hebrew words are based on a three letter root. The root here is nun [נ], gimel [ג], ayin [ע]. From this root, nouns and verbs are formed by the use of different prefixes, suffixes and vocalization marks.

There are **verbs** in the Tanach which are based on this root. An example is.

Isaiah 6:7 (NIV) *With it **he touched** my mouth and said, "See, this has touched your lips; your guilt is taken away and your sin atoned for."*

The verb *"to touch"* is based on the same root but the vocalization is different when the word is a verb. In the above verse, the verb is נָגַע. This is **exactly** the form of the verb in modern Hebrew which is in the third person masculine singular in the past tense. In other words, it means *"he touched"*.

The noun form of the root is נֶגַע and it is this form that is in Isaiah 53:8. This noun is translated plague but is also occurs as a stroke, wound, bruise or disease in the Tanach. So how do we translate this particular Hebrew phrase? In order to do so, we <u>have</u> to add some words that are not there in the Hebrew. It could be as follows:

> From [the] transgression [of] my people, a plague [is] on them

The only verb added to this translation is *"is"* which has no Hebrew equivalent as the present tense of the verb *"to be"* is not used. Accordingly, if this translation is legitimate, the verse is simply stating that as a result of their transgressions, they have suffered as described in Deuteronomy.

Deuteronomy 28:20-22 (RSV) *The LORD will send upon you curses, confusion, and frustration, in all that you undertake to do, until you are destroyed and perish quickly, on account of the evil of your doings, because you have forsaken me. The LORD will make the pestilence cleave to you until he has consumed you off the land which you are entering to take possession of it. The LORD will smite you with consumption, and with fever, inflammation, and fiery heat, and with drought, and with blasting, and with mildew; they shall pursue you until you perish.*

---

51 Gesenius inaugurated in Semitic language studies a modern philological approach such as had been developed in Indo-European linguistics. His Hebrew grammar (1815; edited and enlarged by E. Kautzsch; 2nd English edition revised according to the 28th German edition by A.E. Cowley, 1910) and his Hebrew and Chaldee (i.e., Aramaic) dictionary (1810–13; Eng. trans., 1959) taught generations of scholars, and have been kept alive into the 21st century in various editions and translations. Gesenius also laid the basis for Semitic epigraphy, collecting and deciphering the Phoenician inscriptions known in his time [taken from http://www.britannica.com/EBchecked/topic/232032/Wilhelm-Gesenius]

So was *"He"* Stricken?

As indicated in footnote 48, the literal rendering of נֶגַע לָמוֹ is *'stroke to him'* . Wilhelm Gesenius (1786-1842) [51] correctly concluded that the Hebrew לָמוֹ [lamo] is almost without exception translated as *"them"*.

This is a clear example of the nation being regarded as a single entity. It is interesting to note, however, that the Septuagint [52] translates Isaiah 53:8b as follows:

$$\dot{\alpha}\pi\grave{o} \ \tau\hat{\omega}\nu \ \dot{\alpha}\nu o\mu\iota\hat{\omega}\nu \ \tauo\hat{\upsilon} \ \lambda\alpha o\hat{\upsilon} \ \mu o\upsilon \ \mathring{\eta}\chi\theta\eta \ \epsilon\mathring{\iota}\varsigma \ \theta\acute{\alpha}\nu\alpha\tau o\nu$$

The literal translation is:

because of the transgression of my people <u>he</u> was led to death.

Of course, the singular *"he"* does not necessarily mean that the passage is speaking of an individual or of the nation as a single entity. The equivocal plural-singular form highlights the enigmatic nature of this passage and again underlines the multifaceted informational content in the way the passage can be translated. I stress it is neither one thing nor the other but BOTH.

---

[52] The translation of the Hebrew Scriptures in Koine Greek begun in Alexandria in the third century BCE and completed in 132 BCE. The Septuagint contains more books than the contemporary Hebrew Canon including those that are now part of the Apocrypha which is still included in the Roman Catholic Bible.

This Text of Isaiah 53:8b in the Isaiah Scroll found at Qumran

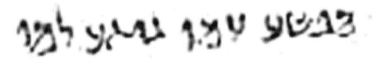

A. The Phrase as it appears in the Isaiah Scroll

מפשע עמו נוגע למו

B. A Printed Version for Comparison

מִפֶּשַׁע עַמִּי נֶגַע לָמוֹ

C. The Masoretic Text for Comparison

A Comparison of Texts

From the above figure, we can see that there are some differences between the Masoretic text and the Hebrew text in the Isaiah Scroll found in Qumran in 1947. This scroll probably pre-dates the final form of the Masoretic text by at least 800 years. It certainly pre-dates the Christian era. Firstly, we notice is that the Isaiah Scroll does not have any vocalization marks. Consequently, one cannot be certain how it was pronounced although it might be transliterated as:

mi-pesha amo nuga lamo.

Secondly, the noun [נֶגַע transliterated nayga] in the Masoretic text **appears as a verb [נוגע transliterated nuga]** in the Qumran text. This verb is in the past tense and is third person masculine singular. It is also a passive form of the verb (Pu'al). In modern Hebrew, it simply means *"he was afflicted".*[53]

However, it does not tell us who the *"he"* is.

---

[53] See, for example, 201 Hebrew Verbs (1970) New York: Barron's Educational Series, page 200

Thirdly, and perhaps most important of all, עַמִּי (ami; my people) in the Masoretic text is עַמּוֹ (amo; his people) in the Isaiah scroll. The significance of this change cannot be overstated. The translation of the text pre-dating the Masoretic text and the Christian era states plainly, *"from [the] transgression [of] his people, he was afflicted for them"*.

The point is this: it matters not who is speaking these words. Rabbi Singer maintains that it is the kings of the nations writing a report in stunned amazement. Perhaps so, but the simple fact is *"he"* has suffered for the sins of *"his"* own people. Whoever, the *"he"*, is, *"he"* is a representative of *"his"* people.

Obviously Jesus qualifies as that representative.

2 Corinthians 5:21 (NIV) *God made him who had no sin to be sin for us, so that in him we might become the righteousness of God.*

It does not, however, preclude the possibility that a righteous remnant, within the nation as a whole, might suffer for the sins of their own people.

Remarkably, this is alluded to by Rabbi Singer.

> According to rabbinic thought, however, when Isaiah speaks of the "servant," the prophet is not speaking of all the Jewish people. Rather, the "servant" in these uplifting prophetic hymns refers to the righteous remnant of Israel, the most pious of the nation. The faithful members of Israel who willingly suffer for Heaven's sake are identified in Tanach as God's servant. These are the devout that call upon the name of the Lord (43:7), bear witness to His unity (43:11), and are therefore charged to bring back the rest of Jacob (49:5)... In rabbinic thought, all of God's faithful, gentiles included (Zechariah 13:8-9), endure suffering on behalf of God (Isaiah 40:2; Zechariah 1:15). Thus, Jewish leaders of the past, such as Moses and Jeremiah, Rabbi Akiva, as well as future eschatological figures, such as the messiah ben Joseph and the messiah ben David, are held up in rabbinic literature as individuals who exemplify the "servant" who willingly suffers on behalf of Heaven.[54]

---

[54] http://www.outreachjudaism.org/articles/rabbinic-53.html

The next verse in the fourth servant song is as follows.

Isaiah 53:9 (NIV) *He was assigned a grave with the wicked and with the rich in his death, though he had done no violence, nor was any deceit in his mouth.*

Apparently, there is another problem of translation here. The word *"death"* is actually in a plural form in the Masoretic text. This is shown below:

$$\text{וְאֶת־עָשִׁיר בְּמֹתָיו}$$

This is transliterated v'et ashir b'motaiv and is literally *"and the rich (man) in his deaths"*. It is therefore difficult to see how this relates to one man. There is, however, something of a conundrum here. As written in the Masoretic text, the word "motaiv" [מֹתָיו] is in the plural form, whereas the word "ashir" [עָשִׁיר] is singular. In order to try to solve this conundrum we need to revisit alternative and more ancient texts.

Isaiah 53:9a in the Septuagint

In the Septuagint translation, which was essentially completed in the second century BCE, we read the following:

$$\text{καὶ τοὺς πλουσίους ἀντὶ τοῦ θανάτου}$$

The word translated *"death"* [i.e. θανάτου] is a masculine singular noun. The exact form of this word is used throughout the Septuagint translation of the Tanach. Two interesting example of this are:

Deuteronomy 21:22-23 (NIV) *If a man guilty of a capital offense is put to death [θανάτου] and his body is hung on a tree, you must not leave his body on the tree overnight. Be sure to bury him that same day, because anyone who is hung on a tree is under God's curse.*

Psalm 23:4 (NIV) *Even though I walk through the valley of the shadow of death [θανάτου], I will fear no evil, for you are with me …*

Every example of the use of θανάτου in the Septuagint is likewise in the singular. This is not surprising. It does not, however, preclude the possibility of the *"he"* being representative of a people as well as an individual. In English, we occasionally use the word *"deaths"*. For example, and relevant to our discussion, we speak of the six million going to their *"death"* or *"deaths"* in the Holocaust. There are a few examples of the word *"deaths"* in the Tanach.

Jeremiah 16:4 (KJV) *They shall die of grievous **deaths** …*

Ezekiel 28:8 (KJV) *They shall bring thee down to the pit, and thou shalt die the **deaths** of them that are slain in the midst of the seas.*

In each case, the Greek word translated *"deaths"* in the Septuagint is θανάτῳ. This is in a plural form (i.e. their death or deaths). It is not the word used in the Septuagint translation of Isaiah 53:9a [θανάτου]. There is also an example of *"deaths"* in the New Testament.

2 Corinthians 11:23 (KJV) *… in labors more abundant, in stripes above measure, in prisons more frequent, in **deaths** oft …*

The Greek word used here is θανάτοις which is the masculine plural form and literally means *"deaths"*. This word form does not occur at all in the Septuagint.

To summarize, the use of the Greek word [θανάτου] in the Septuagint translation of Isaiah 53:9a demonstrates unequivocally the multi-faceted nature of this servant song. This Greek word can allow for *"death"* to be both individual and corporate. If either of the two plural variants had been used [θανάτῳ or θανάτοις], this would have precluded the possibility of a single individual fulfilling this prophetic passage.

Isaiah 53:9a in the Isaiah Scroll found at Qumran

Remarkably, this ancient text (see footnote 8) carries the Hebrew word במתו [*his tomb*] rather than בְּמֹתָיו [*in his deaths*]. Thus, the literal and official [55] English translation of this phrase in the Qumran scroll is the following:

… and with *rich people his tomb* [56]

Apparently, Ibn Ezra [57] also alluded to this as long ago as the 12th Century based on his understanding of the use of the Hebrew word במות [bamot] which can be used for the raised earth over a grave.

---

[55] The Israel Museum Jerusalem
[56] http://dss.collections.imj.org.il/chapters_pg. English translations by Professors Peter Flint and Eugene Ulrich [Variants from Masoretic text are shown on the website in italics]
[57] Rabbi Abraham Ben Meir Ibn Ezra (1089–1164)

From the New Testament, we understand that Jesus may have been assigned a grave with the wicked but he was buried in the new tomb of a rich man, Joseph of Arimathea.[58] On the other hand, the righteous remnant of Jewish people throughout the centuries has suffered all manner of deaths and burials. Many, particularly in the Holocaust, were children. They had done no violence nor was there any deceit in their mouths.

Children going to their death in Auschwitz

The next verse in the fourth servant song is as follows.

Isaiah 53:10 (NIV) *Yet it was the LORD's will to crush him* [59] *and cause him to suffer, and though the LORD makes his life a guilt offering, he will see his offspring and prolong his days, and the will of the LORD will prosper in his hand.*

This is true for Jesus and it is true for the people of Israel. The anti-Semitic cry of *"Christ killer"* which has haunted the Jewish people over the centuries betrays a total ignorance of the reason why Jesus died. **It was the LORD's will to crush him** and we shall have occasion to return to this theme in the next chapter.

But why would God the Father want to crush his son and cause him to suffer? The most famous verse in the New Testament gives a clear answer.

---

[58] Matthew 27:57-60
[59] It is important to note here that the one who is crushed is a *"him"* and not a *"them"*.

John 3:16-17 (KJV) *For God so loved the world, that he gave his only begotten Son, that whosoever believeth in him should not perish, but have everlasting life. For God sent not his Son into the world to condemn the world; but that the world through him might be saved.*

For God so loved the World [60]

Jesus gave his life that we might be forgiven of our sins. He is the *Lamb of God who takes away the sins of the world.*[61] As we will see in later chapters, Jesus' blood is the seal of the New Covenant which is for both Jew and Gentile. If this is true, Jesus had to die. This was God's intention from the beginning.[62]

However, if the words in Isaiah 53:10, namely, *"yet it was the LORD's will to crush him",* can be applied to the nation of Israel (and I believe that this is perfectly legitimate), **we HAVE to conclude that it was the Lord's will to crush them and to cause them to suffer.** Again we will return to this theme in the next chapter when we consider Gethsemane. Suffice to say now that this is the clear testimony of Scripture.

---

[60] For God so loved the World by Danica Wixom. This beautiful artwork can be seen in full color and purchased on the website: http://fineartamerica.com/featured/for-god-so-loved-the-world-danica-wixom.html
[61] John 1:29
[62] Revelation 13:8

For example:

Isaiah 42:23-25 (NIV) *Which of you will listen to this or pay close attention **in time to come**? Who handed Jacob over to become loot and Israel to the plunderers? Was it not the LORD, **against whom we have sinned**? For they would not follow his ways; they did not obey his law. So he poured out on them his burning anger, the violence of war. It enveloped them in flames, yet they did not understand; it consumed them, but they did not take it to heart.*

It is worth noting that this terrible passage is at the end of the chapter that includes the first servant song. God has just castigated his servant for being blind and deaf [63] and the above verses are the inevitable consequence. We will return to these verses in later chapters of this book but we need to remember that the Lord has a purpose in this crushing of his own people. Although the chapter division is very unhelpful, the prophet Isaiah continues.

Isaiah 43:1-2 (NIV) *But now, this is what the LORD says - he who created you, O Jacob, he who formed you, O Israel: "Fear not, for I have redeemed you; I have summoned you by name; you are mine. When you pass through the waters, I will be with you; and when you pass through the rivers, they will not sweep over you. When you walk through the fire, you will not be burned; the flames will not set you ablaze.*

"The flames will not set you ablaze"

---

[63] **Isaiah 42:19-20 (NIV)** Who is blind but my servant, and deaf like the messenger I send? Who is blind like the one committed to me, blind like the servant of the LORD? You have seen many things, but have paid no attention; your ears are open, but you hear nothing

These two verses which have brought comfort to thousands of Christians and Jews begin with the words *"But now"*. The *"now"* is the time to come when this terrible truth of Jewish suffering will become clearly apparent to the nations of the world. As we will see in later chapters, although it does not answer all the questions, because of the suffering the Jewish people, they have been enabled to return to their land. Accordingly, the Lord goes on to comfort his people in chapter 43 of the book of Isaiah.

Isaiah 43:4-7 (NIV) *Since you are precious and honored in my sight, and because I love you, I will give men in exchange for you, and people in exchange for your life. Do not be afraid, for I am with you; I will bring your children from the east and gather you from the west. I will say to the north, 'Give them up!' and to the south, 'Do not hold them back.' Bring my sons from afar and my daughters from the ends of the earth - everyone who is called by my name, whom I created for my glory, whom I formed and made.*

This leads us to the next verse in the fourth servant song.

Isaiah 53:11 (NIV) *After the suffering of his soul, he will see the light [of life] and be satisfied; by his knowledge my righteous servant will justify many, and he will bear their iniquities.*

It is imperative to see the multi-faceted nature of the *"servant"* in this verse. The term HAS to mean both nation and individual. Let's divide this verse into three sections.

1. After the suffering of his soul, he will see the light [of life] and be satisfied.
2. By his knowledge my righteous servant will justify many.
3. He will bear their iniquities.

Without doubt, the first part of this verse speaks of resurrection. To whom does it apply? If it is true that it was the Lord's will to crush his son [64] and the people of Israel, this section has to apply to BOTH.

Historically, this is the only conclusion.

---

[64] It is important to note in Isaiah 53 that the servant is not just the passive object of actions from the Lord or his persecutors—but also an active participant, a willing "subject". He took our infirmities and carried our sorrows (v. 4). We considered him only a passive victim *"we considered him stricken by God, smitten by him and afflicted"* (vs. 4b). Though he clearly was afflicted, pierced, crushed, later we read that he *"poured out his life until death, and he bore the sin of many and made intercession..."* (v. 12). The servant's active engagement in redemptive suffering is important for us to appreciate.

T'kumah: The National Resurrection of Israel

The most important truth, however, of the Christian faith is that Jesus rose from the dead. This is explicitly stated by the Apostle Paul in the first letter to the Corinthians.

1 Corinthians 15:13-20 (RSV) *But if there is no resurrection of the dead, then Christ has not been raised; if Christ has not been raised, then our preaching is in vain and your faith is in vain. We are even found to be misrepresenting God, because we testified of God that he raised Christ, whom he did not raise if it is true that the dead are not raised. For if the dead are not raised, then Christ has not been raised. If Christ has not been raised, your faith is futile and you are still in your sins. Then those also who have fallen asleep in Christ have perished. If for this life only we have hoped in Christ, we are of all men most to be pitied. But in fact Christ has been raised from the dead, the first fruits of those who have fallen asleep.*

The resurrection of the dead is a Jewish concept and we will consider this in greater detail in later chapters. However, can we apply these words to the resurrection of the state of Israel out of the ashes of the Holocaust? I believe we can. The obvious passage to turn to is in the prophecy of Ezekiel.

Ezekiel 37:1-5 (NIV) *The hand of the LORD was upon me, and he brought me out by the Spirit of the LORD and set me in the middle of a valley; it was full of bones. He led me to and fro among them, and I saw a great many bones on the floor of the valley, bones that were very dry. He asked me, "Son of man, can these bones live?" I said, "O Sovereign LORD, you alone know." Then he said to me, "Prophesy to these bones and say to them, 'Dry bones, hear the word of the LORD! This is what the Sovereign LORD says to these bones: I will make breath enter you,* **and you will come to life**.

The Prophet continues

Ezekiel 37:6-10 (NIV) *I will attach tendons to you and make flesh come upon you and cover you with skin; I will put breath in you, and you will come to life. Then you will know that I am the LORD.'" So I prophesied as I was commanded. And as I was prophesying, there was a noise, a rattling sound, and the bones came together, bone to bone. I looked, and tendons and flesh appeared on them and skin covered them, but there was no breath in them. Then he said to me, "Prophesy to the breath; prophesy, son of man, and say to it, 'This is what the Sovereign LORD says: Come from the four winds, O breath, and breathe into these slain, that they may live.'" So I prophesied as he commanded me, and breath entered them; they came to life and stood up on their feet - a vast army.*

Mass Grave at Bergen Belsen

A Vast Army

The Prophet continues

Ezekiel 37:11-14 (NIV) *Then he said to me: "Son of man, **these bones are the whole house of Israel**. They say, 'Our bones are dried up and our hope is gone; we are cut off.' Therefore prophesy and say to them: 'This is what the Sovereign LORD says: O my people, **I am going to open your graves and bring you up from them; I will bring you back to the land of Israel**. Then you, my people, will know that I am the LORD, when I open your graves and bring you up from them. **I will put my Spirit in you and you will live**, and I will settle you in your own land. Then you will know that I the LORD have spoken, and I have done it, declares the LORD.'"*

The return to the Land and the re-establishment of the nation of Israel is a resurrection. They have seen the light [of life] and are satisfied.

The second part of the verse (Isaiah 53:11) suggests that *"by his knowledge, my righteous servant will justify many"*. Rabbi Singer suggests that this cannot apply to Jesus because Christians believe that it is Jesus' blood that justifies.[65] Of course, he is only partly correct.

Romans 5:9 (NIV) *Since we have now been justified by his blood, how much more shall we be saved from God's wrath through him!*

---

[65] Rabbi Tovia Singer (1996) In-depth Study Guide to the "Let's Get Biblical!" Tape Series, page 39.

But the apostle Paul speaks of justification in other places in his letters with emphases added in emboldened text.

Roman 3:22-24 (NIV) *This righteousness from God comes through faith in Jesus Christ to all who believe. There is no difference, for all have sinned and fall short of the glory of God, and are* **justified freely by his grace** *through the redemption that came by Christ Jesus.*

1 Corinthians 6:11 (NIV) *And that is what some of you were. But you were washed, you were sanctified, you were* **justified in the name of the Lord Jesus Christ and by the Spirit of our God.**

Galatians 2:15-16 (NIV) *We who are Jews by birth and not 'Gentile sinners' know that a man is not justified by observing the law, but by faith in Jesus Christ. So we, too, have put our faith in Christ Jesus that we may be* **justified by faith** *in Christ and not by observing the law, because by observing the law no-one will be justified.*

So, is it possible that by his knowledge he justified many? Consider these words of the Apostle Paul.

Romans 8:29-30 (NIV) *For those God* **foreknew** *he also predestined to be conformed to the likeness of his Son, that he might be the firstborn among many brothers. And those he predestined, he also called; those he called, he also* **justified***; those he justified, he also glorified.*

God's knowledge is pre-requisite to justification. It is no use arguing that this verse speaks of God rather than the suffering servant. If Jesus is the suffering servant then we can conclude along with the Apostle Paul,

Colossians 2:2-3 (NIV) *My purpose is that they may be encouraged in heart and united in love, so that they may have the full riches of complete understanding, in order that they may know the mystery of God, namely, Christ,* **in whom are hidden all the treasures of wisdom and knowledge.**

Rabbi Singer is somewhat *"clutching at straws"* to suggest that Jesus is disqualified here because it is **only** his blood that brings justification and vindication [his word] to the world.[66] He goes on to suggest that the prophet Isaiah is referring to *"the Almighty's Servant Israel who, by their knowledge is witness to the world that there are no other gods"*. But my question to him is this - how does **this** knowledge **justify** many?

---

[66] Ibid

The final part of this verse in the fourth servant song (Isaiah 53:11) is *"he will bear their iniquities"*. We have already considered at length that the people of Israel have suffered the consequences of their own sins.

However, it might still be argued that their suffering has been exacerbated by the iniquity of the nations particularly as expressed in anti-Semitism. As has been stated previously, this does not and cannot lead to atonement for the nations of the world if that is the meaning contained in this verse.

On the other hand, the Messiah, supported by some classical Jewish exegesis, has born the sin of the world on his shoulders. In the New Testament we read the following.

1 Peter 2:24 (RSV) *He himself bore our sins in his body on the tree, that we might die to sin and live to righteousness. By his wounds you have been healed.*

Hebrews 9:27-28 (RSV) *And just as it is appointed for men to die once, and after that comes judgment, so Christ, having been offered once to bear the sins of many, will appear a second time, not to deal with sin but to save those who are eagerly waiting for him.*

This leads us to the final verse of the fourth servant song.

Isaiah 53:12 (NIV) *Therefore I will give him a portion among the great, and he will divide the spoils with the strong, because he poured out his life unto death, and was numbered with the transgressors, for he bore the sin of many, and made intercession for the transgressors.*

As we have seen, these words certainly refer to Jesus. At this moment he is praying for you, for me AND for the nation of Israel.

Romans 8:33-34 (RSV) *Who shall bring any charge against God's elect? It is God who justifies; who is to condemn? Is it Christ Jesus, who died, yes, who was raised from the dead, who is at the right hand of God, who indeed intercedes for us?*

These words have to apply to the people of Israel. They are first and foremost the Lord's chosen people.

Deuteronomy 7:6 (RSV) *For you are a people holy to the LORD your God; the LORD your God has chosen you to be a people for his own possession, out of all the peoples that are on the face of the earth.*

Jesus is interceding for us

Jesus continues to pray and to weep for the slain of his people.[67] His prayers will be answered because, in the prophetic sense, this final verse of the fourth servant song will one day refer to the nation of Israel. Isaiah has a vision of the redeemed Israel in chapter 60.

Isaiah 60:10-11 (NIV) *Foreigners will rebuild your walls, and their kings will serve you. Though in anger I struck you, in favor I will show you compassion. Your gates will always stand open; they will never be shut, day or night, so that men may bring you the wealth of the nations.*

Isaiah 60:21-22 (NIV) *Then will all your people be righteous and they will possess the land for ever. They are the shoot I have planted, the work of my hands, for the display of my splendor. The least of you will become a thousand, the smallest a mighty nation. I am the LORD; in its time I will do this swiftly.*

---

[67] **Hebrews 7:26 (NIV)** Therefore he is able to save completely those who come to God through him, because he always lives to intercede for them. This verse is speaking of Jesus as our great high priest. He has a permanent priesthood as well as being the king seated on David's throne (Luke 1:32-33). He is the fulfillment of the vision of Zechariah who sees the crown placed on the head of the high priest Yeshua (Zechariah 6:12-13). There is, after all, harmony between the two.

Conclusion

In this introductory chapter, we have spent some time considering the identification of the suffering servant in the book of Isaiah. We have clearly seen that the term *"servant"* can be applied to the nation as a whole, to individuals within the nation and to one individual in particular who is the Messiah.

To take the entrenched position that it is either one (i.e. Jesus) or the other (i.e. the nation of Israel) does violence to the beauty, inherent consistency and the depth of information contained within the verses. For Jewish people and for the Christian world to recognize this multifaceted aspect will facilitate a fruitful dialogue and allow for greater understanding of each for the other. We can stand face to face.

Romans 15:7-9 (NIV) *Accept* (i.e. receive) *one another, then, just as Christ accepted you, in order to bring praise to God. For I tell you that* **Christ has become a servant of the Jews** *on behalf of God's truth,* **to confirm the promises made to the patriarchs** *so that the Gentiles may glorify God for his mercy, as it is written: "Therefore I will praise you among the Gentiles; I will sing hymns to your name."*

This study has also laid the theological groundwork for an understanding of the Fountain of Tears. And it is to this we now turn.

CHAPTER TWO
Gethsemane

Yet it was the LORD's will to crush him and cause him to suffer.
Isaiah 53:10

Capernaum Roman Olive Press [1]

The name Gethsemane is derived from the Aramaic (Gaṯ-Šmānê), meaning *"oil press"*. People have used olive presses since Greeks first began pressing olives over 5000 years ago.[2] The above photograph was taken in Capernaum and shows an Olive press from the time of Jesus. No doubt there were many on the Mount of Olives, particularly in the Garden called Gethsemane. First the olives are ground into an olive paste using large millstones. The olive paste is often left under these stones for 30 to 40 minutes to allow enough time for the small olive oil drops to coalesce into larger ones. The olive press then applies pressure to the resulting olive paste to separate the liquid oil from water and other solid material. Crushing the olives was a necessary beginning of a process that would eventually lead to the production of high quality olive oil.

Gethsemane was a place of crushing. It was here that Jesus went with his disciples after the "last" supper and where Judas came with the guards and where Jesus was betrayed and arrested. From this place, he was confined in Herod's palace, tried and eventually crucified. It was here in the Garden of Gethsemane that Jesus struggled over a "cup"

---

[1] Photo by David Shankbone (Wikimedia Commons)
[2] http://en.wikipedia.org/wiki/Olive_oil_extraction

Matthew 26:36-39 (RSV) *Then Jesus went with them to a place called Gethsemane, and he said to his disciples, "Sit here, while I go yonder and pray." And taking with him Peter and the two sons of Zebedee, he began to be sorrowful and troubled. Then he said to them, "My soul is very sorrowful, even to death; remain here, and watch with me." And going a little farther he fell on his face and prayed, "My Father, if it be possible, let this cup pass from me; nevertheless, not as I will, but as thou wilt."*

The Identity of the Cup

Jesus had just celebrated a Passover meal with his disciples. They had reclined at table and heard the story of the Exodus from Egypt. They would have celebrated the festival in a way not dissimilar to the ancient tradition that is still enjoyed by Jewish families. Today there is unleavened bread and, specifically four cups, of wine which are drunk at different moments in the evening. Two are drunk before the meal and two are drunk after the meal. It is very significant; therefore, that Jesus takes the cup after supper and adds a depth of meaning that had never been done previously.

Luke 22:20 (NIV) *In the same way, after the supper he took the cup, saying, "This cup is the new covenant in my blood, which is poured out for you."*

The four cups of Passover are connected to four promises that God makes to his people in the Exodus.

Exodus 6:6-7 (NIV) *Therefore, say to the Israelites: 'I am the LORD, and I will bring you out from under the yoke of the Egyptians. I will free you from being slaves to them, and I will redeem you with an outstretched arm and with mighty acts of judgment. I will take you as my own people, and I will be your God'.*

The first cup is linked to *"I will bring you out from under the yoke of the Egyptians"*. The second cup is linked to *"I will free you from being slaves to them"*. The final cup is linked to *"I will take you as my own people, and I will be your God."* The third cup (i.e. the cup after supper) is linked to this amazing promise *"I will redeem you with an outstretched arm and with mighty acts of judgment."* It is known as the cup of redemption or salvation.

Psalm 116:12-14 (NIV) *How can I repay the LORD for all his goodness to me? I will lift up the **cup of salvation** and call on the name of the LORD. I will fulfil my vows to the LORD in the presence of all his people.*

So was this the cup that Jesus struggled with in the Garden? I think it was. It is interesting to note that the next words in Psalm 116 are as follows.

Psalm 116:15-16 (NIV) *Precious in the sight of the LORD is the death of his saints. O LORD, truly I am your servant.*

The cup after supper was symbolic of Jesus' blood which was to be the seal of the New Covenant that God was about to make with the house of Israel and the house of Judah.

Jeremiah 31:31-32 (RSV) *Behold, the days are coming, says the LORD, when I will make a new covenant with the house of Israel and the house of Judah, not like the covenant which I made with their fathers when I took them by the hand to bring them out of the land of Egypt, my covenant which they broke, though I was their husband, says the LORD.*

Just as the Mosaic Covenant was sealed in blood [3] so also the New had to be sealed in blood, Jesus' blood. To take the cup of salvation into his hands was to submit to his death which was to be precious in the sight of God. Peter came to understand this.

1 Peter 1:18-19 (RSV) *You know that you were ransomed from the futile ways inherited from your fathers, not with perishable things such as silver or gold, but with the precious blood of Christ, like that of a lamb without blemish or spot.*

The submission by Jesus to the will of the Father in Gethsemane also carried the recognition that Jesus was truly the Lord's servant (Psalm 116:16). Consequently, since the suffering servant in the prophecy of Isaiah was to be crushed (bruised and hurt) so in this place of crushing, Jesus was also being crushed, bruised and hurt. It is remarkable; therefore, that in the equivalent passage in Luke it says this:

Luke 22:41-46 (NIV) *He withdrew about a stone's throw beyond them, knelt down and prayed, "Father, if you are willing, take this cup from me; yet not my will, but yours be done." An angel from heaven appeared to him and strengthened him. And being in anguish, he prayed more earnestly, and **his sweat was like drops of blood falling to the ground.** When he rose from prayer and went back to the disciples, he found them asleep, exhausted from sorrow. "Why are you sleeping?" he asked them.*

Just as olive oil is extracted from the crushed olives, so Jesus was sweating, as it were, drops of blood. He is perfectly aware of what is in front of him. He knows he is going to be betrayed, beaten and violently killed. He knows what it will cost to lift the Cup of Salvation and although he struggles, he submits to the Father's will. And, as we have seen, it was the Father's will to crush him. [4] Furthermore, there is another meaning of the cup in the Scriptures. The Bible speaks of the cup of God's wrath.

Isaiah 51:17 (NIV) *Awake, awake! Rise up, O Jerusalem, you who have drunk from the hand of the LORD the **cup of his wrath**, you who have drained to its dregs the goblet that makes men stagger.*

---

[3] Exodus 24:7-8
[4] Isaiah 53:10

Our God is a God of love but he is also a God of justice. He cannot let sin go unpunished. As the Apostle Paul writes:

Romans 1:18-19 (RSV) *For the wrath of God is revealed from heaven against all ungodliness and wickedness of men who by their wickedness suppress the truth. For what can be known about God is plain to them, because God has shown it to them.*

God is a God of justice but he is also a God of love. He has made a way.

Romans 5:8-10 (RSV) *But God shows his love for us in that while we were yet sinners Christ died for us. Since, therefore, we are now justified by his blood, much more shall we be saved by him from the wrath of God. For if while we were enemies we were reconciled to God by the death of his Son, much more, now that we are reconciled, shall we be saved by his life*

Isaiah 53:5 (NIV) *But he was pierced for our transgressions, he was crushed for our iniquities; the punishment that brought us peace was upon him, and by his wounds we are healed.*

Jesus takes the cup of salvation which is also the cup of God's wrath. Gethsemane is the place of crushing; it is also the place from where Jesus goes to his death. I develop some of these themes further and the reader is referred to chapter 12 which is entitled *"Comfort My People, An In-Depth Study of Isaiah Chapter 40 Verses 1 and 2"* on page 230.

The Crushing of the Nation of Israel

Jeremiah 8:21-22 and 9:1 (NIV) *Since my people are crushed, I am crushed; I mourn, and horror grips me. Is there no balm in Gilead? Is there no physician there? Why then is there no healing for the wound of my people? Oh, that my head were a spring of water and my eyes a fountain of tears! I would weep day and night for the slain of my people.*

It is extremely interesting that the NIV translation of this passage uses the word *"crushed"* in the last verse of chapter 8 of Jeremiah. Although, it is not the same word as that used in Isaiah 53, the meaning that all the various Hebrew words convey is crushing, bruising and hurting. These verses in Jeremiah are the immediate context for the prophet's prayer that his eyes would become a fountain of tears.

It is important to realize that Jeremiah is crying out to God before Jerusalem has been devastated by the Babylonian forces. The prophet is aware that thousands of people will perish and many will be carried off into captivity. Consequently, we must look more closely at chapter 8 of the prophecy. It is an amazing chapter in the context of our study. Of course, the immediate context of Jeremiah chapter 8 is the last verse of Jeremiah chapter 7!

Jeremiah 7:34 (RSV) *And I will make to cease from the cities of Judah and from the streets of Jerusalem the voice of mirth and the voice of gladness, the voice of the bridegroom and the voice of the bride; for the land shall become a waste.*

God has decided that the nation is going to face disaster. They have turned away from him and they have to face his wrath.[5] It hasn't happened yet but it is coming. Little by little, the people of Jerusalem are being crushed. Here are some verses in chapter 8.

Jeremiah 8:9-13 (NIV) *The wise will be put to shame; they will be dismayed and trapped. Since they have rejected the word of the LORD, what kind of wisdom do they have? Therefore I will give their wives to other men and their fields to new owners. From the least to the greatest, all are greedy for gain; prophets and priests alike, all practice deceit. They dress the wound of my people as though it were not serious. "Peace, peace," they say, when there is no peace. Are they ashamed of their loathsome conduct? No, they have no shame at all; they do not even know how to blush. So they will fall among the fallen; they will be brought down when they are punished, says the LORD. "'I will take away their harvest, declares the LORD. There will be no grapes on the vine. There will be no figs on the tree, and their leaves will wither. What I have given them will be taken from them.'"*

Little by little, their prosperity and possessions are being taken away. While they are dismayed (Jeremiah 8:9), they do not seem to be able to respond appropriately. They are crying peace when there is no peace. However, the mood begins to change.

Jeremiah 8:14-15 (NIV) *"Why are we sitting here? Gather together! Let us flee to the fortified cities and perish there! For the LORD our God has doomed us to perish and given us poisoned water to drink, because we have sinned against him. We hoped for peace but no good has come, for a time of healing but there was only terror.*

---

[5] **Jeremiah 7:28-29 (NIV)** Therefore say to them, 'This is the nation that has not obeyed the LORD its God or responded to correction. Truth has perished; it has vanished from their lips. Cut off your hair and throw it away; take up a lament on the barren heights, for the LORD has rejected and abandoned this generation that is under his wrath.

Why this change of mood? All of a sudden the people realize that the enemy is at the door but it is now too late.

Jeremiah 8:17 (NIV) *"See, I will send venomous snakes among you, vipers that cannot be charmed, and they will bite you," declares the LORD.*

Jeremiah is beside himself. Let us remind ourselves of these verses:

Jeremiah 8:21-22 and 9:1 (NIV) *Since my people are crushed, I am crushed; I mourn, and horror grips me. Is there no balm in Gilead? Is there no physician there? Why then is there no healing for the wound of my people? Oh, that my head were a spring of water and my eyes a fountain of tears! I would weep day and night for the slain of my people.*

The Crushing of the Jewish People during the 1930s

This gradual crushing of the Jewish people was to be repeated in the 1930's with the election of the Adolf Hitler as Chancellor in 1933. It began subtly but gathered momentum from that moment on. It follows a pattern not dissimilar to that described in Jeremiah chapter 8.

Hitler elected Chancellor of Germany in 1933

1. The wise will be put to shame (Jeremiah 8:9)

Beginning in 1933, Germans were encouraged **not** to use Jewish doctors and lawyers. Jewish civil servants, teachers and those employed by the mass media were sacked. Hostility towards the Jewish people was reflected in the decision made by many shops and restaurants not to serve the Jewish population. In some parts of Germany, Jews were banned from public parks, swimming pools and public transport.

2. Therefore I will give their wives to other men and their fields to new owners (Jeremiah 8:10)

In 1935, the Nuremberg Laws of Citizenship and Race were introduced. Under this new law, Jews could no longer be citizens of Germany. It was also made illegal for Jews to marry Aryans. Thus, potential wives were given to other men.

Mixed Marriages Forbidden

Furthermore, between 1933 and 1938, Jewish people were under increasing pressure to transfer their property into German ownership. By 1938, 60 to 70% of all Jewish businesses had been liquidated. Subsequently, every Jew was required to value and register their remaining assets. After Kristallnacht in November 1938, legislation was passed that sought to exclude Jews from the economic life of Germany. All remaining Jewish businesses were put under government control with the goal of sale to Germans with a substantial portion of the sales price going to the government.

3. "Peace, peace," they say, when there is no peace (Jeremiah 8:11)

The policy of appeasement by the allies during the 1930s is a fact of history. Nobody wanted war and everything was done to avoid it. Initially, the policy of appeasement allowed the British and French to ignore the imminent threat and to produce a fake peace which ultimately was to lead to many deaths. Appeasement led Hitler to believe that no one would oppose his expansionist policies and allowed Germany time to increase its navy, army, and air force. The reoccupation of the Rhineland and the annexation of the Czech Sudetenland all helped to strengthen the German position in Europe. It would lead to Germany taking over most of Europe with relative ease in a matter of months.

Neville Chamberlain's return from Munich in 1938

4. What I have given them will be taken from them (Jeremiah 8:13)

Kristallnacht took place between November 9th and 10th 1938. The date was chosen in honor of Martin Luther's birthday. Over 7,500 Jewish shops were destroyed and 400 synagogues were burnt down. Ninety-one Jews were killed and an estimated 20,000 were sent to various concentration camps.

Kristallnacht

The Evian Conference, July 1938

5. "Why are we sitting here? Gather together! Let us flee …
(Jeremiah 8:14)

After Kristallnacht, the number of Jews wishing to leave Germany increased dramatically. It has been calculated that between 1933 and 1939, about half the Jewish population of Germany (250,000) left the country. A higher number of Jews would have left but anti-Semitism was not restricted to Germany and many countries were reluctant to take them. In particular, the Evian Conference had already taken place in July 1938. The conference was convened by US President Franklin D. Roosevelt to discuss the issue of increasing numbers of Jewish refugees fleeing Nazi persecution. For eight days, from 6th to 13th July, representatives from 32 countries met at Evian in France. The Jews of Austria and Germany were very hopeful, believing that this international conference would provide them a safe haven.

Remarkably, Hitler responded to the news of the conference by saying that if the other nations would agree to take the Jews, he would help them leave. However, the conference was an abject failure. The United States and Britain refused take in substantial numbers of Jews and most of the other countries at the conference followed suit.

6. God has doomed us to perish … (Jeremiah 8:14)

The ultimate result of the Evian conference was that the Jews had no escape and were to be subject to what was known as Hitler's *"Final Solution to the Jewish Question"*. The words of Jeremiah were to be fulfilled to the letter, namely; *"We hoped for peace but no good has come, for a time of healing but there was only terror"* (Jeremiah 8:15).

Where was God in all of this?

As we have considered at length in the introduction to this book, the Suffering Servant of Isaiah is fulfilled in the life of Jesus and in the life of the Nation as a whole. Although it is very difficult to understand, it was the LORD's will to crush him (them) and cause him (them) to suffer (Isaiah 53:10). Christians can rejoice in the purpose of Jesus' death. However, it is exquisitely painful to think that there was a purpose in the crushing of the Jewish people in the Holocaust. As Jeremiah cries out:

Jeremiah 8:18-20 (NIV) *O my Comforter in sorrow, my heart is faint within me. Listen to the cry of my people from a land far away: "Is the LORD not in Zion? Is her King no longer there?" "Why have they provoked me to anger with their images, with their worthless foreign idols?" "The harvest is past, the summer has ended, and we are not saved."*

Throughout the 1930's, the Jewish people were crushed. Like Jesus in the Garden, they were to be arrested, imprisoned and violently killed. Like the Babylonians, God used the Nazis to fulfil his ultimate purposes. But also like the Babylonians, the Nazis were also going to drink the cup of God's wrath.

Jeremiah 25:15-17 (NIV) *This is what the LORD, the God of Israel, said to me: "Take from my hand this cup filled with the wine of my wrath and make all the nations to whom I send you drink it. When they drink it, they will stagger and go mad because of the sword I will send among them." So I took the cup from the LORD's hand and made all the nations to whom he sent me drink it.*

Although, it is impossible to understand fully, God's ultimate purposes for the nation of Israel were to be fulfilled for, out of the ashes of the Holocaust, the nation would be re-established. We will consider this in much greater detail in later chapters. I suppose it could now be summed up in these very familiar words in Psalm 23.

Psalm 23:4-5 (KJV) *Yea, though I walk through the valley of the shadow of death, I will fear no evil: for thou art with me; thy rod and thy staff they comfort me. Thou preparest a table before me in the presence of mine enemies: thou anointest my head with oil; my cup runneth over.*

CHAPTER THREE

Father, Forgive them

Luke 23:33-34 (KJV) *And when they were come to the place, which is called Calvary, there they crucified him, and the malefactors, one on the right hand, and the other on the left. Then said Jesus, Father, forgive them; for they know not what they do. And they parted his raiment, and cast lots.*

The Survivor clutches his Heart and leans into the Stones

The Order of the Seven Statements of Jesus

Although there is a general consensus, we cannot be completely dogmatic about the order of the seven sayings that Jesus made at the crucifixion. These seven are derived from a synthesis of all four Gospels.

1. Matthew's Account

There is only one of the seven statements recorded in Mathew's account of the Crucifixion, namely,

Matthew 27:46 (NIV) *About the ninth hour Jesus cried out in a loud voice, "Eloi, Eloi, lama sabachthani?" which means, "My God, my God, why have you forsaken me?"*

Jesus had been on the cross for at least six hours before this cry was heard. Matthew also records that between the 6th hour and the 9th hour, darkness was over the entire land.[1] Following this cry, Jesus was offered a drink of wine vinegar which may have been in response to the cry *"I thirst"* although that is not mentioned. Shortly after this Jesus dies and, in the words of Matthew, Jesus gave up his spirit.

2. Mark's Account

The situation in Mark's account is essentially identical to Matthew's. However, Mark gives us the following information.

Mark 15:25 (NIV) *It was the third hour when they crucified him.*

It is likely that the third hour was the equivalent of 9 am in the morning but, like Matthew's account, the only explicit reference to the seven last statements is,

Mark 15:34 (NIV) *And at the ninth hour Jesus cried out in a loud voice, "Eloi, Eloi, lama sabachthani?" which means, "My God, my God, why have you forsaken me?"*

According to Mark's account, this sets this statement at approximately 3 pm in the afternoon and, as we shall in a later chapter, this reference has great significance for the Fountain of Tears.

3. Luke's Account

Luke provides more detail. Again, we infer from Luke's account that Jesus was crucified for an unspecified period, presumably 3 hours, before darkness came over the whole land.[2] Before this unusual and unexpected darkness, Jesus had already made two statements.

Luke 23:33-34 (NIV) *When they came to the place called the Skull, there they crucified him, along with the criminals - one on his right, the other on his left. Jesus said, "Father, forgive them, for they do not know what they are doing." And they divided up his clothes by casting lots.*

We can conclude that this is the first statement. Later, one of the criminals, who had been cursing Jesus according to Matthew and Mark's account,[3] became much more reflective. He turns to Jesus.

---

[1] Matthew 26:45
[2] Luke 23:44
[3] Matthew 27:34, Mark 15:32

Luke 23:42-43 (NIV) *Then he said, "Jesus, remember me when you come into your kingdom." Jesus answered him, "I tell you the truth, today you will be with me in paradise."*

The three hours of darkness follow this second statement and at the end of this period, Jesus dies after crying out the last of the seven statements.

Luke 23:46 (NIV*)* *Jesus called out with a loud voice, "Father, into your hands I commit my spirit." When he had said this, he breathed his last.*

4. John's Account

There is an interesting issue that requires our attention.

John 19:14 (NIV) *It was the day of Preparation of Passover Week, about the sixth hour. "Here is your king," Pilate said to the Jews.*

John suggests that Jesus is with Pilate about the sixth hour. This appears to disagree with the synoptic gospel accounts that Jesus has already been crucified for three hours before darkness came over the entire land between the sixth to the ninth hour. How do we resolve this apparent contradiction?

Some has suggested that there are two clocks in operation here, one Jewish and one Roman.[4] According to the Roman clock, about the sixth hour would be 6.00 am in the morning. However, another straightforward explanation is to recognize that there are TWO sets of 12 hour periods, one corresponding to day and another corresponding to night. The sixth hour of the night would be approximately midnight. This timing schedule is intimated in the Book of Acts.

Acts 2:15 (NKJV) *For these are not drunk, as you suppose, since it is only the third hour **of the day.*** [5]

Acts 23:23 (NKJV) *And he called for two centurions, saying, "Prepare two hundred soldiers, seventy horsemen, and two hundred spearmen to go to Caesarea at the third hour **of the night**..*[6]

The sixth hour **in the day** according to Jewish chronology was noon. It is therefore very significant to refer to the ancient prophecy of Amos.

---

[4] This has some credibility as the Biblical day begins at sunset and the Roman day begins at midnight.
[5] Acts 2:15 (NIV) It's only nine in the morning!
[6] Acts 23:235 (NIV) At nine tonight.

Amos 8:9-10 (RSV) *"And on that day," says the Lord GOD, "I will make the sun go down **at noon**, and darken the earth in broad daylight. I will turn your feasts into mourning, and all your songs into lamentation; I will bring sackcloth upon all loins, and baldness on every head; I will make it like the mourning for an only son, and the end of it like a bitter day.*

Biblical prophecy may have multiple fulfillments and we shall have occasion to return to this one, in particular. However, there is little doubt, in my mind, that this passage in Amos was fulfilled during the crucifixion.[7] The context of this prophecy is a religious feast and Passover must qualify for this. It is also a time of mourning for an only son. The prophet Zechariah states:

Zechariah 12:10 (NIV) *They will look on me, the one they have pierced, and they will mourn for him as one mourns for an only child, and grieve bitterly for him as one grieves for a firstborn son.*

Grieving for a First-born Son [8]

---

[7] It will be fulfilled again.
[8] Reconciliation—Sculpture by Rick Wienecke [http://www.castingseeds.com/reconciliation.html]

John suggests that this prophecy was fulfilled at the crucifixion.[v] So although, John does not specifically mention the darkness in his account, everything that he does say is consistent with the timing of the crucifixion that is contained in the synoptic gospels. Furthermore, John was standing at the foot of the cross with Mary, the mother of Jesus and hears the statement that was made directly to them.

John 19:26-27 (NIV) *When Jesus saw his mother there, and the disciple whom he loved standing nearby, he said to his mother, "Dear woman, here is your son," and to the disciple, "Here is your mother." From that time on, this disciple took her into his home.*

We are not able to conclude whether this is either the second or the third statement made by Jesus as we cannot know for certain whether Jesus spoke to John before or after he spoke to the thief. Although, as has been mentioned, John does not speak of the darkness, he goes on to tell us.

John 19:28-30 (NIV) *Later, knowing that all was now completed, and so that the Scripture would be fulfilled, Jesus said, "I am thirsty." A jar of wine vinegar was there, so they soaked a sponge in it, put the sponge on a stalk of the hyssop plant, and lifted it to Jesus' lips. When he had received the drink, Jesus said, "It is finished." With that, he bowed his head and gave up his spirit.*

Only someone close to the crucifixion could possibly have heard these words. They would have only been whispered. Accordingly, we may conclude that these are the fifth and sixth statements as Jesus dies immediately after asking God to receive his spirit.

Conclusion

Accepting that it is impossible to know for certain whether Jesus spoke to John before or after he spoke to the thief, it is reasonable to suggest that the order of the seven recorded statements made by Jesus from the Crucifixion are:

1. Father, forgive them, they know not what they do
2. Today you will be with me in Paradise
3. Mother, this is your son, son this is your mother
4. My God, my God, why have you forsaken me?
5. I thirst
6. It is finished
7. Into your hands, I commit my spirit.

---

[9] **John 19:37 (NIV)** Another scripture says, "They will look on the one they have pierced."

A Covenant of Forgiveness

The First Panel of the Fountain of Tears

We can be confident that the first statement made by Jesus that is recorded in the New Testament is *"Father forgive them, they know not what they do"*. He is surrounded by cursing.

Mark 15:29-32 (RSV) *And those who passed by derided him, wagging their heads, and saying, "Aha! You who would destroy the temple and build it in three days, save yourself, and come down from the cross!" So also the chief priests mocked him to one another with the scribes, saying, "He saved others; he cannot save himself. Let the Christ, the King of Israel, come down now from the cross, that we may see and believe." Those who were crucified with him also reviled him.*

Who is being Forgiven?

As we have discussed in the introduction, over millennia, the Jewish people have been accused of being the *"Christ killers"*. This betrays a total ignorance of the reason why Jesus died. Jesus is the Lamb of God who takes away the sin of the world. He dies at Passover and his blood is the seal of the New Covenant. He had to be rejected by his own people. This is most eloquently expressed in the interaction between Jesus and Peter.

Matthew 16:21-23 (RSV) *From that time Jesus began to show his disciples that he must go to Jerusalem and suffer many things from the elders and chief priests and scribes, and be killed, and on the third day be raised. And Peter took him and began to rebuke him, saying, "God forbid, Lord! This shall never happen to you." But he turned and said to Peter, "Get behind me, Satan! You are a hindrance to me; for you are not on the side of God, but of men."*

That Jesus would fulfill the role of the suffering servant[10] was a total mystery to his disciples. Peter had just declared him to be the Messiah[11] so the expectation was that he would be proclaimed King in Jerusalem and free the nation from Roman occupation. Jesus had no such allusions. He came to die and to give his life as a ransom for many.[12] Furthermore, it was the Lord's will to crush him and to cause him to suffer. We need to look again at this verse in Isaiah 53.

Isaiah 53:10 (NIV) *Yet it was the LORD's will to crush him and cause him to suffer, and though the LORD makes his life a guilt offering, he will see his offspring and prolong his days, and the will of the LORD will prosper in his hand.*

The fact that Jesus becomes a guilt offering is very significant.[13] We read about the guilt offering in the book of Leviticus.

Leviticus 5:17-18 (RSV) *If any one sins, doing any of the things which the LORD has commanded not to be done, though he does not know it, yet he is guilty and shall bear his iniquity. He shall bring to the priest a ram without blemish out of the flock, valued by you at the price for a guilt offering, and the priest shall make atonement for him for the error which he committed unwittingly, and he shall be forgiven.*

Furthermore, the blood of the guilt offering had to be shed.

Leviticus 7:2 (NIV) *The guilt offering is to be slaughtered in the place where the burnt offering is slaughtered, and its blood is to be sprinkled against the altar on all sides.*

---

[10] Messiah, Son of Joseph

[11] Matthew 16:16

[12] Matthew 20:28

[13] This is most clearly expressed in the New International Version of the Bible. The other English translations generally speak of an offering for sin. However, the Hebrew word transliterated Ah-Sham is found in the text of the Hebrew Bible and this word refers to guilt and is also used in passages in Leviticus describing the guilt offering (also known in more ancient versions as the trespass offering).

Just as in Egypt, the blood of the Passover lamb was a sign. The lamb was slain at twilight on 14th Nisan and the blood was applied to doorposts and lintel.

Exodus 12:13 (NIV) *The blood will be a sign for you on the houses where you are; and when I see the blood, I will pass over you.*

Jesus dies at the right time and in the right place. His blood is shed on the upright and the cross piece and when God sees the blood (and our trust in its efficacy), his wrath passes over us and we are saved. Jesus' blood is also a sin offering.

Hebrews 13:11-12 (NIV) *The high priest carries the blood of animals into the Most Holy Place as a sin offering, but the bodies are burned outside the camp. And so Jesus also suffered outside the city gate to make the people holy through his own blood.*

So, what is the fundamental difference between the sin offering and the guilt offering? A sin offering is required for bearing false witness and for general ceremonial uncleanness. For example, a person would become ceremonially unclean if he (or she) were to touch the carcass of unclean animals or a dead human body. In addition, the swearing of a false oath, whether for good or for evil, requires a sin offering.

However, the necessity of the sin offering also requires an acknowledgement of sin and repentance on behalf of the individual. There can only be an acknowledgment of sin when there is a realization that we HAVE actually sinned. I am reminded of the words in the first letter of John.

1 John 1:5-10 (RSV) *This is the message we have heard from him and proclaim to you, that God is light and in him is no darkness at all. If we say we have fellowship with him while we walk in darkness, we lie and do not live according to the truth; but if we walk in the light, as he is in the light, we have fellowship with one another, and the blood of Jesus his Son cleanses us from all sin. If we say we have no sin, we deceive ourselves, and the truth is not in us. If we confess our sins, he is faithful and just, and will forgive our sins and cleanse us from all unrighteousness. If we say we have not sinned, we make him a liar, and his word is not in us.*

The Terrible Oath

Some have said that the nation of Israel is under a curse because of the terrible oath that they swore in response to Pilate's frustration.

Matthew 27:24-25 (NIV) *When Pilate saw that he was getting nowhere, but that instead an uproar was starting, he took water and washed his hands in front of the crowd. "I am innocent of this man's blood," he said. "It is your responsibility!" All the people answered, "Let his blood be on us and on our children!"*

It is no use suggesting that the Jewish people were innocent and that it was the Romans who actually killed Jesus. To a certain extent, that Jesus would be rejected by his own people was inevitable since it was the Lord's will to cause him to suffer. The nation of Israel became, as it were, a collective priesthood fulfilling the will of God in the death of his Son.

Exodus 19:5-6 (NIV) *Although the whole earth is mine, you will be for me a kingdom of priests and a holy nation.*

Of course, they did not know what they were doing and the guilt offering is for sin that is unknown. It is particularly true of sins regarding the tabernacle and associated holy things.

Leviticus 5:15 (NIV) *When a person commits a violation and sins unintentionally in regard to any of the LORD's holy things, he is to bring to the LORD as a penalty a ram from the flock, one without defect and of the proper value in silver, according to the sanctuary shekel. It is a guilt offering.*

Unlike, false witness and ceremonial uncleanness, the fact is no-one can know if they have erred with respect to the holy things. As someone has said:

> *"I didn't know" was not an acceptable excuse. They had to still make sacrifice to atone for their sin. So the priest shall make atonement for him regarding his ignorance in which he erred and did not know it: Ignorance can be sin. It is no excuse; often it is sin and must be atoned for."* [14]

I think we can turn again to Isaiah 53:10.

Isaiah 53:10 (NIV) *Yet it was the LORD's will to crush him and cause him to suffer, and though **the LORD makes his life a guilt offering**, he will see his offspring and prolong his days, and the will of the LORD will prosper in his hand.*

---

[14] David Guzik http://www.enduringword.com/commentaries/0305.htm

The Lord made his life a guilt offering. It is simply because no-one knew what they were actually doing. Jesus cries out *"Father forgive them, they know not what they do"*. In essence, Jesus is saying to the Father, *"I am giving my life as a guilt offering"*. I also think that the words of the following psalm were in the mind of Jesus.

Psalm 130 (RSV) *Out of the depths I cry to thee, O LORD! Lord, hear my voice! Let thy ears be attentive to the voice of my supplications! If thou, O LORD, shouldst mark iniquities, Lord, who could stand? But there is forgiveness with thee, that thou mayest be feared. I wait for the LORD, my soul waits, and in his word I hope; my soul waits for the LORD more than watchmen for the morning, more than watchmen for the morning. O Israel, hope in the LORD! For with the LORD there is steadfast love, and with him is plenteous redemption. And he will redeem Israel from all his iniquities.*

The New Covenant is a Covenant of Forgiveness

At the Fountain of Tears, we speak about a covenant based on forgiveness. Is this scriptural? The answer has to be *"yes"*. Let us consider the outworking of the New Covenant as described in Jeremiah chapter 31.

Jeremiah 31:31-34 (NIV) *"The time is coming," declares the LORD, "when I will make a new covenant with the house of Israel and with the house of Judah. It will not be like the covenant I made with their forefathers when I took them by the hand to lead them out of Egypt, because they broke my covenant, though I was a husband to them," declares the LORD. "This is the covenant that I will make with the house of Israel after that time," declares the LORD. "I will put my law in their minds and write it on their hearts. I will be their God, and they will be my people. No longer will a man teach his neighbor, or a man his brother, saying, 'Know the LORD,' because they will all know me, from the least of them to the greatest," declares the LORD. "For I will forgive their wickedness and will remember their sins no more".*

The New Covenant is primarily made with the people of Israel (i.e. Israel and Judah). It is a renewal or replacement of the covenant that God made with Israel when he brought them out of Egypt. This is the Mosaic covenant, sealed in blood, [15] when the Lord gave the law to Moses on Mount Sinai. The Jewish people commemorate this event each year during the Festival of Shavuot (Weeks; Pentecost).

---

[15] **Exodus 24:7-8 (NIV)** Then he took the Book of the Covenant and read it to the people. They responded, "We will do everything the LORD has said; we will obey." Moses then took the blood, sprinkled it on the people and said, "This is the blood of the covenant that the LORD has made with you in accordance with all these words."

Acts 2:1-4 (RSV) *When the day of Pentecost had come, they were all together in one place. And suddenly a sound came from heaven like the rush of a mighty wind, and it filled all the house where they were sitting. And there appeared to them tongues as of fire, distributed and resting on each one of them. And they were all filled with the Holy Spirit and began to speak in other tongues, as the Spirit gave them utterance.*

It is no coincidence that the Holy Spirit fell at Pentecost. This time the Law was not written on stone but written on human hearts through the administration of the Spirit. Shortly after the day of Pentecost, Peter spoke to the leaders of Israel as follows:

Acts 3:17-21 (NIV) *Now, brothers, **I know that you acted in ignorance, as did your leaders.** But this is how God fulfilled what he had foretold through all the prophets, saying that his Christ would suffer. Repent, then, and turn to God, so that your sins may be wiped out, that times of refreshing may come from the Lord, and that he may send the Christ, who has been appointed for you - even Jesus. He must remain in heaven until the time comes for God to restore everything, as he promised long ago through his holy prophets.*

In other words, Peter could now pray *"Father forgive them, they knew not what they were doing".*

The New Covenant is for Jew and Gentile

Peter was absolutely shocked. Several years after that momentous Pentecost when they were filled with the Holy Spirit, he is in the house of Cornelius.

Acts 10:44-45 (RSV) *While Peter was still saying this, the Holy Spirit fell on all who heard the word. And the believers from among the circumcised who came with Peter were amazed, because the gift of the Holy Spirit had been poured out even on the Gentiles.*

This was totally unexpected and it created a real problem for the emergent believing community that up until this time was exclusively of the House of Israel. However, the giving of the Holy Spirit to Jew and Gentile is the outworking of the promise of blessing that God gave to Abraham.[16] This was also clearly the conclusion of the Council of Jerusalem (Acts 15) and the argument that Paul addressed in his letter to the Galatians.

---

[16] Genesis 18:18

Acts 15:8-9 (RSV) *And God who knows the heart bore witness to them, giving them the Holy Spirit just as he did to us; and he made no distinction between us and them, but cleansed their hearts by faith.*

Galatians 3:14 (NIV) *He redeemed us in order that the blessing given to Abraham might come to the Gentiles through Christ Jesus, so that, by faith, we might receive the promise of the Spirit.*

All covenants are sealed in blood. So, where is the blood of the New Covenant? As we have been reminded in the previous chapter:

Matthew 26:27-28 (NIV) *Then he took the cup, gave thanks and offered it to them, saying, "Drink from it, all of you. This is my blood of the covenant, which is poured out for many for the forgiveness of sins.*

The New Covenant is a covenant of forgiveness and this is true for Jews and Gentiles. However, with respect to the House of Israel and the House of Judah, there is a prophetic aspect to the covenant, namely,

Jeremiah 31:34 (RSV) *And no longer shall each man teach his neighbor and each his brother, saying, 'Know the LORD,' for they shall all know me, from the least of them to the greatest, says the LORD; for I will forgive their iniquity, and I will remember their sin no more."*

The words are explicit. The entire House of Israel (also encompassing Judah) will know the Lord. Everyone will know him from the least to the greatest. The words could not be clearer and they are re-iterated by the Apostle Paul.

Romans 11:25-27 (NIV) *I do not want you to be ignorant of this mystery, brothers, so that you may not be conceited: Israel has experienced a hardening in part until the full number of the Gentiles has come in.* ***And so all Israel will be saved****, as it is written: "The deliverer will come from Zion; he will turn godlessness away from Jacob. And this is my covenant* ***with them*** *when I take away their sins" .*

Paul is combining two ancient prophecies in Jeremiah 31 and Isaiah 59

Isaiah 59:20-21 (RSV) *And he will come to Zion as Redeemer, to those in Jacob who turn from transgression, says the LORD. And as for me, this is my covenant with them, says the LORD: my spirit which is upon you, and my words which I have put in your mouth, shall not depart out of your mouth, or out of the mouth of your children, or out of the mouth of your children's children, says the LORD, from this time forth and for evermore.*

The covenant that Isaiah speaks of has to be the New Covenant as it involves the administration of the Spirit. And this promise resonates throughout the Tanach and in particular, in the prophecy of Ezekiel.

Ezekiel 36:24-28 (RSV) *For I will take you from the nations, and gather you from all the countries, and bring you into your own land. I will sprinkle clean water upon you, and you shall be clean from all your uncleanness, and from all your idols I will cleanse you. A new heart I will give you, and a new spirit I will put within you; and I will take out of your flesh the heart of stone and give you a heart of flesh. And I will put my spirit within you, and cause you to walk in my statutes and be careful to observe my ordinances. You shall dwell in the land which I gave to your fathers; and you shall be my people, and I will be your God.*

Ezekiel sets this prophecy into the distant future. The administration of the Spirit on the House of Israel as a whole will only take place when the nation has been gathered back into the land.

"If I forgive, will they be forgotten?"

The Holocaust Survivor's Dilemma

As we have seen, through the New Covenant, not only does God forgive sin but, remarkably, he remembers our sin no more. In other words, God forgives and forgets. It is therefore incumbent upon those who receive God's forgiveness to forgive others. This situation is unusual in the Tanach although there are some notable examples. In particular, there is no doubt that Joseph forgives his brothers for all the wrong that they had done to him. When Jacob died, the brothers come to Joseph filled with fear. They remind him of Jacob's request that Joseph should be forgiving.

Genesis 50:17-20 (RSV) *Say to Joseph, Forgive, I pray you, the transgression of your brothers and their sin, because they did evil to you.' And now, we pray you, forgive the transgression of the servants of the God of your father." Joseph wept when they spoke to him. His brothers also came and fell down before him, and said, "Behold, we are your servants." But Joseph said to them, "Fear not, for am I in the place of God? As for you, you meant evil against me; but God meant it for good, to bring it about that many people should be kept alive, as they are today.*

Joseph revealing himself to his Brothers[17]

It is not surprising that the suffering servant is likened to Joseph[18] who is rejected by his own brothers. Joseph is sent to his death but rises to become a savior in Egypt.[19] He is given the name Zaphenath-paneah which can mean *"Savior of the World"* according to the Septuagint translation.

Joseph weeps for his brothers but he also reminds them that it is God's prerogative to forgive. In other words, he has already prayed the prayer, *"Father, forgive them for they know not what they do".* God is sovereign and what they intended for harm, God allowed for the ultimate good. I am reminded of the words in Isaiah.

---

[17] Sculpture by Rick Wienecke [http://www.castingseeds.com/josephreveal.html]
[18] Messiah, Son of Joseph
[19] Genesis 41:45

Isaiah 55:8-11 (NIV) *For my thoughts are not your thoughts, neither are your ways my ways ... so is my word that goes out from my mouth: It will not return to me empty, but will accomplish what I desire and achieve the purpose for which I sent it.*

Forgiveness and the Holocaust

In a remarkable article entitled *"Is Forgiveness Possible? A Jewish Perspective"* written by Rabbi Albert Friedlander, he states:

> *Throughout this past half century, our neighbours have enjoined us to 'forgive and forget'. In 1985, after the Bitburg Incident when Chancellor Kohl and President Reagan stood at the grave of SS officers in Germany, the British press carried long debates on the subject of forgiveness. When I was asked to speak for the Jewish community, I reported a frequently retold incident in my life:*
>
> *'Can we forgive? Who are we to usurp God's role? Once, at a Kirchentag in Nurenberg, I talked about the anguish of Auschwitz. A young girl rushed up to me after the lecture. 'Rabbi, she said, I wasn't there, but can you forgive me?' and we embraced and cried together. Then an older man approached me. 'Rabbi', he said, I was a guard at a concentration camp. Can you forgive me?' 'No, I said. I cannot forgive. It is not the function of rabbis to give absolution, to be pardoners.'*
>
> *Between the New Year and the Day of Atonement, we try to go to any person whom we have wronged and asked forgiveness. 'But you cannot go to the six million. They are dead I cannot speak for them. Nor can I speak for God. But you are here at a church conference. God's forgiving grace may touch you but I am not a mediator, pardoner or spokesperson for God.'*
>
> *A number of my Christian colleagues were unhappy with my stance. An Oxford Chaplain with great respect for the Jewish community still felt he had to enunciate the Christian principle that one must forgive. He concluded that our refusal to forgive might lead to a recurrence of the Holocaust. A refusal to forgive is seen as a fatal human weakness. However, throughout rabbinic literature, there is awareness that an act of forgiveness is a relationship between humans requiring action from both sides. First, there must be repentance and the attempt to undo the evil committed. Forgiveness, difficult as it is, is a proper response by the victim. It is not always possible if the hurt is too deep and enduring.*

Both sides will then suffer: one carries the pain inflicted; and the other carries an awareness of an unfulfilled expiation. However, can the 'class action' of pardoning a nation take place at all? In Judaism, we see this as the prerogative of God. Nevertheless, we are approached and asked as a people to forgive. What can we do? [20]

The Rabbi is essentially repeating the words of Joseph. He cannot take the place of God whose prerogative is forgiveness.[21] The Rabbi also tells his hearers that he also cannot represent the six million who were the actual victims of the Nazi atrocity. He reminds us that *"forgiveness is a relationship between humans requiring action from both sides"*. There must be repentance on the part of the victimizer as well as forgiveness on the part of the victim.

So what can the holocaust survivor do? He does not want the perished to be forgotten, so true forgiveness remains unfinished business. When Joseph revealed himself to his brothers, there was repentance and reconciliation. One day, God will show himself to be holy through the entire nation of Israel in the sight of the entire world.

Ezekiel 39:7-8 (NIV) *I will make known my holy name among my people Israel. I will no longer let my holy name be profaned, and the nations will know that I the LORD am the Holy One in Israel. It is coming! It will surely take place, declares the Sovereign LORD. This is the day I have spoken of.*

This event will parallel the unveiling of Joseph. The nations of the world will be startled at what takes place. Even though the Christian world recognizes that the God we believe in is the God of Abraham, Isaac and Jacob,[22] it will still come as a total shock that he continues to be the God of Israel.

But there will also be another unveiling. Joseph is a picture of Jesus. Jesus has been dressed in Egyptian garb and he has been estranged from his brothers for millennia. There is a purpose in this mystery because God loves the world and the blindness that has come, in part, to the nation of Israel has allowed the good news to go out into the entire world. Paul is adamant.

---

[20] http://www.bbc.co.uk/history/worldwars/genocide/forgive_01.shtml
[21] Psalm 130:4
[22] Exodus 3:15

Romans 11:12 (NIV) *But if their transgression means riches for the world, and their loss means riches for the Gentiles, how much greater riches will their fullness bring!*

The *"fullness"* of Israel involves the outpouring of the Holy Spirit as on the day of Pentecost. God's purposes in redemption will have come full circle.

Ezekiel 39:27-29 (NIV) *When I have brought them back from the nations and have gathered them from the countries of their enemies, I will show myself holy through them in the sight of many nations. Then they will know that I am the LORD their God, for though I sent them into exile among the nations, I will gather them to their own land, not leaving any behind. I will no longer hide my face from them, for I will pour out my Spirit on the house of Israel, declares the Sovereign LORD.*

Like Joseph, the Lord will no longer hide his face from them and he will also pour out his Spirit on them. They will all know him, from the least to the greatest [23] and from them, one day, this will be heard as they cry out to him on behalf of the nations *"Father forgive them, they did not know what they were doing"*. What the nations had intended for harm, God intended for good, the saving of many lives.

---

[23] Jeremiah 31:34

CHAPTER FOUR

Today you will be with me in Paradise

The Second Panel of the Fountain of Tears

Luke 23:39-43 (NIV) *One of the criminals who hung there hurled insults at him: "Aren't you the Christ? Save yourself and us!" But the other criminal rebuked him. "Don't you fear God," he said, "since you are under the same sentence? We are punished justly, for we are getting what our deeds deserve. But this man has done nothing wrong." Then he said, "Jesus, remember me when you come into your kingdom." Jesus answered him, "I tell you the truth, today you will be with me in paradise."*

Crucifixion

Crucifixion was often performed to terrorize and dissuade the onlookers from perpetrating the crimes punishable by it. Victims were left on display after death as warnings so that others who attempt dissent might be forewarned. Crucifixion was usually intended to provide a death that was particularly slow, painful (hence the term excruciating, literally *"out of crucifying"*), gruesome, humiliating, and public, using whatever means were most expedient for that goal. Crucifixion methods varied considerably with location and time period.

The length of time required to reach death could range from a matter of hours to several days, depending on exact methods, the prior health of the condemned and environmental circumstances.

Death could result from any combination of causes, including blood loss, hypovolemic shock, or sepsis following infection, caused by the scourging that sometimes preceded the crucifixion, or by the process of being nailed itself, or eventual dehydration.

A theory attributed to Pierre Barbet holds that, when the whole body weight was supported by the stretched arms, the cause of death was asphyxiation. He conjectured that the condemned would have severe difficulty inhaling, due to hyper-expansion of the chest muscles and lungs. The condemned would therefore have to draw himself up by his arms, leading to exhaustion, or have his feet supported by tying or by a wood block. When no longer able to lift himself, the condemned would die within a few minutes. Legs were often broken to hasten death through severe traumatic shock and fat embolism.[1]

Crucifixion and the Torah

In the Torah, capital offenses (of which there were many) were punishable by death although crucifixion is not mentioned as a form of execution. It is possible; however, that crucifixion may be alluded to in the following passage:

Deuteronomy 21:22-23 (RSV) *And if a man has committed a crime punishable by death and he is put to death, and you hang him on a tree, his body shall not remain all night upon the tree, but you shall bury him the same day, for a hanged man is accursed by God; you shall not defile your land which the LORD your God gives you for an inheritance.*

The most obvious interpretation of this passage is the historical practice recorded several times in the Tanach of warriors or kings that were killed in battle. Sometimes their bodies were hung on trees. An example was the king of Ai.

Joshua 8:29 (NIV) *He [Joshua] hung the king of Ai on a tree and left him there until evening. At sunset, Joshua ordered them to take his body from the tree and throw it down at the entrance of the city gate. And they raised a large pile of rocks over it, which remains to this day.*

The removal of the body was in fulfillment to the commandment recorded in Deuteronomy (shown above).

---

[1] http://en.wikipedia.org/wiki/Crucifixion

A New Testament Interpretation

Both the Apostles Paul and Peter allude to the passage in Deuteronomy in their redemptive assessment of the crucifixion of Jesus.

Galatians 3:13 (NIV) *Christ redeemed us from the curse of the law by becoming a curse for us, for it is written: "Cursed is everyone who is hung on a tree."*

1 Peter 2:24 (NIV) *He himself bore our sins in his body on the tree, so that we might die to sins and live for righteousness; by his wounds you have been healed.*

We do not know what type of tree or stake that Jesus and the thieves were fixed to. Almost certainly it was not like the crucifix that is often displayed in medieval art. It may have been in the shape of a "T" or it could even have been a tree – even an olive tree. What we do know, however, is that Jesus (with the assistance of Simon of Cyrene) carried the *"cross"*. This could well have been the *"crosspiece"* that was to be fixed to the upright (stake or tree) that was permanently positioned in the place of execution.

The passage in Peter (1 Peter 2:24) is significant because it links the crucifixion of Jesus with the suffering of the servant in Isaiah 53.

Isaiah 53:5 (NIV) *But he was pierced for our transgressions, he was crushed for our iniquities; the punishment that brought us peace was upon him, and by his wounds we are healed.*

This is the New International Version's interpretation of this passage. The words translated *"he was pierced"* are transliterated **hu micholal** is probably more accurately translated *"he was defiled"*. However, the Greek word used in the Septuagint translation of Isaiah 53:5 (translated between the 3rd and 2nd century BCE in Alexandria) is also used in:

1 Samuel 31:3 (NIV) *The fighting grew fierce around Saul, and when the archers overtook him, they **wounded** him critically.*

This gives credence to the possibility that the word does carry the connotation of wounding by piercing. The KJV, of course, translates the phrase, *"He was wounded for our transgressions"*. The other passage that *might* speak of piercing is in Psalm 22.

Psalm 22:16 (NIV) *Dogs have surrounded me; a band of evil men has encircled me, they have pierced my hands and my feet.*

Unfortunately, this verse Is surrounded in controversy. The verse, which is Psalm 22:17 in the Tanach, reads *"like a lion my hands and my feet"* in the Masoretic Text which was copied, edited and distributed by a group of Jews known as the Masoretes between the 7th and 10th centuries CE. However, this rendering of the Hebrew phrase lacks any appropriate verb. In the Aramaic Targum we read *"they bite like a lion my hands and my feet"* and in the Septuagint we read *"they have dug [or pierced] my hands and feet"*. This last translation is also supported by the Dead Sea Scrolls.[2] As we will see, Psalm 22 maybe the most descriptive passage in the Tanach describing the agonies of the suffering experienced by Jesus AND by the Jewish people in the Holocaust.

Humiliation

While a crucifixion was an execution, it was also a humiliation, by making the condemned as vulnerable as possible. Although artists have depicted the figure on a cross with a loin cloth, it is likely that victims were crucified completely naked. This was also the experience of many of the millions who perished in the Holocaust and this aspect is alluded to in Psalm 22.

Psalm 22:17-18 (NIV) *I can count all my bones; people stare and gloat over me. They divide my garments among them and cast lots for my clothing.*

As I write this, I can see, in my mind's eye, the emaciated bodies of the living dead in the liberated camps such as Bergen Belsen. In particular, after arriving at the Death Camps, all personal belongings including clothes were removed, divided and re-distributed within the Third Reich. These verses, of course, were fulfilled in the Crucifixion of Jesus.

The Crucifixion of the Jewish People

[2] http://en.wikipedia.org/wiki/They_have_pierced_my_hands_and_my_feet

Mark 15:24 (NIV) *And they crucified him. Dividing up his clothes, they cast lots to see what each would get.*

The Gospel of John is much more explicit.

John 19:23-24 (RSV) *When the soldiers had crucified Jesus they took his garments and made four parts, one for each soldier; also his tunic. But the tunic was without seam, woven from top to bottom; so they said to one another, "Let us not tear it, but cast lots for it to see whose it shall be." This was to fulfil the scripture, "They parted my garments among them, and for my clothing they cast lots."*

Humiliation for the Jewish People, however, did not just begin within the Death Camps. Following Hitler's rise to power and with the implementation of the Nuremburg laws, Jewish people were increasingly victimized. We may be familiar with the ridicule given by the Nazis to Hasidic Jews within the ghetto. This is also alluded to in Psalm 22.

Psalm 22:6-8 (NIV) *But I am a worm and not a man, scorned by men and despised by the people. All who see me mock me; they hurl insults, shaking their heads: "He trusts in the LORD; let the LORD rescue him. Let him deliver him, since he delights in him."*

And also in Isaiah:

Isaiah 50:6 (NIV) *I offered my back to those who beat me, my cheeks to those who pulled out my beard; I did not hide my face from mocking and spitting.*

"I did not hide my face from mocking and spitting"

117

Again, this was the experience of Jesus. He predicted:

Mark 10:33-34 (NIV) *"We are going up to Jerusalem," he said, "and the Son of Man will be betrayed to the chief priests and teachers of the law. They will condemn him to death and will hand him over to the Gentiles, who will mock him and spit on him, flog him and kill him. Three days later he will rise."*

And this was fulfilled:

Mark 14:65 (RSV) *And some began to spit on him, and to cover his face, and to strike him, saying to him, "Prophesy!" And the guards received him with blows.*

The Two Thieves

Jesus was not alone. He was crucified between two thieves.

Luke 23:33 (RSV) *And when they came to the place which is called The Skull, there they crucified him, and the criminals, one on the right and one on the left.*

They are described as *"criminals"* but we have no idea of their crimes. Barabbas, who was released in place of Jesus, had been involved in murder and in an insurrection.[3] It is possible that these men, crucified with Jesus, were also involved but this is speculation. They knew, however, that there was some just cause for their execution.

Luke 23:41 (RSV) *And we indeed justly; for we are receiving the due reward of our deeds; but this man has done nothing wrong.*

Something had happened to this particular thief in these last moments before death. Matthew's account of the crucifixion is worth considering.

Matthew 27:38-45 (NIV) ***Two robbers were crucified with him, one on his right and one on his left.*** *Those who passed by hurled insults at him, shaking their heads and saying, "You who are going to destroy the temple and build it in three days, save yourself! Come down from the cross, if you are the Son of God!" In the same way the chief priests, the teachers of the law and the elders mocked him. "He saved others," they said, "but he can't save himself! He's the King of Israel! Let him come down now from the cross, and we will believe in him. He trusts in God. Let God rescue him now if he wants him, for he said, 'I am the Son of God.'"* ***In the same way the robbers who were crucified with him also heaped insults on him.*** *From the sixth hour until the ninth hour darkness came over all the land.*

---

[3] Mark 15:7; Luke 23:19

Jesus' Left Hand is turned down in Response to the Cursing

We can see from this passage that, at the very beginning of the crucifixion, BOTH criminals hurled insults at Jesus. Something happened to one of the criminals. What exactly was it? Personally, I think he had heard something. Let us remind ourselves of the context and what it was that Jesus said.

Luke 23:33-34 (RSV) *When they came to the place called The Skull, there they crucified him, and the criminals, one on the right and one on the left. And Jesus said, "Father, forgive them; for they know not what they do."*

Almost certainly, the criminals heard these words. They were the closest to Jesus after all and the offer of forgiveness was for them as well. They hurled insults at Jesus but they did not know what they were doing. One of the thieves realized this and became silent.

We were both Thieves

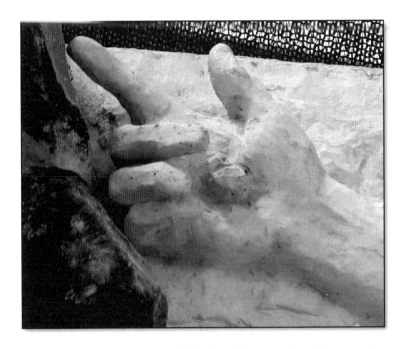

Jesus reaches out to the Thief asking to be Remembered

The Recognition

What did the criminal come to understand in these last moments of life? He uses the words *"Lord"* and *"Kingdom"*. This is an amazing insight. One moment he is cursing and the next moment he is recognizing that Jesus is Lord and that he is a king. He also recognized that Jesus was innocent.

Luke 23:41 (NIV) *"We are punished justly, for we are getting what our deeds deserve. But this man has done nothing wrong."*

This is an amazing admission. The criminal recognizes that he deserved to die for his crimes.

The Acknowledgement

When all is said and done, forgiveness only requires the acknowledgement of guilt (sin) on our part.

Jeremiah 3:12-13 (NIV) *'Return, faithless Israel,' declares the LORD, 'I will frown on you no longer, for I am merciful,' declares the LORD, 'I will not be angry forever. **Only acknowledge your guilt ...** '*

Acknowledgment of guilt is probably the hardest thing to do but it opens the door to paradise. The Covenant of Forgiveness is also a Covenant of Grace.

The Kingdom

The criminal also reckoned that Jesus was going to establish the kingdom. IF the criminals were involved with Barabbas, they would also have participated in the insurrection. This was against Roman occupation. The Jewish people (the disciples included) believed that the coming of the Messiah would usher in the Kingdom of Israel. Even after the resurrection and the extra 40 days of teaching, the disciples come to Jesus on the Mount of Olives:

Acts 1:6-7 (RSV) *So when they had come together, they asked him, "Lord, will you at this time restore the kingdom to Israel?" He said to them, "It is not for you to know times or seasons which the Father has fixed by his own authority.*

The problem for the insurrectionists and the disciples was when the kingdom of God would actually be restored to Israel. Jesus was hailed the King of Israel, he was crucified under a sign declaring him King of the Jews but he was dying on a cross.

In those moments before death, the disappointment of the thief, expressed in those initial insults, was transformed into hope. *"Lord, remember me* **when** *you come into your kingdom".* Jesus replies*, "I tell you the truth, today you will be with me in paradise."*

"Death was always before us"

Paradise

Whatever, Jesus understood about Paradise, the essential fact in this interaction is wherever the criminal was going to be after his death, he was going to be with Jesus.

The use of the word translated *"paradise"* in Scripture carries the idea of a garden. Perhaps the most enigmatic use of paradise in the New Testament are the words of the Apostle Paul:

2 Corinthians 12:3-4 (RSV) *And I know that this man was caught up into Paradise, whether in the body or out of the body I do not know, God knows, and he heard things that cannot be told, which man may not utter.*

Paul is intentionally evasive. He has no wish to speak of his own experiences. In fact, he says that what the man experienced and I think we can be fairly confident that he is speaking of himself; he was not permitted to speak about such things. This I think is very significant. We should be very cautious about testimonies that give explicit details about after-death and out-of-body experiences.

If Paul was not permitted to speak of such things, one might conclude that no-one is. If Paradise is the place that the departed spirits of believers go after death, when did Paul die? Although one cannot be dogmatic about this, according to the New Testament, Paul was once stoned. This took place in the city of Lystra.

Acts 14:19-20 (RSV) *But Jews came there from Antioch and Iconium; and having persuaded the people, they stoned Paul and dragged him out of the city, **supposing that he was dead**. But when the disciples gathered about him, he rose up and entered the city; and on the next day he went on with Barnabas to Derbe.*

The other use of the term *"Paradise"* in the New Testament is in the book of Revelation.

Revelation 2:7 (RSV) *He who has an ear, let him hear what the Spirit says to the churches. To him who conquers I will grant to eat of the tree of life, which is in the paradise of God.*

This alludes to OT usage where the word *'Pardes'* (a transliteration of a Persian word) occurs in Song of Solomon 4:13 (translated *"orchard"* in the KJV), Ecclestiastes.2:5 (translated *"orchards"* In the KJV), and Nehemiah 2:8 (translated *"forest"* in the KJV).

The original Persian meaning of the word is *"park"*. In Second Temple era Judaism, *'paradise'* came to be associated with the Garden of Eden and prophecies regarding the restoration of Eden.

The Septuagint uses the Greek word **παράδεισος** transliterated paradeisos around 30 times, both of Eden, (Genesis 2:8 etc.) and of Eden restored (Ezekiel 28:13, 36:35) etc.

Being with Jesus

Whatever, Jesus meant by Paradise, and we CANNOT know with certainty, the thief was promised that he would be with Jesus there. This reminds me of other words of Jesus:

John 14:1-3 (RSV) *Let not your hearts be troubled; believe in God, believe also in me. In my Father's house are many rooms; if it were not so, would I have told you that I go to prepare a place for you? And when I go and prepare a place for you, I will come again and will take you to myself, that where I am you may be also.*

"Let not your hearts be troubled"

"Mother, this is your Son" [1]

---

[1] Pencil drawing by Rick Wienecke

CHAPTER FIVE

Mother, this is your son ...

John 19:25-27 (RSV) *Standing by the cross of Jesus were his mother, his mother's sister, Mary the wife of Clopas, and Mary Magdalene. When Jesus saw his mother, and the disciple whom he loved standing near, he said to his mother, "Woman, behold, your son!" Then he said to the disciple, "Behold, your mother!" From that hour the disciple took her to his own home.*

The Third Panel of the Fountain of Tears

1. Natural Relationships

A. Mary, Mother of Jesus

Four women are standing at the foot of the cross but it is only one that Jesus notices. Probably the person he was closest to was Mary (Miriam) his mother. It was she who carried him when he was a child. God entrusted the raising of his son to this woman and, in a way, this was a great risk. For Jesus to be the perfect sacrifice for sin, he had to be without sin. This means that he kept the Law in its entirety throughout his entire life. The scripture says:

Hebrews 4:15 (RSV) *For we have not a high priest who is unable to sympathize with our weaknesses, but one who in every respect has been tempted as we are, yet without sin.*

Before his Bar Mitzvah, Jesus was under the tutelage and guidance of his parents and, in particular, his mother. I do not believe that we have sufficiently credited Mary with her total observance to Torah. In one particular aspect, we catch a glimpse of this in the Gospel of Luke.

Luke 2:39 (NIV) *When Joseph and Mary had done everything required by the Law of the Lord, they returned to Galilee to their own town of Nazareth.*

We do not know when Joseph died but there is no mention of him after Jesus began his public ministry apart from one rather cryptic reference in the Gospel of John.

John 6:42 (RSV) *They said, "Is not this Jesus, the son of Joseph, whose father and mother we know?*

One might assume from this passage that Joseph was still alive. However, there is no mention of him at significant events which took place during the Jesus' public ministry. A clear example is the Wedding at Cana.

John 2:1-2 (RSV) *On the third day there was a marriage at Cana in Galilee, and the mother of Jesus was there; Jesus also was invited to the marriage, with his disciples.*

It seems that Mary has been involved in the preparation of the wedding. She is the one who comes to Jesus to tell him that they have run out of wine. Jesus response to her is *"Dear woman …"* (John 2:4 NIV) and he uses the same word from the crucifixion. It is a little unclear as to whether the word was a term of affection. What he actually says to Mary from the crucifixion is *"Woman, behold your son"*. The word he must have used would have been the Hebrew or Aramaic equivalent of the Greek word transliterated *"gunai"* which is a general word for woman or wife. Maybe there is, in this, a reflection that there was something of an unnatural relationship between Jesus and Mary.

B. John, the Beloved Disciple

It is consistent and characteristic of the Apostle John that, in the fourth Gospel, he is never described by name. He is always *"another disciple"* (e.g. John 18:15) but, most often, *"the disciple whom Jesus loved"* (e.g. John 21:20). It appears that the most important thing as far as John was concerned was not who he was but that Jesus loved him. Years later John was also to write:

1 John 4:9-10 (RSV) *In this the love of God was made manifest among us, that God sent his only Son into the world, so that we might live through him. In this is love, not that we loved God but that he loved us and sent his Son to be the expiation for our sins.*

But there is much more that we can discover about John. His father's name was Zebedee and his brother was James (Ya'acov). The family business was fish and it was successful. His father had hired men working for him (Mark 1:20). The question before us is *"who was his actual mother"?* Can we know? The amazing answer is that we can know. The mother of James and John features rather a lot in the Gospel accounts. For example,

Matthew 20:20 (NIV) *Then the mother of Zebedee's sons came to Jesus with her sons and, kneeling down, asked a favor of him.*

The Gospel of Matthew also places her in close proximity to the cross.

Matthew 27:55-56 (RSV) *There were also many women there, looking on from afar, who had followed Jesus from Galilee, ministering to him; among whom were Mary Magdalene, and Mary the mother of James and Joseph, **and the mother of the sons of Zebedee.***

The parallel account in the Gospel of Mark is:

Mark 15:40-41 (NIV) *Some women were watching from a distance. Among them were Mary Magdalene, Mary the mother of James the younger and of Joses, **and Salome**. In Galilee these women had followed him and cared for his needs. Many other women who had come up with him to Jerusalem were also there.*

From this we can deduce that the name of the mother of John was Salome. But there is more!

John 19:25 (RSV) *Standing by the cross of Jesus were his mother, **and his mother's sister,** Mary the wife of Clopas, and Mary Magdalene.*

While we can deduce that Mary, the wife of Cleopas, was also the mother of James (Ya'acov) the younger and Joses (Yosef), the most amazing thing we can also know from this passage is that Salome (Shulamit), the mother of John, was also the sister of Mary, the mother of Jesus. John and Jesus were actually first cousins. Almost certainly they were of a similar age. Almost certainly they would have grown up together and would have been very close. It also explains why Mary could be entrusted to his care and, of course, the care of Salome, Mary's sister. Ultimately, the care of his mother was put into the hands of her blood relatives.

2. Unnatural Relationships

A. The Burden of Guilt

The memory of the perished is put on the shoulders of the Holocaust survivor. They are his blood relatives. For the rest of his life, he will carry the memory of them wherever he goes. But this is not the only thing that he carries. He has survived the Holocaust where they have perished. He was unable to save the members of his own family. If he could have, he would have carried his mother to safety. She was snatched away with no one to help. The survivor carries the burden of guilt.

Psalm 38:4 (NIV) *My guilt has overwhelmed me like a burden too heavy to bear.*

If Christians sometimes struggle with the concept of God's disfavor, how much more must the Jewish people and the nation of Israel struggle with the whole idea of the Holocaust in which 6 million of their own people perished. Thus, another part of the mantle that Jewish people carry is the struggle to reconcile the Holocaust with the possibility of being in the disfavor of God.

It has also been the experience of some Jewish people coming to the Fountain of Tears. Confronted with the crucifixion of Jesus, some have been convicted of guilt that somehow the involvement of Jewish people in the death of Jesus has led to their suffering. This is another part of the burden that the Jewish people may carry. Nevertheless, it is recorded in the book of Isaiah that the suffering servant would deal with this issue and bring this unnatural relationship to an end.

The Mantle of the Perished

Isaiah 53:10 (NIV) *Yet it was the LORD's will to crush him and cause him to suffer, and though the LORD makes his life a **guilt offering**, he will see his offspring and prolong his days, and the will of the LORD will prosper in his hand.*

Matthew 11:28-30 (RSV) *Come to me, all who labor and are heavy laden, and I will give you rest. Take my yoke upon you, and learn from me; for I am gentle and lowly in heart, and you will find rest for your souls. For my yoke is easy, and my burden is light.*

B. The Lord and his People

Although it is an unnatural relationship, God himself declares that he is not only a father to Israel but he is also like a mother. We particularly see this aspect when we consider the journey that the children of Israel made in the desert. Moses was increasingly burdened by the difficulty of leading his people. God reassured him:

Deuteronomy 1:30-31 (RSV) *The LORD your God who goes before you will himself fight for you, just as he did for you in Egypt before your eyes, and in the wilderness, where you have seen how the LORD your God bore you, as a man bears his son, in all the way that you went until you came to this place.'*

The father is carrying his son. This is an illustration of God's eternal love for his people. He is committed to carrying them and loving them:

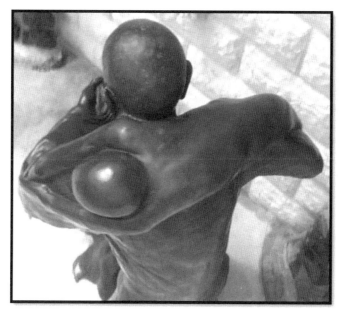

A Heavy Yoke to Bear

Hosea 11:1-4 (RSV) *When Israel was a child, I loved him, and out of Egypt I called my son. The more I called them, the more they went from me; they kept sacrificing to the Baals, and burning incense to idols. Yet it was I who taught Ephraim to walk, I took them up in my arms; but they did not know that I healed them. I led them with cords of compassion, with the bands of love, and I became to them as one, who eases the yoke on their jaws, and I bent down to them and fed them.*

These words in the prophecy of Hosea reflect the words of Jesus that we read previously. He lifts the yoke and the burden and takes it upon himself. Most of the illustrations in the Bible depict God as Father, but there are also passages which speak of a mother's love. Perhaps the most remarkable is found in the book of Isaiah:

"I could not save my own mother"

Mother this is your Son …

Isaiah 49:14-16 (NIV) *But Zion said, "The LORD has forsaken me, the Lord has forgotten me." "Can a mother forget the baby at her breast and have no compassion on the child she has borne? Though she may forget, I will not forget you! See, I have engraved you on the palms of my hands; your walls are ever before me.*

**Naomi and Ruth: An Unnatural Relationship
between Jew and Gentile** [2]

C. Jew and Gentile

Historically, the Jewish people have kept themselves to themselves. Even though they were called to be a light to the Gentiles, they have been kept in isolation. And yet it is God's intention to bring together Jew and Gentile. Perhaps this is the most unnatural relationship of all.

The Bible makes it very clear that disobedience by the children of Israel would lead to their dispersion to the ends of the Earth. The apostle Paul also makes clear that through their disobedience, salvation has come to the Gentiles to provoke Israel to jealousy. Unfortunately, the history of the church reminds us that, in the main, Gentiles have failed in their mission.

Nevertheless, it **is** the Gentiles who will be the instruments in God's hands to facilitate the restoration of the nation and the return of the children of Israel to their land. In a sense, God has commissioned the Gentiles to carry the Jewish people.

Isaiah 49:21-22 (NIV) *Then you will say in your heart, 'Who bore me these? I was bereaved and barren; I was exiled and rejected. Who brought these up? I was left all alone, but these - where have they come from?'" This is what the Sovereign LORD says: "See, I will beckon to the Gentiles, I will lift up my banner to the peoples; they will bring your sons in their arms and carry your daughters on their shoulders.*

---

[2] Sculpture by Rick Wienecke [http://www.castingseeds.com/naomiandruth.html] Also shown in this sculpture is Orpa who turns her back on Naomi and returns to Moab. She is a picture of the church that sees no place for the people of Israel in God's plan and purpose.

Another picture of the unnatural relationship between Jews and Gentile is Paul's use of the olive tree analogy in Romans chapter 11. Israel is depicted as the natural branches; the Gentiles are the wild olive branches. The grafting in of the Gentiles is an indication of this unnatural relationship that will fulfill God's purposes for humanity.

Romans 11:24 (NIV) *After all, if you were cut out of an olive tree that is wild by nature, and contrary to nature were grafted into a cultivated olive tree, how much more readily will these, the natural branches, be grafted into their own olive tree!*

The Nature of the Olive Tree

I believe there is a great deal of confusion regarding the nature of the olive tree into which the Gentiles have been grafted. Is the tree Israel? In other words, when Gentiles come to faith, are they grafted into Israel? Replacement theologians go one step further and state that the Church is now Israel and that all the blessings and promises that God has made to the Nation have been transferred to the Church. It is my opinion that this is a total denial of God's faithfulness. As the Apostle Paul states categorically:

Romans 11:1 (NIV) *I ask then: Did God reject his people? By no means!*

So, what is the nature of the olive tree which belongs to them according to Paul? It is actually quite straightforward. The people of Israel are the natural olive branches; the Gentiles are the wild olive branches. So what or who is the ROOT. Jesus uses a different horticultural analogy in John chapter 15

John 15:5-6 (RSV*) I am the vine, you are the branches. He who abides in me, and I in him, he it is that bears much fruit, for apart from me you can do nothing. If a man does not abide in me, he is cast forth as a branch and withers; and the branches are gathered, thrown into the fire and burned.*

If Gentiles are grafted into anything, they are grafted into Jesus. Jesus is described as the ROOT and offspring of David (Jesse). As we have considered previously, he is THE branch.

Isaiah 11:10 (NIV) *In that day the Root of Jesse will stand as a banner for the peoples; the nations will rally to HIM, and his place of rest will be glorious.*

This is quoted by Paul in the book of Romans.

Romans 15:12 (NIV) *And again, Isaiah says, "The Root of Jesse will spring up, one who will arise to rule over the nations; the Gentiles will hope in HIM."*

In other words, the root is a *"HIM"*. It is noteworthy, that the last statement that Jesus makes in the Bible is not in the Gospels but in Revelation.

Revelation 22:16 (RSV) *I Jesus have sent my angel to you with this testimony for the churches. I am the root and the offspring of David, the bright morning star.*

We shall have occasion to return to this verse in the next chapter but the point is this: The root is Jesus and if the root is holy (and he is), then so are the branches (Romans 11: 16). This is true for both Israel (the natural branches) and the Gentiles (the wild Olive branches).

Paul gives a warning to the Gentile believers.

Romans 11:21-22 (NIV) *For if God did not spare the natural branches, he will not spare you either. Consider therefore the kindness and sternness of God: sternness to those who fell, but kindness to you, provided that you continue in his kindness. Otherwise, you also will be cut off.*

This reflects exactly the words of Jesus in John 15:6 shown above. If anyone does not remain in Jesus, he becomes a discarded branch that is thrown away and burned. These words raise very important questions but they are beyond the scope of this study.

Paul also speaks about this unnatural relationship in his letter to the Ephesians.

Ephesians 3:4-6 (NIV) *In reading this, then, you will be able to understand my insight into the mystery of Christ, which was not made known to men in other generations as it has now been revealed by the Spirit to God's holy apostles and prophets. This mystery is that through the gospel the Gentiles are heirs together with Israel, members together of one body, and sharers together in the promise in Christ Jesus.*

The Gentiles do not become Israel but they can be heirs together WITH Israel. Israel and the Gentiles are members together of one body and they have a share together in the promises that God has made. As Paul has written elsewhere

2 Corinthians 1:20-22 (RSV) *For all the promises of God find their Yes in him. That is why we utter the Amen through him, to the glory of God. But it is God who establishes us with you in Christ, and has commissioned us; he has put his seal upon us and given us his Spirit in our hearts as a guarantee.*

It is possible that we might read these words understanding that the *"us"* are the Jewish people (in this case, Paul, representative of the believing remnant of Israel) and the *"you"* are the Gentiles (in this case, the people of Corinth). The fact is this, what guarantees the fulfillment of the promises is the gift of the Holy Spirit.

The Story of Ruth

It is very significant that the book of Ruth is read by the Jewish people at Shavuot (the Feast of Weeks; Pentecost). The story of Ruth is a wonderful example of God's plan to bring Jew and Gentile together. Elimelech and his wife Naomi with their two sons, Mahlon and Kilion flee to Moab to escape the famine in Bethlehem. While in Moab, the two sons marry Moabite wives, Orpah and Ruth. All the men in the family die and Naomi decides to go back to Bethlehem. She pleads with her two daughters-in-law to stay in Moab. Orpah leaves but Ruth clings to Naomi and says these immortal words.

Ruth 1:16-17 (RSV) *But Ruth said, "Entreat me not to leave you or to return from following you; for where you go I will go, and where you lodge I will lodge; your people shall be my people, and your God my God; where you die I will die, and there will I be buried. May the LORD do so to me and more also if even death parts me from you."*

Naomi returns to Bethlehem but she considers that her life is now very bitter.

Ruth 1:20-22 (RSV) *She said to them, "Do not call me Naomi, call me Mara, for the Almighty has dealt very bitterly with me. I went away full, and the LORD has brought me back empty. Why call me Naomi, when the LORD has afflicted me and the Almighty has brought calamity upon me?" So Naomi returned, and Ruth the Moabitess her daughter-in-law with her, who returned from the country of Moab. And they came to Bethlehem at the beginning of barley harvest.*

One of the reasons, Ruth is read at Shavuot is because the story of Ruth unfolds between Passover and Pentecost. Among other things, both of these festivals are harvests. Passover occurs at the barley harvest and Pentecost occurs at the wheat harvest that follows some 50 days later.

Ruth 2:23 (RSV) *So she kept close to the maidens of Boaz, gleaning until the end of the barley and wheat harvests; and she lived with her mother-in-law.*

This is also an outworking of the injunction to care for the poor and the alien contained in the Torah particularly in the passage describing the Festival of Shavuot.

Leviticus 23:16-17, 22 (NIV) *Count off fifty days up to the day after the seventh Sabbath, and then present an offering of new grain to the LORD. From wherever you live, bring two loaves made of two-tenths of an ephah of fine flour, baked with yeast, as a wave offering of firstfruits to the LORD ... When you reap the harvest of your land, do not reap to the very edges of your field or gather the gleanings of your harvest. Leave them for the poor and the alien. I am the LORD your God.*

Boaz is faithful and takes the place of kinsman redeemer, purchasing the property of Elimelech as well acquiring Ruth the Moabitess as his wife. The end of the story is remarkable in the context of this chapter.

Ruth 4:13-17 (RSV) *So Boaz took Ruth and she became his wife; and he went in to her, and the LORD gave her conception, and she bore a son. Then the women said to Naomi, "Blessed be the LORD, who has not left you this day without next of kin; and may his name be renowned in Israel! He shall be to you a restorer of life and a nourisher of your old age; for your daughter-in-law who loves you, who is more to you than seven sons, has borne him." Then Naomi took the child and laid him in her bosom, and became his nurse. And the women of the neighborhood gave him a name, saying, "A son has been born to Naomi." They named him Obed; he was the father of Jesse, the father of David.*

Naomi had lost everything but through Ruth's devotion and Boaz' faithfulness, Naomi was brought out of her bitterness. It is as though Ruth becomes a surrogate mother for Naomi. It is as though Ruth says to Naomi, ***"Mother, this is your son"***. By so doing, Ruth was to become part of the ancestral line both of David and Jesus.[3]

This truth is made all the more remarkable because of another passage in the Torah.

Deuteronomy 23:3 (NIV) *No Ammonite or Moabite or any of his descendants may enter the assembly of the LORD, even down to the tenth generation.*

Ruth was a descendent of a Moabite. King David was a 4th generation descendent of a Moabite. How can this be? Something has to happen to this commandment contained in the book of Deuteronomy.

I think a clue is to be found in the 15th and 16th chapters of the prophecy of Isaiah which are described as an oracle concerning Moab. The prophet sees that Moab is destroyed and fugitives are fleeing. In the midst of all of this, there is an amazing promise.

---

[3] Matthew 1:5

Isaiah 16:5 (NIV) *In love a throne will be established; in faithfulness a man will sit on it - one from the house of David - one who in judging seeks justice and speeds the cause of righteousness.*

In other words, because of the love of God, there is hope for Moab (a picture of the Gentiles). This is also because of the one who is to come and who will sit on David's throne seeking justice and bringing righteousness.[4] Thus, God is in the business of creating the most unlikely unnatural relationships. He loves the Jewish people but his love extends to the whole of humanity. His eternal purpose is to unite Jew and Gentile.

Ephesians 2:13-15 (RSV) *Now in Christ Jesus you who once were far off have been brought near in the blood of Christ. For he is our peace, who has made us both one, and has broken down the dividing wall of hostility, by abolishing in his flesh the law of commandments and ordinances, that he might create in himself one new man in place of the two, so making peace.*

Jesus fulfilled the requirements of all the law and this has to include the law that would forbid the descendants of Moabites from becoming part of God's people. As we have seen in Leviticus 23, during Shavuot, the priest was to wave two loaves of leavened bread before the Lord. Some have seen in this a picture of Jew and Gentile that have been brought together. Paul puts it like this.

Ephesians 2:15-18 (NIV) *His purpose was to create in himself one new man out of the two, thus making peace, and in this one body to reconcile both of them to God through the cross, by which he put to death their hostility. He came and preached peace to you who were far away and peace to those who were near.* **For through him we both have access to the Father by one Spirit.**

This is another reason why it is very appropriate for the book of Ruth to be read at Shavuot. On the day of Pentecost, the Holy Spirit was poured out to write the Law on the hearts of both Jews and Gentiles. It is through the New Covenant that Gentiles are grafted in to the believing community of God's people. Jew and Gentile become one in Jesus through the administration of the Holy Spirit.

Replacement Theology

Many sincere evangelical Christians do not accept that the Lord has any continuing purpose for the people of Israel. They believe that all the promises made to the Israel have been transferred to the Church. This, of course, is theologically inconsistent. Paul is adamant.

---

[4] See also Psalm 9; Isaiah 11:1-5; Isaiah 42:1-7

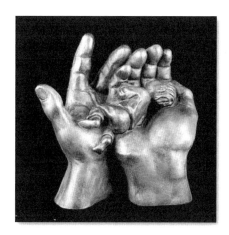

"Mother, this is your Son" [5]

Romans 9:3-5 (RSV) *For I could wish that I myself were accursed and cut off from Christ for the sake of my brethren, my kinsmen by race. They are Israelites, and to them belong the sonship, the glory, the covenants, the giving of the law, the worship, and the promises; to them belong the patriarchs, and of their race, according to the flesh, is the Christ. God who is over all be blessed for ever. Amen.*

The chapters 9, 10 and 11 in his letter to the Romans are a logical continuation of his argument that nothing can separate from the love of God from those that he has chosen.[6] If this is true, how do we understand Israel, they are the chosen ones after all.[7] Everything belongs to them (note the present tense in the verses above). How come they did not welcome the Messiah with open arms?

This, in a nutshell, is the mystery of Israel and over the next three chapters, Paul explains the inexplicable.

Romans 11:25 (KJV) *I would not, brethren, that ye should be ignorant of this mystery, lest ye should be wise in your own conceits; that blindness in part is happened to Israel, **until** the fullness of the Gentiles be come in.*

The word *"until"* is very significant. Accordingly, replacement theology could be defined as theological conceit. The fact is this: because of their blindness (which is God ordained) the gospel has gone out into the world. Jesus clearly predicted this.

---

[5] The Sculpture by Rick Wienecke is actually entitled "The Calling" [http://www.castingseeds.com/calling.html]. This author, however, sees in the piece the fulfilment of God's call to the Gentiles to carry the Jewish people home as expressed in Isaiah 49:22.

[6] Romans 8:33-39

[7] Deuteronomy 7:6

Acts 1:8 (RSV) *But you shall receive power when the Holy Spirit has come upon you; and you shall be my witnesses in Jerusalem and in all Judea and Samaria and to the end of the earth.*

The actual trigger for the gospel to move out into the world was the invasion of Jerusalem by the Roman armies under Titus. Jesus forewarned his disciples of the days leading up to the destruction of the Temple in 70 CE.

Luke 19:41-44 (NIV) *As he approached Jerusalem and saw the city, he wept over it and said, "If you, even you, had only known on this day what would bring you peace - but now it is hidden from your eyes. The days will come upon you when your enemies will build an embankment against you and encircle you and hem you in on every side. They will dash you to the ground, you and the children within your walls. They will not leave one stone on another, because you did not recognize the time of God's coming to you.*

These are truly amazing words. Jesus weeps over Jerusalem because he knows that the nation would not be able to recognize him (even the time of God coming to them). This was hidden from their eyes. God was sovereign over the fact that the nation of Israel had eyes but could not see and ears that could not hear.[8] Later, Jesus returns to the theme of the desolation of Jerusalem.

Luke 21:20-21 (RSV) *But when you see Jerusalem surrounded by armies, then know that its desolation has come near. Then let those who are in Judea flee to the mountains, and let those who are inside the city depart, and let not those who are out in the country enter it.*

The siege of Jerusalem began in the spring of 70 CE. This gave the believers ample time to flee. They took the gospel with them initially into Judea and Samaria and then, ultimately, to the end of the earth. Those who did not believe were left behind and more than a million perished at the hands of the Romans.

Luke 21:24 (RSV) *They will fall by the edge of the sword, and be led captive among all nations; and Jerusalem will be trodden down by the Gentiles, until the times of the Gentiles are fulfilled.*

Again, the word *"until"* is very significant. Jesus looks into the distant future and sees the time when Jerusalem would once again be the capital of Israel. This has happened in our day. Although we cannot be dogmatic, it is possible that the times of the Gentiles were fulfilled in June 1967 when the Israel Defense Force re-unified Jerusalem.

---

[8] Isaiah 42:18-20

Following the fulfillment of the times of the Gentiles (i.e. the fullness of the Gentiles), all Israel will be saved. Paul puts it like this.

Romans 11:11-12 (NIV) *Again I ask: Did they stumble so as to fall beyond recovery? Not at all! Rather, because of their transgression, salvation has come to the Gentiles **to make Israel envious.** But if their transgression means riches for the world, and their loss means riches for the Gentiles, how much greater riches will their fullness bring!*

The above translation in the NIV is simply terrible. The KJV translates it like this.

Soldiers at the Wall in 1967

Romans 11:11-12 (KJV) *I say then, have they stumbled that they should fall? God forbid: but rather through their fall salvation is come unto the Gentiles, for **to provoke them to jealousy**. Now if the fall of them be the riches of the world, and the diminishing of them the riches of the Gentiles; how much more their fullness?*

There is a world of difference between *"envy"* (NIV) and *"jealousy"* (KJV). In particular, envy is a sin[9] and it may be defined as wanting something (or someone) that does **not** belong to you. Another word for *"envy"* is *"covetousness"*. Envy is breaking the 10th commandment. On the other hand, jealousy is wanting something (or someone) back that **actually** belongs to you. According to Paul, the Gentiles have been saved to provoke the nation of Israel to jealousy. We need to help them re-appropriate what belongs to them – even their Messiah.

Generally speaking, the institutional church has done a very poor job in doing this (with some notable exceptions). Perhaps the greatest heresy of all is to suggest, through replacement theology, that the church has supplanted Israel in God's plan and purposes. Sometimes you will hear the church being described as the *"New Israel"* even though this term does not exist anywhere in scripture. Paul does refer, however, to *"the Israel of God"* in his letter to the Galatians. Again the NIV is unhelpful here.

---

[9] See Mark 7:21-23; 1 Peter 2:1

Galatians 6:15-16 (NIV) *Neither circumcision nor uncircumcision means anything; what counts is a new creation. Peace and mercy to all who follow this rule, even to the Israel of God.*

Galatians 6:15-16 (KJV) *For in Christ Jesus neither circumcision availeth anything, nor uncircumcision, but a new creature. **And** as many as walk according to this rule, peace be on them, **and** mercy, **and** upon the Israel of God.*

The Greek of verse 16 is as follows.

$$\text{καὶ ὅσοι τῷ κανόνι τούτῳ στοιχήσουσιν, εἰρήνη ἐπ' αὐτοὺς καὶ ἔλεος καὶ ἐπὶ τὸν Ἰσραὴλ τοῦ θεοῦ.}$$

I have highlighted the Greek word καὶ which simply means *"and"*. Unlike the NIV, the KJV does justice to this Greek text and the three *"ands"* are there. What Paul is saying in this verse is that grace and mercy are on all those that follow this rule as well as (i.e. and) on the Israel of God. The Israel of God is the believing remnant of Israel.

The foolishness of considering the church to be Israel is best highlighted in the following verses in chapter 11 of Romans. Again I quote them in the KJV because I think this translation conveys the heart of Paul's argument better than the other versions.

Romans 11:30-32 (KJV) *For as ye in times past have not believed God, yet have now obtained mercy through their unbelief: Even so have these also now not believed, that through your mercy they also may obtain mercy. For God hath concluded them all in unbelief, that he might have mercy upon all.*

Accordingly, the onus is on the Gentiles to show mercy to the nation of Israel. This truth sends Paul into raptures.

Romans 11:33-36 (NIV) *O the depth of the riches both of the wisdom and knowledge of God! How unsearchable are his judgments, and his ways past finding out! For who hath known the mind of the Lord? Or who hath been his counselor? Or who hath first given to him, and it shall be recompensed unto him again? For of him, and through him, and to him, are all things: to whom be glory forever. Amen.*

Paul's logic spills over into chapter 12.

Romans 12:1 (NIV) *Therefore, I urge you, brothers, **in view of God's mercy**, to offer your bodies as living sacrifices, holy and pleasing to God - this is your spiritual act of worship.*

Paul continues his argument through the remaining chapters of his letter to the Romans. Jew and Gentile are to live together in harmony.

Romans 15:7-13 (NIV) *Accept one another, then, just as Christ accepted you, in order to bring praise to God. For I tell you that Christ has become a servant of the Jews on behalf of God's truth, to confirm the promises made to the patriarchs so that the Gentiles may glorify God for his mercy, as it is written: "Therefore I will praise you among the Gentiles; I will sing hymns to your name." Again, it says, "Rejoice, O Gentiles, with his people." And again, "Praise the Lord, all you Gentiles, and sing praises to him, all you peoples." And again, Isaiah says, "The Root of Jesse will spring up, one who will arise to rule over the nations; the Gentiles will hope in him." May the God of hope fill you with all joy and peace as you trust in him, so that you may overflow with hope by the power of the Holy Spirit.*

Replacement theology is a denial of this relationship and God's eternal purpose. Replacement theology is the ultimate unnatural relationship.

CHAPTER SIX

My God, My God, Why have You Forsaken Me?

Matthew 27:46-49 (NIV) *About the ninth hour Jesus cried out in a loud voice, "Eloi, Eloi, lama sabachthani?" which means, "My God, my God, why have you forsaken me?" When some of those standing there heard this, they said, "He's calling Elijah." Immediately one of them ran and got a sponge. He filled it with wine vinegar, put it on a stick, and offered it to Jesus to drink. The rest said, "Now leave him alone. Let's see if Elijah comes to save him."*

The Fourth Panel of the Fountain of Tears

Throughout his life, Jesus had the closest possible relationship with God who he always called Father. But now, at the highest point of his suffering, he was not able to find him. He felt abandoned. All he was able to do was to call out the words of the ancient Jewish psalm that he would have known by heart. It is an amazing psalm for it probably describes the pain he was suffering in greater detail than in any other place in the entire Bible. We will need to look at every word. In particular, the few words spoken by Jesus that are recorded in the Gospels can be set in the context of the first two verses of Psalm 22.

Psalm 22:1-2 (NIV) *My God, my God, why have you forsaken me? Why are you so far from saving me, so far from the words of my groaning? O my God, I cry out by day, but you do not answer, by night, and am not silent.*

Jesus has been crucified for over six hours by the time he utters these words of abandonment. He has cried out by *"day"* and by *"night"* when the darkness covered the land for those three hours. In fact, we can see that the darkness actually contributes to the total fulfillment of this psalm.

Jesus is groaning in agony, Jesus is crying out but seemingly the heavens are closed up. It is as though the Father has turned his back on the Son he loves so much.

Before we move on, we need to note that in the Hebrew text the actual first verse of this psalm includes this: *To the chief musician, set to 'The Deer of the Dawn', a psalm of David.* This is from the Hebrew:

לַמְנַצֵּחַ עַל־אַיֶּלֶת הַשַּׁחַר מִזְמוֹר לְדָוִד׃

The Hebrew words [אַיֶּלֶת הַשַּׁחַר] translated *"Deer of the Dawn"* can be transliterated *"Ayelet HaShachar"*.[1] This could have been the melody to which the psalm was originally sung. The word *"Ayelet"* is the compound form of *"Ayalah"* which is a female deer, hind or doe.[2] *"HaShachar"* is translated *"the dawn"*. The gentle animal is being hounded to death by bulls (verse 12), lions (verse 13) and dogs (verse 16). The word *"ayalah"* is also alluded to in verse 19:

Psalm 22:19 (NIV) *But you, O LORD, be not far off; O **my strength**, come quickly to help me.*

The word translated *"my strength"* is transliterated as *"ayalooti"* and is the only time this word is used in the entire Tanach. The psalmist is asking for strength because, like a gentle doe, he has none.

From the Hebrew text, we can know for certain that this is a psalm written by David but there is no clear indication, unlike some of his other psalms, as to why and when he wrote it. If he is speaking about himself, we can only speculate as to his situation. He is desperate and he feels totally abandoned. It is this writer's opinion that he may have written this after he was driven from Jerusalem during Absalom's rebellion. David weeps over Jerusalem as he leaves the city via the Mount of Olives.

---

[1] The words "Ayelet HaShachar" may be foreign to our ears but this is not true for Jewish people. It is the name of a kibbutz, a Jewish Study Centre for young women and several musical groups. The name Ayelet is also a girl's name although it is not in common usage.
[2] The masculine form is "Ayal".

2 Samuel 15:30 (RSV) *But David went up the ascent of the Mount of Olives, weeping as he went, barefoot and with his head covered; and all the people who were with him covered their heads, and they went up, weeping as they went.*

Thus, David and all the people are weeping as they slowly process up the Mount of Olives. David is also being cursed as well being pelted with stones. He even suggests that it may be the Lord who is the author of the curse.

2 Samuel 16:7-10 (NKJV) *Also Shimei said thus when he cursed: "Come out! Come out! You bloodthirsty man, you rogue! The LORD has brought upon you all the blood of the house of Saul, in whose place you have reigned; and the LORD has delivered the kingdom into the hand of Absalom your son. So now you are caught in your own evil, because you are a bloodthirsty man!" Then Abishai the son of Zeruiah said to the king, "Why should this dead dog curse my lord the king? Please, let me go over and take off his head!" But the king said, "What have I to do with you, you sons of Zeruiah? So let him curse, because the LORD has said to him, 'Curse David.' Who then shall say, 'Why have you done so?'"*

Abishai, one of David's mighty men suggests that Shimei is a dog, albeit a dead one. Maybe this is in David's mind when he writes:

Psalm 22:20 (NIV) *Deliver my life from the sword, my precious life from the power of the dogs.*

And David is also deserted and betrayed by his friend Hushai.[3]

2 Samuel 16:16-18 (NKJV) *And so it was, when Hushai the Archite, David's friend, came to Absalom, that Hushai said to Absalom, "Long live the king! Long live the king!" So Absalom said to Hushai, "Is this your loyalty to your friend? Why did you not go with your friend?" And Hushai said to Absalom, "No, but whom the LORD and this people and all the men of Israel choose, his I will be, and with him I will remain.*

It might be that he words of Isaiah also apply to David in his distress.

Isaiah 53:3 (NIV) *He was despised and rejected by men, a man of sorrows, and familiar with suffering. Like one from whom men hide their faces he was despised, and we esteemed him not.*

---

[3] Jesus was deserted by his friends and betrayed by one in particular.

However, David still has the hope of vindication.

2 Samuel 16:12 (NKJV) *It may be that the LORD will look on my affliction, and that the LORD will repay me with good for his cursing this day.*

This hope and expectation is reflected in the next verses of Psalm 22.

Psalm 22:3-5 (NIV) *Yet you are enthroned as the Holy One; you are the praise of Israel. In you our fathers put their trust; they trusted and you delivered them. They cried to you and were saved; in you they trusted and were not disappointed.*

At this point, it is interesting to note that *"Ayelet HaShachar"* is also the name of the morning star (i.e. the first light of dawn). This is the very last thing that Jesus says about himself:

Revelation 22:16 (NIV) *I, Jesus, have sent my angel to give you this testimony for the churches. I am the Root and the Offspring of David, and the bright Morning Star.*

Furthermore, the apostle Peter suggests:

2 Peter 1:19 (NIV) *And we have the word of the prophets made more certain, and you will do well to pay attention to it, as to a light shining in a dark place, until the day dawns and the morning star rises in your hearts.*

So Psalm 22 has to be in two parts. Verses 1 to 21 describes in detail the suffering of the afflicted one. This is the darkness of his soul. Verses 22 to 31, however, are very optimistic. The day has dawned and the morning star has risen. We will study the second part of the psalm in greater detail when we consider the theme of resurrection in later chapters.

As we have said, the first part of Psalm 22 is probably the most graphic description in the entire Bible of what took place at the crucifixion. When Jesus cries out *"My God, My God, why have you forsaken me?"* it is not just the first verse that is in his mind. Every verse must be significant. For example:

Psalm 22:6-8 (NIV) *But I am a worm and not a man, scorned by men and despised by the people. All who see me mock me; **they hurl insults, shaking their heads:** "He trusts in the LORD; let the LORD rescue him. Let him deliver him, since he delights in him."*

These words were fulfilled to the letter at the crucifixion.

Matthew 27:39-40 (NIV) *Those who passed by hurled insults at him, shaking their heads and saying, "You who are going to destroy the temple and build it in three days, save yourself! Come down from the cross, if you are the Son of God!"*

The next verses of the psalm are also very significant.

Psalm 22:9-11 (NIV) *Yet you brought me out of the womb; you made me trust in you even at my mother's breast. From birth I was cast upon you; from my mother's womb you have been my God. Do not be far from me, for trouble is near and there is no-one to help.*

I have no doubt that Jesus knew this entire psalm by heart. He is living (and dying) every word of this psalm in his crucifixion. After so many hours of suffering, he is reminded of his mother. It is as though he snaps out of his terrible suffering and looks down from the cross and sees his mother and his close friend standing close by. We have considered this in the previous chapter but it is good to be reminded in the context of this amazing psalm.

John 19:26-27 (RSV) *When Jesus saw his mother, and the disciple whom he loved standing near, he said to his mother, "Woman, behold, your son!" Then he said to the disciple, "Behold, your mother!" And from that hour the disciple took her to his own home.*

John remains the faithful friend and he is there to help. However, he is nearly lost in the crowd of hostile witnesses to this execution.

Psalm 22:12-13 (NIV) *Many bulls surround me; strong bulls of Bashan encircle me. Roaring lions tearing their prey open their mouths wide against me.*

The next verses in Psalm 22 are truly remarkable when we consider the order of the words spoken during the crucifixion.

Psalm 22:14-15 (NIV) *I am poured out like water, and all my bones are out of joint. My heart has turned to wax; it has melted away within me. My strength is dried up like a potsherd, and my tongue sticks to the roof of my mouth; you lay me in the dust of death.*

We will look at this passage in greater detail in the next chapter when we consider the words *"I thirst"*. The next verse of the psalm is as follows.

Psalm 22:16 (NIV) *Dogs have surrounded me; a band of evil men has encircled me, they have pierced my hands and my feet.*

Unfortunately, this verse is surrounded in controversy. The verse, which is Psalm 22:17 in the Tanach, reads *"like a lion my hands and my feet"* in the Masoretic Text. As I have already mentioned, this rendering of the Hebrew phrase lacks any appropriate verb. In the Aramaic Targum[4] we read *"they bite like a lion my hands and my feet"* and in the Septuagint we read *"they have dug [or pierced] my hands and feet".* This last translation is also supported by the Dead Sea Scrolls. [5]

The Masoretic text was compiled during the Christian era and it needs to be born in mind that most of the Old Testament translations that are currently used worldwide are largely based on the Masoretic text. On the other hand, the Septuagint was the Greek translation of the Hebrew Scriptures that was compiled (by some 70 scholars) initially in Alexandria and begun in the third Century BCE. [6]

Although, the translation of the Septuagint continued into the Christian era, the Tanach that was available to the writers of the New Testament obviously predated the Christian era. These texts were available in Greek (the earliest Septuagint) and Hebrew (similar to the scrolls found in the Essene community by the Dead Sea). This might explain some of the differences that exist particularly where the writers of New Testament quote passages from the Tanach. The controversy surrounding the verses continues unabated and we consider this in greater detail in the following section. It is this writer's opinion that the rabbinic rendering of Psalm 22:16[17] makes the application of this verse to the Jewish people more problematic and is, therefore, counter-productive.

---

[4] The Targums are Aramaic paraphrases of the Hebrew Scriptures.
[5] http://en.wikipedia.org/wiki/They_have_pierced_my_hands_and_my_feet
[6] http://en.wikipedia.org/wiki/Septuagint

A Rabbinic Interpretation of Psalm 22

As we have mentioned in earlier chapters, a wonderful resource for Christians who have a passion for the Bible is *Messiah Truth*.[7] This might surprise some but the fact is this; the vast majority of Christian believers are largely ignorant of the biblical context of passages in the Tanach that are prophetic and can, rightly so in the opinion of this author, be applied to Jesus. *Messiah Truth* is an organization that has been established to counter Christian missionary arguments. An appreciation of their material, however, only enriches our understanding of the word of God. Accordingly, we wish to refer to this material regarding current rabbinic understanding of Psalm 22.[8]

It is interesting to this author to realize that *Messiah Truth* does not give us any clues as to the *actual* writer of the Psalm. They write:

> *The Jewish perspective rests on the context as well as on the consistency of the themes described in this psalm with those found elsewhere within the Hebrew Bible. The overall theme of Psalms 22 depicts the plight of the Jew who, as an individual, prays for an end to Israel's long exile from its land and from the Temple in Jerusalem. A reading of this psalm in the original Hebrew or in a correct translation reveals that King David is its author (Ps 22:1) and that he is the "voice" throughout. David describes his own pain, anguish, and longing during those times when he was a fugitive from his enemies. Consequently, this is an historical rather than a messianic psalm. When he refers to himself as a worm (Ps 22:7[6]), a helpless creature, whose only salvation can come from G-d, it becomes abundantly clear that the author does not consider himself to be someone who can provide salvation, and certainly not one who is divine!*

We can see from this passage that there is a suggestion made by *Messiah Truth* that the psalm was written after the Jewish Exile into Babylon. This denies the veracity of the statement in the Hebrew Scriptures that this is a Psalm written by David. Paradoxically, however, David, is seen as the *"voice"* of the psalm as he, also, became an exile. This, in passing, lends credence to the possibility of David writing the psalm as a result of the conspiracy of his son Absalom. For *Messiah Truth*, the psalm is historic rather than messianic. In other words, a rabbinic interpretation of Psalm 22 allows for the possibility that a king (in this case David) can be seen as representative of the suffering of the people of Israel. *Messiah Truth* offers an intriguing question.

---

[7] http://www.messiahtruth.com/
[8] http://www.messiahtruth.com/psa22.html

148

A comparison of the Christian and Jewish perspectives on Psalms 22 indicates that both cannot be simultaneously valid interpretations The question is, "Which of these two views is consistent with the Hebrew Bible (and Israel's history)?"

This is the heart of the issue which we are addressing in this study. Rather than taking extreme positions, I would wish to maintain that there is a powerful and parallel connection between the suffering of the Jewish people throughout the ages (and, in particular, the Holocaust) with the suffering of Jesus, another king and a representative of the nation of Israel.

Messiah Truth goes on to consider the first verse of the Psalm and I would also refer readers to the article for a complete appreciation of the attempt to demonstrate that the words quoted in the New Testament have suffered somewhat through transliteration from Hebrew into Aramaic into Greek. This attempt, however, is essentially pointless because *Messiah Truth* concedes that the text in the New Testament is valid taking into account the double transliteration process. What follows, however, is very significant for the purposes of this study. *Messiah Truth* concludes:

> *However, placing this verse into the mouth of a dying Jesus creates more theological difficulties for the Christian paradigm than it solves. For example, King David makes the following statement: Psalms 37:25(KJV) I have been young, and [now] am old; yet I have not seen the righteous forsaken, nor his seed begging bread. This would imply that Jesus was not righteous, i.e., a sinner, since he complained to G-d about being forsaken.*

Unfortunately, this betrays an ignorance of the Christian understanding of Jesus' death which could be summed up in the following verse from the first letter of Peter:

1 Peter 3:18 (NIV) *For Christ died for sins once for all, the righteous for the unrighteous, to bring you to God.*

However, there is another very important issue here. It is evident that it is possible to confuse the **actuality** of being forsaken with a **perception** of being forsaken. In other words, does depravation actually mean that we are forsaken by God? If this were true, then no righteous person would ever suffer depravation of any kind.

However, David the psalmist also says:

Psalm 34:17-20 (NIV) *The righteous cry out, and the LORD hears them; he delivers them from all their troubles. The LORD is close to the broken-hearted and saves those who are crushed in spirit. A righteous man may have many troubles, but the LORD delivers him from them all; he protects all his bones, not one of them will be broken.*

We will obviously have occasion to return to this verse. But the question before us is this: *"Does God actually forsake his people"?* Moses spoke to the people of Israel:

Deuteronomy 31:6 (RSV) *Be strong and of good courage, do not fear or be in dread of them: for it is the LORD your God who goes with you; he will not fail you or forsake you.*

However, the same chapter in the book of Deuteronomy we read this:

Deuteronomy 31:16-18 (NIV) *And the LORD said to Moses: "You are going to rest with your fathers, and these people will soon prostitute themselves to the foreign gods of the land they are entering. **They will forsake me** and break the covenant I made with them. On that day I will become angry with them and forsake them**; I will hide my face from them,** and they will be destroyed. Many disasters and difficulties will come upon them, and on that day they will ask, 'Have not these disasters come upon us because our God is not with us?' **And I will certainly hide my face** on that day because of all their wickedness in turning to other gods.*

Thus, the consequence of <u>our</u> forsaking God is that he will hide his face from us. Furthermore, it is self-evident that if we do not forsake God, continue to trust him and call out to him, he will never forsake us or hide his face from us.

When David is in trouble (which is inevitable for everyone), he perceives that God has forsaken him. *"My God, My God, why have you forsaken me?"* But the fact is simply this; God had not forsaken him for the psalm goes on to say this:

Psalm 22:24 (NIV) *For he has not despised or disdained the suffering of the afflicted one; **he has not hidden his face from him but has listened to his cry for help.***

I re-iterate; it is clear from Scripture that the consequences of our forsaking God is that God will hide his face from us. However, according to Psalm 22:24, in the case of the *"afflicted one"* whether it be David, Jesus or even the people of Israel, it may have seemed that God had hidden his face, but in actuality, the *"afflicted one"* was **not** forsaken.

It is therefore, extremely significant that Jesus, in the high point of his suffering, cries out the same complaint. The question for Christian (and Jewish) theologians to consider is whether God (the Father) actually turned his back (figuratively speaking) on his beloved son. If, as we believe, Jesus may be seen as the representative *"afflicted one"* of Psalm 22, he was not forsaken. Jesus as representative of his people also joins them in this lament:

Isaiah 49:14-16 (NIV) *But Zion said, "The LORD has forsaken me, the Lord has forgotten me." "Can a mother forget the baby at her breast and have no compassion on the child she has borne? Though she may forget, I will not forget you! See, I have engraved you on the palms of my hands; your walls are ever before me.*

This verse also betrays the total futility of the Jewish concerns over the translation of Psalm 22:16 (or Psalm 22:17 in the Tanach) which we will consider in greater detail.

Worms and Maggots

Please bear with this writer with respect to this issue. It might appear to be unrelated but I but I believe there is incredible truth to be discovered here.

Psalm 22:6-8 (NIV) *But I am a worm and not a man, scorned by men and despised by the people. All who see me mock me; they hurl insults, shaking their heads: "He trusts in the LORD; let the LORD rescue him. Let him deliver him, since he delights in him."*

Messiah Truth makes some very interesting points about this verse.

> *In the Christian scenario, it would be Jesus calling himself a worm ... David uses this metaphor as he writes about the plight of his own people. Does the worm metaphor fit Jesus? Would anyone, other than pagans who worship worms, use this metaphor to characterize a divine being?*

This is a remarkable statement but again it betrays the fact that the writer of *Messiah Truth* has absolutely no concept of the incarnation and the substitutionary atonement with all that this means. Within this section of his treatise, *Messiah Truth* quotes Bildad the Shuhite in the book of Job but it is worth quoting a few more verses to establish a context.

Job 25:4-6 (NIV) *How then can a man be righteous before God? How can one born of woman be pure? If even the moon is not bright and the stars are not pure in his eyes, how much less man, who is but a maggot - a son of man, who is only a worm!"*

Now it would be very dangerous to consider anything that Bildad says as definitive, but there is a significant element of truth here. However, it is worth noting at this point the actual Jewish rendition of this verse that is quoted in *Messiah Truth*.

Job 25:6 (*Messiah Truth*) *How much less, man, who is a worm, and the son of man, who is a maggot!"*

The writer of *Messiah Truth* is rightly concerned with correct translation of the Hebrew Scriptures so we need to consider this verse. If you look closely you will see that there is a reversal taking place. In the NIV translation, man is a maggot and the son of man is a worm. In the Jewish rendition quoted in *Messiah Truth*, man is a worm and the son of man is a maggot! Which is true and is it significant in our study of Psalm 22?

The Hebrew of this verse is:

$$\text{אַף כִּי־אֱנוֹשׁ רִמָּה וּבֶן־אָדָם תּוֹלֵעָה:}$$

This may be transliterated as "Af ki enosh rimah oo ben adam towleyah". The word *"enosh"* is an archaic form for *"man"* used in the book of Job and also in Isaiah and Jeremiah. It is thought to be derived from Enosh, the son of Seth mentioned in Genesis. The words *"ben adam"* are literally *"son of man"*. We can easily see that Enosh (man) is a *"rimah"* and ben adam (son of man) is a *"towleyah"*.

The question before us is what word is used in Psalm 22:6? The Hebrew for this verse is:

$$\text{וְאָנֹכִי תוֹלַעַת וְלֹא־אִישׁ}$$

The writer of the psalm is therefore equated with the "son of man". He is the *"towleyah"* of Job 25:6 and the *"towlah-at"* in Psalm 22:6. The word *"rimah"* may also be translated worm or maggot but that is irrelevant to our discussion.

The point that I wish to emphasize is this, whatever the psalmist calls himself (i.e. worm in both the English and Jewish texts) is equated by Bildad as *"son of man"*. The rendition suggested by *Messiah Truth* is at best inconsistent. It is therefore very significant to note that the term that Jesus most often uses about himself in the Gospels is *"Son of Man"*. For example:

Luke 19:9-10 (NIV) *Jesus said to him, "Today salvation has come to this house, because this man, too, is a son of Abraham. For the Son of Man came to seek and to save what was lost."*

Another very significant example of the use of the term *"Son of Man"* is found in the book of Daniel:

Daniel 7:13-14 (RSV) *I saw in the night visions, and behold, with the clouds of heaven there came one **like a son of man**, and he came to the Ancient of Days and was presented before him. And to him was given dominion and glory and kingdom, that all peoples, nations, and languages should serve him; his dominion is an everlasting dominion, which shall not pass away, and his kingdom one that shall not be destroyed.*

Jesus applies this passage to himself:

Matthew 26:62-64 (NIV) *Then the high priest stood up and said to Jesus, "Are you not going to answer? What is this testimony that these men are bringing against you?" But Jesus remained silent. The high priest said to him, "I charge you under oath by the living God: Tell us if you are the Christ, the Son of God." "Yes, it is as you say," Jesus replied. "But I say to all of you: In the future you will see the Son of Man sitting at the right hand of the Mighty One **and coming on the clouds of heaven.**"*

We are aware of the response.

Matthew 26:65-68 (NIV) *Then the high priest tore his clothes and said, "He has spoken blasphemy! Why do we need any more witnesses? Look, now you have heard the blasphemy. What do you think?" "He is worthy of death" they answered. Then they spat in his face and struck him with their fists. Others slapped him and said, "Prophesy to us, Christ. Who hit you?"*

In declaring himself to be the *"Son of Man"*, he is also declaring himself to be the *"worm"* of Job 25:6 and, in particular, Psalm 22:6. However, as *Messiah Truth* rightly suggests:

Jewish Humiliation by the Nazis

This reference to a worm as a metaphor for people is not unique within the Hebrew Bible. Isaiah likens the Jewish people to a worm: **Isaiah 41:14 Fear not, O worm of Jacob, the number of Israel; "I have helped you," says the L-rd, and your redeemer, the Holy One of Israel.**

The word for *"worm"* is *"towlah-at".* Thus, Psalm 22:6 applies both to the *"voice"* of the psalm who is also the *"Son of Man"* **and** to the people of Israel. It is worth considering these verses again in this light.

Psalm 22:6-8 (NIV) *But I am a worm and not a man, scorned by men and despised by the people. All who see me mock me; they hurl insults, shaking their heads: "He trusts in the LORD; let the LORD rescue him. Let him deliver him, since he delights in him."*

Unfortunately, the writer of *Messiah Truth* completely misses the point. This is also true when we turn again to this most controversial verse of all.

Psalm 22:16 (NIV) *Dogs have surrounded me; a band of evil men has encircled me, they have pierced my hands and my feet.*

The Jewish rendition of this verse makes no sense. *Messiah Truth* writes it (equivalent to Psalm 22:17) as follows:

Psalm 22:17 (*Messiah Truth Version*) *For dogs have surrounded me; a band of evildoers encompassed me; like a lion* **[they are at]** *my hands and my feet.*

With great respect to *Messiah Truth*, their rendering betrays the impossibility of the translation because the words *"they are at"* are an addition that is not in the Hebrew. They are added because the verse makes no sense without the extra words (the verb in particular). I do not wish to enter this discussion at great length but refer the reader to an article by Tim Hegg.[9]

The main point in this controversy is whether there is actually a verb in the original Hebrew which has become translated by the Rabbis as *"like a lion"*. Certainly, the verb is not the regular biblical Hebrew word that would be translated *"pierced"*. The original verb might be better translated *"dug"* as it is an archaic form of the verb *"to dig"*. This would make perfect sense. Dogs dig in the dirt and the surrounding dogs are digging at hands and feet. But in all this controversy, an obvious point is being overlooked. Whether there is a verb present or not, our focus of attention is to the hands and feet of the afflicted one.

Luke 24:39-40 (NIV) *Look at my hands and my feet. It is I myself! Touch me and see; a ghost does not have flesh and bones, as you see I have." When he had said this, he showed them his hands and feet.*

And there is something more to say. Let us assume, for one minute, that there is no verb. Let us assume that the correct translation is *"like a lion, my hands and feet"*. What the afflicted one is saying is that his hands and feet are like a lion. This of course makes no grammatical sense because the afflicted one is not a lion … or is he?

Revelation 5:5 (NIV) *Then one of the elders said to me, "Do not weep! See, the Lion of the tribe of Judah, the Root of David, has triumphed.*

The Lion of Judah [10]

---

9   http://www.torahresource.com/EnglishArticles/Ps22.16.pdf
10 The Lion of Judah—Sculpture by Rick Wienecke

The Shaved Head and the Striped Clothes

The Tattoo on the Arm of Jesus

The main point that I wish to make is this, we believe the suffering of the king with his perceived sense of being forsaken is representative of the suffering of the Jewish people in the Holocaust. In addition, his hands and feet were nailed to a cross. The arms of the Jewish people were tattooed.

Sonderkommandos are put to Work [10]

---

[10] http://en.wikipedia.org/wiki/Sonderkommando

Jewish Children displaying their Tattoos at Liberation

The tattoo became a permanent reminder of the suffering of Holocaust survivors from Auschwitz. The hair of shaved heads would re-grow, the striped clothes would be burnt but the tattoo would always remain. In the early days of the state of Israel, even in the height of summer, Holocaust survivors would wear long sleeves to hide the marks of their suffering.

Visitors to the Fountain of Tears will see that the figure representing Jesus also has his head shaved and his arm tattooed. For Rick, this was the most difficult aspect of the sculpting. The fact is this; there is total identification in this word between Jesus and those that perished in the Holocaust. We know because of the testimony of some of the Sonderkommandos that many entering the gas chambers cried out *"My God, my God why have you forsaken me?"* The psalm is part of Jewish liturgy. Everything that we have said which relates to Jesus' experience in his crucifixion became the experience of those that perished in the Holocaust.

Some have asked why Rick chose the number 1534. His explanation is a simple one. The addition of one and five makes six which represents the six million. The addition of three and four makes seven which represents the seven last statements that Jesus makes from the Crucifixion.

Some have suggested other meanings. One day a friend of Rick's suggested that it could be chapter and verse. Considering that the tattoo was a permanent mark, he looked at the Gospel of Mark, chapter 15, verse 34.

It says this:

Mark 15:34 (NIV) *And at the ninth hour Jesus cried out in a loud voice, "Eloi, Eloi, lama sabachthani?" which means,* **"My God, my God, why have you forsaken me?"**

Could it be that God himself has engraved his word into this work? We have no wish to be presumptuous but, for Rick, it was a wonderful confirmation.

As far as I can tell, there is no rabbinic controversy over **the text** of next verse in Psalm 22:

Psalm 22:17-18 (NIV*)* *I can count all my bones; people stare and gloat over me. They divide my garments among them and cast lots for my clothing.*

John 19:23-24 (RSV) *When the soldiers had crucified Jesus they took his garments and made four parts, one for each soldier; also his tunic. But the tunic was without seam, woven from top to bottom; so they said to one another, "Let us not tear it, but cast lots for it to see whose it shall be." This was to fulfil the scripture, "They parted my garments among them, and for my clothing they cast lots."*

Messiah Truth makes the following interesting comment regarding the **context** of this verse:

> *The previous verse, Psalms 22:18[17], is critical to a correct understanding of the true context of this verse. Psalms 22:18[17] describes the person whose clothes are being divided as counting his bones while those who are taking his garments look on gloating. This starving man is so skinny that his bones are visible and can be counted. The "voice" here is still King David, as it is throughout the psalm, and he uses the act of taking and dividing his garments as a metaphorical reference to the desires of his enemies to take away his mantle of royalty and make it their own.*

For *Messiah Truth* to consider that this was David's experience in the removal of metaphorical robes of royalty is a rather desperate measure to remove any messianic connotation. It also does violence to the fact that this was also the experience of all those who died in the Holocaust.

We have also discussed the humiliation of crucifixion In a previous section. One of the significant aspects to the crucifixion of Jesus was the fact that none of his bones were broken.

John 19:33-37 (RSV) *But when they came to Jesus and saw that he was already dead, they did not break his legs. But one of the soldiers pierced his side with a spear, and at once there came out blood and water. He who saw it has borne witness - his testimony is true, and he knows that he tells the truth that you also may believe. For these things took place that the scripture might be fulfilled, "Not a bone of him shall be broken." And again another scripture says, "They shall look on him whom they have pierced."*

We therefore repeat the verses, taken from one of David's other psalms.

Psalm 34:19-20 (NIV) *A righteous man may have many troubles, but the LORD delivers him from them all; he protects all his bones, not one of them will be broken.*

I can count all my bones - Dachau Survivors

The second part of Psalm 22 will also be the experience of people of Israel. We will return to this theme in later chapters. David was restored as King over all Israel. Jesus was resurrected and continues as the legitimate King of the Jews. The nation of Israel has also been restored and one day both King and people will be re-united.

Isaiah 42:16 (NIV*) I will lead the blind by ways they have not known, along unfamiliar paths I will guide them; I will turn the darkness into light before them and make the rough places smooth. These are the things I will do; I will not forsake them.*

The dark days of the Holocaust are over, a new day has dawned; the morning star has appeared in the sky, in other words ***"Ayelet haShachar".***

**The Fountain of Tears is
a Dialogue of Suffering**

CHAPTER SEVEN

I Thirst

John 19:28-29 (NIV) *Later, knowing that all was now completed, and so that the Scripture would be fulfilled, Jesus said, "I am thirsty." A jar of wine vinegar was there, so they soaked a sponge in it, put the sponge on a stalk of the hyssop plant, and lifted it to Jesus' lips.*

The Fifth Panel of the Fountain of Tears

Knowing that all was now completed

As we have seen, although we do not know the exact order of the words of Jesus spoken by him from his crucifixion, it is obvious from the above verse that he speaks the words *"I thirst"* towards the end of his ordeal. We know from the following verses in John's Gospel that it is shortly after this cry that Jesus declares *"it is finished"*. We shall look at this statement in more detail in a the next chapter.

However, Jesus was aware that by the time he recognized his thirst, he had actually accomplished all that the Father had given him to do. He **knew** that everything was now completed. His crucifixion had lasted many hours and, during this time, he had been cut off from the intimate fellowship that he had always enjoyed with the one that he had always called Father. This separation, which we discussed in the earlier chapter, had now brought Jesus to a point where he now recognized his own suffering. In particular, he was acutely aware that he was very thirsty.

So that the Scripture would be fulfilled

One of the very interesting things about these verses is the fact that Jesus said *"I am thirsty"* (or indeed *"I thirst"*) so that the Scriptures (i.e. verses in the Tanach) would be fulfilled. What verses might these be? We have already discussed the fact that Psalm 22 is probably the clearest depiction of the crucifixion in the entire Bible. In this Psalm, the afflicted one describes his condition.

Psalm 22:14-15 (NIV) *I am poured out like water, and all my bones are out of joint. My heart has turned to wax; it has melted away within me. My strength is dried up like a potsherd, and my tongue sticks to the roof of my mouth; you lay me in the dust of death.*

Thus, from the very outset, Jesus, in his crucifixion, is fulfilling the suffering of the afflicted one as described in this Psalm (see previous chapter). He feels that he has been abandoned by God; he is searching and looking up to find his Father but he cannot reach him. Furthermore, if it is true (and I believe it is) that, in Jesus' death, we see a very particular fulfillment of the sacrifice of the Passover lamb on the 14th day of Nisan, the shedding of his blood on the execution stake has to be the most significant aspect of his suffering. Jesus is establishing the New Covenant based on forgiveness.

Luke 22:20 (NIV) *In the same way, after the supper he took the cup, saying, "This cup is the new covenant in my blood, which is poured out for you.*

As the Apostle Peter says:

1 Peter 1:18-19 (RSV) *You know that you were ransomed from the futile ways inherited from your fathers, not with perishable things such as silver or gold, but with the precious blood of Christ, like that of a lamb without blemish or spot.*

And the Apostle Paul adds:

1 Corinthians 5:7 (NIV) *For Christ, our Passover lamb, has been sacrificed.*

Blood and Water

The Psalmist suggests that he is *"poured out like water"*. Jesus describes the cup as representing his blood that is to be poured out for his disciples. It is therefore not insignificant that the Apostle John describes the following when Jesus had died.

John 19:34-35 (NIV) *Instead, one of the soldiers pierced Jesus' side with a spear, bringing a sudden flow of blood and water. The man who saw it has given testimony, and his testimony is true. He knows that he tells the truth, and he testifies so that you also may believe.*

I believe that the re-enactment and fulfillment of Passover is also alluded to by the fact that hyssop is mentioned (John 19:29) It is on to the stalk of the hyssop plant that the sponge that has been dipped in wine vinegar is attached and raised. It is also using hyssop that the blood is applied to doorposts and lintel by the Israelites in Egypt.

Exodus 12:22-23 (RSV) *Take a bunch of hyssop and dip it in the blood which is in the basin, and touch the lintel and the two doorposts with the blood which is in the basin; and none of you shall go out of the door of his house until the morning. For the LORD will pass through to slay the Egyptians; and when he sees the blood on the lintel and on the two doorposts, the LORD will pass over the door, and will not allow the destroyer to enter your houses to slay you.*

For God had said to Moses:

Exodus 12:13 (RSV) *The blood shall be a sign for you, upon the houses where you are; and when I see the blood, I will pass over you, and no plague shall fall upon you to destroy you, when I smite the land of Egypt.*

In addition, Moses used blood (and presumably hyssop) in the establishment of the covenant that God made with the people of Israel at Sinai.

Exodus 24:8 (NIV) *Moses then took the blood, sprinkled it on the people and said, "This is the blood of the covenant that the LORD has made with you in accordance with all these words."*

It is very significant that these words echo those of Jesus in the upper room. Accordingly, and maybe more than anything else, it has to have been the outpouring of Jesus' own blood that led to his appreciating that *"all was now completed, and so that the Scripture would be fulfilled".*

Romans 5:8-9 (RSV) *But God shows his love for us in that while we were yet sinners Christ died for us. Since, therefore, we are now justified by his blood, much more shall we be saved by him from the wrath of God.*

When God the Father sees the blood of his Son and our faith in its efficacy, the wrath of God passes over us. God will not permit the destroyer to enter our houses and strike us down. It is worth noting, in passing, that the jar from which the soldiers drew the drink offered to Jesus contained a sour wine which was known in Latin as *acetum* (a.k.a. *posca*). This was a typical fermented drink often drunk by Roman soldiers. The word *"acetum"* is connected to the word acetic acid which is the main constituent of vinegar. It will have been derived from red wine similar to that which was used by the disciples in their Passover celebration.

Hyssop and Water

The hyssop plant was also used as a means for applying clean (living) water. This water had been prepared using the ashes of the red heifer which is also described as the purification offering (Numbers 19).

Numbers 19:18 (RSV) *Then a clean person shall take hyssop, and dip it in the water, and sprinkle it upon the tent, and upon all the furnishings, and upon the persons who were there, and upon him who touched the bone, or the slain, or the dead, or the grave.*

This water of cleansing is also alluded to in Psalm 51:

Psalm 51:7-11 (NIV) *Cleanse me with hyssop, and I shall be clean; wash me, and I shall be whiter than snow. Let me hear joy and gladness; let the bones you have crushed rejoice. Hide your face from my sins and blot out all my iniquity. Create in me a pure heart, O God, and renew a steadfast spirit within me. Do not cast me from your presence or take your Holy Spirit from me.*

Here, in this psalm we see a connection between being made clean with water, the renewal of a right spirit and the continuing presence of the Holy Spirit. This is also a promise made to the people of Israel.

Ezekiel 36:24-28 (RSV) *For I will take you from the nations, and gather you from all the countries, and bring you into your own land. I will sprinkle clean water upon you, and you shall be clean from all your uncleanness, and from all your idols I will cleanse you. A new heart I will give you, and a new spirit I will put within you; and I will take out of your flesh the heart of stone and give you a heart of flesh. And I will put my spirit within you, and cause you to walk in my statutes and be careful to observe my ordinances. You shall dwell in the land which I gave to your fathers; and you shall be my people, and I will be your God.*

This is the outworking of the New Covenant that Jesus established through the shedding of his blood. Blood and water are also alluded to in this enigmatic prophecy in the book of Zechariah

Zechariah 9:11 (NIV) *As for you, because of the blood of my covenant with you, I will free your prisoners from the waterless pit.*

This is fulfilled in a later passage.

Zechariah 12:10; 13:1 (NIV) *And I will pour out on the house of David and the inhabitants of Jerusalem a spirit of grace and supplication. They will look on me, the one they have pierced, and they will mourn for him as one mourns for an only child, and grieve bitterly for him as one grieves for a firstborn son … On that day a fountain will be opened to the house of David and the inhabitants of Jerusalem, to cleanse them from sin and impurity.*

Jesus and Living Water

The fact that Jesus is dry, parched, and thirsty provides ample evidence that he has been poured out and has given everything he has to give. However, nowhere in the Gospels does Jesus describe himself as living water. In particular, in the Gospel of John, there are seven *"I ams"* but living water is not one of them. However, in several places, Jesus describes himself as the one who is the source and provider of living water. For example, in chapter 4, Jesus meets the Samaritan woman at the well.

John 4:10-14 (RSV) *Jesus answered her, "If you knew the gift of God, and who it is that is saying to you, 'Give me a drink,' you would have asked him, and he would have given you living water." The woman said to him, "Sir, you have nothing to draw with, and the well is deep; where do you get that living water? Are you greater than our father Jacob, who gave us the well, and drank from it himself, and his sons, and his cattle?" Jesus said to her, "Every one who drinks of this water will thirst again, but whoever drinks of the water* **that I shall give him will never thirst;** *the water that I shall give him will become in him a spring of water welling up to eternal life."*

Jesus declares to the woman that he can give her living water and that water would be reproduced within her to become an everlasting spring. At a literal level, the term *"living water"* was a common Jewish expression for running or flowing water. For example, the Jewish ritual bath (mikveh) was only legitimate if it had a fresh water source and ideally one of flowing water. The living water spoken of by Jesus is also described as the *"gift of God"*. It is this writer's opinion that this is a clear reference to the Holy Spirit.

Luke 11:13 (RSV) *If you then, who are evil, know how to give good gifts to your children, how much more will the heavenly Father give the Holy Spirit to those who ask him!*

This invitation from the lips of Jesus to come and receive living water (i.e. the Holy Spirit) is explicitly repeated during the Feast of Tabernacles.

John 7:37-39 (NIV) *On the last and greatest day of the Feast, Jesus stood and said in a loud voice, "If anyone is thirsty, let him come to me and drink. Whoever believes in me, as the Scripture has said, streams of living water will flow from within him." By this he meant the Spirit, whom those who believed in him were later to receive. Up to that time the Spirit had not been given, since Jesus had not yet been glorified.*

Again, Jesus reiterates the fact that receiving living water from him would invariably lead to the individual becoming a source of water for others. What is significant about this passage is the fact that Jesus clearly equates the living water with the Holy Spirit. Furthermore, this connection is also a fulfillment of Scripture. So where are these passages?

The main passage that seems to be most relevant is the prophecy in Zechariah.

Zechariah14:8-9 (NIV) *On that day living water will flow out from Jerusalem, half to the eastern sea and half to the western sea, in summer and in winter. The LORD will be king over the whole earth. On that day there will be one LORD, and his name the only name.*

It could be argued that during the feast of Tabernacles, Jesus is speaking primarily to the city of Jerusalem. It is on the last and the greatest day of the festival. The priests had been carrying golden jars of water from the pool of Siloam and pouring out their contents at the base of the altar. This occurred every day during the Festival but it reached its climax on the seventh day. This is the context and backdrop of Jesus' declaration. However, the response to this invitation was somewhat equivocal.

John 7:43-44 (RSV) *So there was a division among the people over him. Some of them wanted to arrest him, but no one laid hands on him.*

This passage may also be understood in its eschatological context. Ezekiel 47 describes a future Temple as a water source.

Ezekiel 47:1-5 (RSV) *Then he brought me back to the door of the temple; and behold, water was issuing from below the threshold of the temple toward the east (for the temple faced east); and the water was flowing down from below the south end of the threshold of the temple, south of the altar. Then he brought me out by way of the north gate, and led me round on the outside to the outer gate, that faces toward the east; and the water was coming out on the south side. Going on eastward with a line in his hand, the man measured a thousand cubits, and then led me through the water; and it was ankle-deep. Again he measured a thousand, and led me through the water; and it was knee-deep. Again he measured a thousand, and led me through the water; and it was up to the loins. Again he measured a thousand, and it was a river that I could not pass through, for the water had risen; it was deep enough to swim in, a river that could not be passed through.*

Jesus, in his declaration during Sukkot, may have been re-iterating his understanding that he is the fulfillment of Ezekiel's eschatological temple. This seems to be supported by his assertion described in John's Gospel.

John 2:19-21 (NIV) *Jesus answered them, "Destroy this temple, and I will raise it again in three days." The Jews replied, "It has taken forty-six years to build this temple, and you are going to raise it in three days?" But the temple he had spoken of was his body.*

The Source of Living Water

At the time of the Babylonian occupation, the prophet Jeremiah is in despair about the spiritual condition of his own people

Jeremiah 2:13 (NIV) *My people have committed two sins: They have forsaken me, the spring of living water, and have dug their own cisterns, broken cisterns that cannot hold water.*

If the Bible is consistent, as I believe it is, then God himself is seen as the source of living water which also has to refer to his Spirit. The following verses in this passage in Jeremiah have to be, therefore, very significant.

Jeremiah 2:14-16 (NIV) *Is Israel a servant; a slave by birth? Why then has he become plunder? Lions have roared; they have growled at him. They have laid waste his land; his towns are burned and deserted. Also, the men of Memphis and Tahpanhes have shaved the crown of your head. Have you not brought this on yourselves by forsaking the LORD your God when he led you in the way? Now why go to Egypt to drink water from the Shihor?*

Jeremiah 2:16-19 (NIV) *And why go to Assyria to drink water from the River? Your wickedness will punish you; your backsliding will rebuke you. Consider then and realize how evil and bitter it is for you when you forsake the LORD your God and have no awe of me," declares the Lord, the LORD Almighty.*

It is worth dwelling on these verses which describe the consequences of deserting the one who is the source of living water.[1] Israel is described here as a (the) servant. This is paralleled in the servant songs in the prophecy of Isaiah. However, they have forsaken the source of living water and have created their own cisterns that cannot hold water. I believe that these cisterns are religion. They are described in these verses by drinking water from the rivers of Assyria and Egypt. We cannot obtain living water through religious practice. This is the gift of God. It cannot be earned and is definitely not deserved. It is a gift of grace.

The specific results of deserting the source of living water are many-fold. Lions roar (Psalm 22:13); the land is wasted, and heads are shaved.

Shaved Heads in the Camps

In particular, the people are described as being plundered. This is a recurring theme in scripture and can easily be a study of its own and we shall look at this in greater detail in the next section. In brief, I think that being plundered could be defined as being stripped of all assets.

---

[1] See also Jeremiah 17:13 O LORD, the hope of Israel, all who forsake you will be put to shame. Those who turn away from you will be written in the dust because they have forsaken the LORD, the spring of living water.

The Jewish People were Plundered

Jeremiah 9:1 (NIV) *Oh, that my head were a spring of water and my eyes a fountain of tears! I would weep day and night for the slain of my people.*

This brings out another meaning to this significant verse. Jeremiah prays earnestly that he might become **a source of water** for his people. He is truly the intercessor.

Thirst and the Jewish People

Isaiah 41:17 (NIV) *The poor and needy search for water, but there is none; their tongues are parched with thirst. But I the LORD will answer them; I, the God of Israel, will not forsake them.*

Like the afflicted one in Psalm 22, the Jewish people are described as being parched with thirst. This was their experience in the Holocaust. It is well documented that so many died of thirst within the cattle cars on their journeys to the death camps.

Many died of Thirst in the Cattle Cars

Thus, Jesus suffered the agonies of extreme thirst as did the people of Israel in the Holocaust. This is also alluded to in Psalm 69.

Psalm 69:18-21 (NKJV) *Draw near to my soul, and redeem it; Deliver me because of my enemies. You know my reproach, my shame, and my dishonor; my adversaries are all before You. Reproach has broken my heart and I am full of heaviness; I looked for someone to take pity, but there was none; And for comforters, but I found none. They also gave me gall for my food, And for my thirst they gave me vinegar to drink.*

The word translated *"gall"* is something that which is bitter and poisonous. The source of gall can be animal bile (from the gall bladder) or can be of plant origin such as myrrh [2] or even hemlock.

At Golgotha, at the outset of the crucifixion, Jesus was offered a drink that he refused to take.

Matthew 27:33-34 (NIV) *They came to a place called Golgotha (which means The Place of the Skull). There they offered Jesus wine to drink, mixed with gall; but after tasting it, he refused to drink it.*

Mark 15:22-23 (NIV) *They brought Jesus to the place called Golgotha … they offered him wine mixed with myrrh, but he did not take it.*

Gall, from whatever source, was often used as a sedative. Although gall (particularly myrrh) does have some pain-relieving properties, it is highly unlikely that the Roman soldiers would have used it in this way. More likely, the administration of gall in the wine vinegar would have been used to sedate (i.e. quiet) the victim. This would have made it easier to crucify him as he would be less likely to resist. It might also have been used to prevent some of the struggle and hasten the inevitable outcome of asphyxiation. The question that is before us is to understand why Jesus refused to take anything that would alleviate his suffering. If sedation was the issue, Jesus voluntarily chose to go to his death.

John 10:17-18 (NKJV) *For this reason the Father loves me, because I lay down my life in order to take it up again. No one takes it from me, but I lay it down of my own accord. I have power to lay it down, and I have power to take it up again. I have received this command from my Father."*

---

[2] The word myrrh derives from the Aramaic (murr), meaning "was bitter". Its name entered the English language from the Hebrew Bible where it is called mor [מור] and later as a Semitic loanword was used in the Greek myth of Myrrha, and later in the Septuagint; in the Greek language, the related word μύρον became a general term for perfume (taken from http://en.wikipedia.org/wiki/Myrrh).

Jesus chose to bear the full brunt of what was going to happen to him. He needed to be lucid throughout the process, to be aware of what was going on around him, rather than be under the influence of sedatives. By so doing, he was able to speak to the thief, to John and his mother and also able to pray both for the forgiveness of others and to God himself.

Living Water and the Future

Isaiah 44:3 (NIV) *For I will pour water on the thirsty land, and streams on the dry ground; I will pour out my Spirit on your offspring, and my blessing on your descendants.*

Here again we see the connection between water (presumably living) and the outpouring of the Holy Spirit. A day is coming when this will be the experience of an entire nation for *"they will all know me from the least to the greatest"* (Jeremiah 31:34).

"Give me this water that I may never thirst again"

A time will come when the people of Israel will again cry out *"I thirst"*.

Revelation 7:17 (NIV) *For the Lamb at the center of the throne will be their shepherd; he will lead them to springs of living water. And God will wipe away every tear from their eyes.*

CHAPTER EIGHT

It is Finished

John 19:28-30 (RSV) *After this Jesus, knowing that all was now finished, said (to fulfil the scripture), "I thirst." A bowl full of vinegar stood there; so they put a sponge full of the vinegar on hyssop and held it to his mouth. When Jesus had received the vinegar, he said, "It is finished"; and he bowed his head and gave up his spirit.*

.

The Sixth Panel of the Fountain of Tears

The Final Three Words

Although we are looking at each of these statements in detail, it is worth reflecting on the fact that, in these verses in John's Gospel shown above, we clearly see the connection and order of the final three statements that Jesus made towards the end of his ordeal.

$$\text{τετέλεσται}$$

This Greek word transliterated *"tetelestai"* is only used twice in the entire New Testament and it is only in these verses in John's Gospel. It is used in verse 28 and repeated in verse 30. Jesus knew that all was now completed (*tetelestai*) so he said *"It is finished"* (*tetelestai*). It is an interesting word. In particular, it was used in commercial transactions and stamped on legal documents to say that the bill was paid in full. The word is derived from the Greek root word transliterated *"teleo"* which speaks of completion and finality.

But what exactly did Jesus say?

We have no idea whether Jesus actually spoke the Greek language. It is possible that he did as Koine Greek was the *lingua franca* of the Roman World. This was the language that the New Testament was eventually published in.

However, it may only be the letters of Paul and perhaps the book of the Revelation that were actually originally written in Greek. All of the others, and in particular the Gospels, may have been written in Aramaic or Hebrew or perhaps derived from earlier manuscripts written in these Semitic languages. Without doubt, however, Jesus would have been fluent in Hebrew and Aramaic. So, if he did not say "*tetelestai*" what did he say?

The words *"Tam ve'nishlam"* also mean *"It is finished"*. They are the first two words of the Hebrew phrase, *"Tam ve'nishlam Shevach La'el Boreh Olam"*, which means, *"It is completed and fulfilled, blessed be God, the creator of the world."* It is also worth noting that the acronym for this phrase is also written at the end of sacred Jewish writings such as the books of the Bible. Thus, it is possible that by using these familiar words out of Jewish liturgy, Jesus was declaring that he had completed and fulfilled everything God had purposed since the creation of the world.

1 Peter 1:18-20 (NIV) *For you know that it was not with perishable things such as silver or gold that you were redeemed from the empty way of life handed down to you from your forefathers, but with the precious blood of Christ, a lamb without blemish or defect. He was chosen before the creation of the world, but was revealed in these last times for your sake.*

These words in the letter of Peter seem to indicate that the sacrifice of Jesus was an essential element in God's purposes even before the creation of the world. Accordingly, the words *"Tam ve'nislam Shevach La'el Boreh Olam"* may have been in Jesus' mind although there is no way we can be dogmatic about this.

What we do know is that the word *"tetelestai"* was chosen by the Greek redactors of John's Gospel as an adequate translation of whatever words Jesus actually spoke. As we have already mentioned this word was used in commercial transactions and implicitly carries the concept and meaning of redemption.

The Meaning of Redemption

Throughout the Tanach (and particularly in the book of Isaiah), God is spoken of as Israel's Redeemer.

Isaiah 41:13-14 (RSV) *For I, the LORD your God, hold your right hand; it is I who say to you, "Fear not, I will help you." Fear not, you worm Jacob, you men of Israel! I will help you, says the LORD; your Redeemer is the Holy One of Israel.*

It is worth spending some time considering the implications of this truth. God himself declares that he and he alone is able to redeem the people of Israel. In fact, the Bible makes perfectly clear that, apart from the firstborn son, the people cannot redeem themselves, only animals[1] or property.[2] Furthermore, there is nothing that can be paid or performed that is adequate to redeem a human soul as the Psalmist declares:

Psalm 49:7-9 (NIV) *No man can redeem the life of another or give to God a ransom for him - the ransom for a life is costly, no payment is ever enough that he should live on forever and not see decay.*

But the psalm goes on:

Psalm 49:15 (NIV) *But God will redeem my life from the grave; he will surely take me to himself.*

In the midst of his greatest crisis, Job is able to declare:

Job 19:23-27 (KJV) *Oh that my words were now written! oh that they were printed in a book! That they were graven with an iron pen and lead in the rock for ever! For I know that my redeemer liveth, and that he shall stand at the latter day upon the earth: And though after my skin worms destroy this body, yet in my flesh shall I see God: Whom I shall see for myself, and mine eyes shall behold, and not another; though my reins be consumed within me.*

---

[1] The firstborn of every animal and indeed every firstborn son in any household belonged to the Lord. Every clean animal that could be used in sacrifice, however, could not be bought back. It was to be offered as a sacrifice and the blood was to be applied to the altar. However, God did not require human sacrifice (in fact he declares that it never entered his mind - see Jeremiah 7:31) or the sacrifice of unclean animals. All these, however, had to be bought back, in other words redeemed (see Numbers chapter 18). Redemption was often accomplished with the blood of a lamb. It is also worth noting that Israel is described as God's firstborn son (Exodus 4:22).

[2] See Leviticus chapter 25

These are amazing words for several different reasons. They speak of a future resurrection and we shall have occasion to return to this subject. It is also possible that the *Fountain of Tears* itself is an outworking of these words, engraved in rock forever! More than this, Job comes to the realization that God is his Redeemer who will one day stand upon the earth. If God is the Redeemer, something must happen that will bring about this redemption. Remarkably, the first time the word *"redeem"* is used in Scripture is in the book of Exodus.

Exodus 6:6-7 (NIV) *Therefore, say to the Israelites: 'I am the LORD, and I will bring you out from under the yoke of the Egyptians. I will free you from being slaves to them, and* **I will redeem you with an outstretched arm and with mighty acts of judgment.** *I will take you as my own people, and I will be your God. Then you will know that I am the LORD your God, who brought you out from under the yoke of the Egyptians.*

"I will redeem you with an outstretched arm"

In a mysterious way, the verse in Exodus 6:6 anticipates the outstretched arm. Apparently, God has an arm (as well as hands and feet).

Exodus 24:9-11 (NIV) *Moses and Aaron, Nadab and Abihu, and the seventy elders of Israel went up and saw the God of Israel. Under his feet was something like a pavement made of sapphire, clear as the sky itself. But God did not raise his hand against these leaders of the Israelites; they saw God, and they ate and drank.*

The fact is this; God has done something with an outstretched arm that has brought about redemption for his people. This was true in the deliverance from Egypt but this is just an example of a much greater redemption.

Psalm 130:7-8 (RSV) *O Israel, hope in the LORD! For with the LORD there is steadfast love, and with him is plenteous redemption. And he will redeem Israel from all his iniquities.*

The significance of this verse (along with many others) cannot be overstated. This verse implies that Torah observance alone cannot bring redemption. God has to intervene in the lives of his people to bring about redemption. He has to pay an acceptable price in order to redeem his people from all their sins. In this we see God as a God of justice but he is also a God of compassion.

Isaiah 54:5-8 (RSV) *For your Maker is your husband, the LORD of hosts is his name; and the Holy One of Israel is your Redeemer, the God of the whole earth he is called. For the LORD has called you like a wife forsaken and grieved in spirit, like a wife of youth when she is cast off, says your God. For a brief moment I forsook you, but with great compassion I will gather you. In overflowing wrath for a moment I hid my face from you, but with everlasting love I will have compassion on you, says the LORD, your Redeemer.*

"It is Finished!"

The Significance of these Words for the Jewish People

We are considering the identification of the words *"It is finished"* for the Jewish people in their suffering. In one sense, the slaughter of two-thirds of European Jewry in the Holocaust was not an end but a beginning. Certainly the life that the Jewish people had had before the advent of the Second World War was *"completed"* in the sense that could be no going back to the life that they had once had.

Many of the survivors had lost their identity and there was no obvious place for them to go. But was their suffering in any sense of the word *"redemptive"*?

Isaiah 40:1-2 (NIV) *Comfort, comfort my people, says your God. Speak tenderly to Jerusalem, and proclaim to her that her hard service has been completed, that her sin has been paid for, that she has received from the LORD's hand double for all her sins.*

Isaiah 40:2 (KJV) *Speak ye comfortably to Jerusalem, and cry unto her, that her warfare is accomplished, that her iniquity is pardoned: for she hath received of the LORD's hand double for all her sins.*

"Comfort, Comfort My People"

There are several elements in bringing comfort to the people of Israel typified in our message to the heart of Jerusalem. The tenderness expressed in these words reflects the heart of the Father for his people. The first thing to say by way of comfort is *"your hard service is completed"*. In other words, *"It is complete"*. But exactly what is complete?

The KJV speaks of *"warfare being accomplished".*[3] Suffice to say at this stage that I believe that, since the words are spoken to Jerusalem, these words of Jesus may be very significant.

Luke 21:20-22, 24 (NIV) *When you see Jerusalem being surrounded by armies, you will know that its desolation is near. Then let those who are in Judea flee to the mountains, let those in the city get out, and let those in the country not enter the city for this is the time of punishment in fulfillment of all that has been written ... They will fall by the sword and will be taken as prisoners to all the nations. Jerusalem will be trampled on by the Gentiles until the times of the Gentiles are fulfilled.*

There will come a day when the warfare is accomplished and completed. Has the day arrived? Only time will tell.

The second aspect of our comfort is to declare to Jerusalem *"that her sin has been paid for"* (NIV) or *"that her iniquity is pardoned"* (KJV). We need to be very clear. It is Jesus who has made atonement for sin. We have already understood from Scripture that God alone can redeem his people. This is an eternal truth and this verse can be rightly understood, in my opinion, in the light of the sacrifice of Jesus.

However, is there any sense where the suffering of the Jewish people can be seen as redemptive? The verse (Isaiah 40:2) might be understood as indicating that their sin has been paid for because the people of Israel have received (from the Lord's hand) double for all her sins. This is expressed best, maybe, by the King James Version:

Isaiah 40:2 (KJV) *Her iniquity is pardoned: **for** she hath received of the LORD's hand double for all her sins.*

The word translated *"for"* can legitimately be translated *"because"*. This is an extremely controversial and we will consider all of this in much greater detail in chapter twelve of this book.

---

[3] First I will recompense their iniquity and their sin double. Horsley translates, 'I will recompense, etc., once and again;' literally, the first time repeated: alluding to the two captives-the Babylonian and the Roman. Maurer, 'I will recompense their former iniquities (those long ago committed by their fathers) and their (own) repeated sins' (Jeremiah 16:11-12). The English version gives a good sense, 'First (before 'I bring them again into their land'), I will doubly (i.e., fully and amply, Jeremiah 17:18; Isaiah 40:2) recompense,' etc. (from Jamieson, Fausset, and Brown Commentary, Electronic Database. Copyright (c) 1997 by Biblesoft)

A People Plundered

As I suggested in the last chapter, an aspect of Jewish suffering is to be a people plundered. To plunder is to take the possessions of another by force. Another definition would be to asset strip. Jesus understood what it was to be plundered.

John 19:23-24 (RSV) *When the soldiers had crucified Jesus they took his garments and made four parts, one for each soldier; also his tunic. But the tunic was without seam, woven from top to bottom; so they said to one another, "Let us not tear it, but cast lots for it to see whose it shall be."*

We have already described how the Jewish people were stripped of all assets in the Holocaust. This is also poignantly understood in the attempted return to former homes of Holocaust survivors only to discover the fact that they were now occupied by Gentiles who were formerly their neighbors. Before, during and after the war the Jewish people of mainland Europe were a people plundered. It was complete.

The Pogrom in Kielce Poland in 1946

But we must re-consider again this terrible fact.

Isaiah 42:23-25 (NIV) *Which of you will listen to this or pay close attention in time to come? Who handed Jacob over to become loot and Israel to the plunderers? Was it not the LORD, against whom we have sinned? For they would not follow his ways; they did not obey his law. So he poured out on them his burning anger, the violence of war. It enveloped them in flames, yet they did not understand; it consumed them, but they did not take it to heart.*

These verses lead us again to no other conclusion that God is sovereign, even in the Holocaust. These verses do not allow us to suggest that the Holocaust was an act *against* God himself as some are want to do. I am reminded of the words in the book of Hebrews.

Hebrews 10:29-31 (RSV) *How much worse punishment do you think will be deserved by the man who has spurned the Son of God, and profaned the blood of the covenant by which he was sanctified, and outraged the Spirit of grace? For we know him who said, "Vengeance is mine, I will repay." And again, "The Lord will judge his people." It is a fearful thing to fall into the hands of the living God.*

As I write these words, I am so thankful that God is also a God of Grace. The words that end chapter 42 of Isaiah are immediately followed by these.

Isaiah 43:1-3 (NIV) ***But now,*** *this is what the LORD says - he who created you, O Jacob, he who formed you, O Israel: "Fear not, for I have redeemed you; I have summoned you by name; you are mine. When you pass through the waters, I will be with you; and when you pass through the rivers, they will not sweep over you. When you walk through the fire, you will not be burned; the flames will not set you ablaze. For I am the LORD, your God, the Holy One of Israel, your Savior …*

No Identity and Nowhere to Go

Tho important words to note are the words *"But now"*. If God is sovereign over something as heinous as the Holocaust, he is also sovereign over something as wonderful as the redemption of his suffering people.

Micah 7:18-20 (RSV) *Who is a God like thee, pardoning iniquity and passing over transgression for the remnant of his inheritance? He does not retain his anger for ever because he delights in steadfast love. He will again have compassion upon us, he will tread our iniquities under foot. Thou wilt cast all our sins into the depths of the sea. Thou wilt show faithfulness to Jacob and steadfast love to Abraham, as thou hast sworn to our fathers from the days of old.*

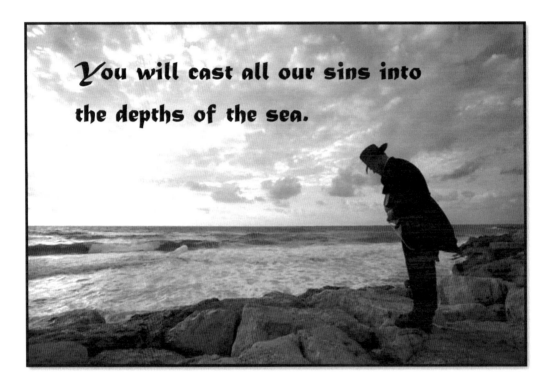

The paradox of punishment and pardon are also to be seen in these verses in the prophecy of Jeremiah.

Jeremiah 30:12-15 (NIV) *This is what the LORD says: "'Your wound is incurable, your injury beyond healing. There is no-one to plead your cause, no remedy for your sore, no healing for you. All your allies have forgotten you; they care nothing for you. I have struck you as an enemy would and punished you as would the cruel, because your guilt is so great and your sins so many. Why do you cry out over your wound, your pain that has no cure? Because of your great guilt and many sins I have done these things to you.*

Jeremiah 30:16 (NIV) *'But all who devour you will be devoured; all your enemies will go into exile. Those who plunder you will be plundered; all who make spoil of you I will despoil. But I will restore you to health and heal your wounds,' declares the LORD, 'because you are called an outcast, Zion for whom no-one cares.'*

Yes, the Holocaust is still an open and festering wound but God promises to bring health and healing. The Jewish people have been the eternal outcast, the despised and rejected.

Promise of Restoration

Ezekiel 34:28-31 (RSV) *They shall no more be a prey to the nations, nor shall the beasts of the land devour them; they shall dwell securely, and none shall make them afraid. And I will provide for them prosperous plantations so that they shall no more be consumed with hunger in the land, and no longer suffer the reproach of the nations. And they shall know that I, the LORD their God, am with them, and that they, the house of Israel, are my people, says the Lord GOD. And you are my sheep, the sheep of my pasture, and I am your God, says the Lord GOD."*

Then it will be truly said **"Tam ve'nislam Shevach La'el Boreh Olam".**

It is finished.

CHAPTER NINE

Into Your Hands I commit my Spirit

The Seventh Panel of the Fountain of Tears

Parallel Accounts of Jesus' death in the Gospels

Matthew 27:50-54 (RSV) *And Jesus cried again with a loud voice and yielded up his spirit. And behold, the curtain of the temple was torn in two, from top to bottom; and the earth shook, and the rocks were split; the tombs also were opened, and many bodies of the saints who had fallen asleep were raised, and coming out of the tombs after his resurrection they went into the holy city and appeared to many. When the centurion and those who were with him, keeping watch over Jesus, saw the earthquake and what took place, they were filled with awe, and said, "Truly this was the Son of God!"*

Mark 15:37-39 (NIV) *With a loud cry, Jesus breathed his last. The curtain of the temple was torn in two from top to bottom. And when the centurion, who stood there in front of Jesus, heard his cry and saw how he died, he said, "Surely this man was the Son of God!"*

Luke 23:44-48 (RSV) *It was now about the sixth hour, and there was darkness over the whole land until the ninth hour, while the sun's light failed; and the curtain of the temple was torn in two. Then Jesus, crying with a loud voice, said, "Father, into thy hands I commit my spirit!" And having said this he breathed his last. Now when the centurion saw what had taken place, he praised God, and said, "Certainly this man was innocent!" And all the multitudes who assembled to see the sight, when they saw what had taken place, returned home beating their breasts.*

John 19:30 (NIV) *When he had received the drink, Jesus said, "It is finished." With that, he bowed his head and gave up his spirit.*

Jesus' reliance on Jewish Liturgy in His Crucifixion

We have considered Psalm 22 as the clearest depiction of Jesus' suffering in the Crucifixion. In the psalm, we sense the abandonment and humiliation, the fact that Jesus lost all his earthly possessions to the plunderers, and that his hands and feet were attacked without mercy by the lions and the dogs.[1] So what is in Jesus' mind when we come to the final words that Jesus spoke at the end of his ordeal? There is only one other place in Scripture where the words *"Into your hands I commit my spirit"* are written.

Psalm 31:1-5 (NIV) *In you, O LORD, I have taken refuge; let me never be put to shame; deliver me in your righteousness. Turn your ear to me; come quickly to my rescue; be my rock of refuge, a strong fortress to save me. Since you are my rock and my fortress, for the sake of your name lead and guide me. Free me from the trap that is set for me, for you are my refuge.* **Into your hands I commit my spirit***; redeem me, O LORD, the God of truth.*

Personally, I have absolutely no doubt that Psalm 31 is in the mind of Jesus as he comes to the end of his ordeal. Every word of this Psalm is the testimony of the Son.

It is worth noting that Jesus adds one word to the phrase as it is expressed in Psalm 31:5. The word is *"Father"*.

Luke 23:46 (NIV) *Jesus called out with a loud voice, "Father, into your hands I commit my spirit." When he had said this, he breathed his last.*

---

[1] I am expressing these thoughts in this way because I want to do justice to the Jewish interpretation of these words.

"Into your hands …"

His first words from the Crucifixion were *"Father, forgive them"*. At the height of His suffering, like the afflicted one in the psalm, he can only cry out *"My God, my God, Why?"* But now at the end of his ordeal, he cries out again *"Father"*. He offers his life not just to God, but to the Father that he has known so well. I believe that he is praying the entire prayer of the psalmist from Psalm 31. He is pleading his case. *"Don't let me be put to shame, deliver me, listen to me, come and rescue me, lead me and guide me."* Most of all he asked to be freed from the trap that his own emaciated body has become. It is no longer the cross, it is no longer the Roman Soldiers, it is no longer the mocking and humiliation, it is now his body. Jesus knew that he was going to be in Paradise. He could no longer wait.

Terror on Every Side

The Parallels between Psalms 31 and 22

Like Psalm 22, Psalm 31 is fulfilled in the death of Jesus. Not surprisingly, there are many parallels between the two psalms.

1. Humiliation and Contempt

Psalm 31:11,13,18 (NIV) *Because of all my enemies, I am the utter contempt of my neighbors; I am a dread to my friends - those who see me on the street flee from me ... For I hear the slander of many; there is terror on every side; they conspire against me and plot to take my life … Let their lying lips be silenced, for with pride and contempt they speak arrogantly against the righteous.*

Psalm 22:6-8 (RSV) *But I am a worm, and no man; scorned by men, and despised by the people. All who see me mock at me, they make mouths at me, they wag their heads; "He committed his cause to the LORD; let him deliver him, let him rescue him, for he delights in him!"*

2. Trust and Deliverance

Psalm 31:14-15 (RSV) *But I trust in thee, O LORD, I say, "Thou art my God." My times are in thy hand; deliver me from the hand of my enemies and persecutors!*

Psalm 22:3-5, 20-22 (NIV) *Yet you are enthroned as the Holy One; you are the praise of Israel. In you our fathers put their trust; they trusted and you delivered them. They cried to you and were saved; in you they trusted and were not disappointed … Deliver my life from the sword, my precious life from the power of the dogs. Rescue me from the mouth of the lions; save me from the horns of the wild oxen.*

3. All my Bones are Out of Joint

Psalm 31: 9-12 (RSV) *Be gracious to me, O LORD, for I am in distress; my eye is wasted from grief, my soul and my body also. For my life is spent with sorrow, and my years with sighing; my strength fails because of my misery, and my bones waste away. I am the scorn of all my adversaries, a horror to my neighbors, an object of dread to my acquaintances; those who see me in the street flee from me.*

Psalm 22:14,17 (NIV) *I am poured out like water, and all my bones are out of joint. My heart has turned to wax; it has melted away within me … I can count all my bones; people stare and gloat over me.*

"Those who see me in the street flee from me"

4. The Perception of Abandonment

Psalm 31:22 (RSV) *I had said in my alarm, "I am driven far from thy sight." But thou didst hear my supplications, when I cried to thee for help.*

Psalm 22:1-2 (NIV) *My God, my God, why have you forsaken me? Why are you so far from saving me, so far from the words of my groaning? O my God, I cry out by day, but you do not answer, by night, and am not silent …*

5. The Certainty that God hears the Cry of the Afflicted

Psalm 31:7, 16-17 (NIV) *I will be glad and rejoice in your love, for you saw my affliction and knew the anguish of my soul … Let your face shine on your servant; save me in your unfailing love. Let me not be put to shame, O LORD, for I have cried out to you.*

Psalm 22:24 (NIV) *For he has not despised or disdained the suffering of the afflicted one; he has not hidden his face from him but has listened to his cry for help.*

6. I Thirst

Psalm 31:12-13 (NIV) *I am forgotten by them as though I were dead; I have become like broken pottery. For I hear the slander of many; there is terror on every side; they conspire against me and plot to take my life.*

Psalm 22:15 (NIV) *My strength is dried up like a potsherd, and my tongue sticks to the roof of my mouth; you lay me in the dust of death.*

7. Eventual Praise

Psalm 31:21 (RSV) *Blessed be the LORD, for he has wondrously shown his steadfast love to me when I was beset as in a besieged city.*

Psalm 22:22 (NIV) *I will declare your name to my brothers; in the congregation I will praise you.*

Other Relevant Aspects in Psalm 31

Today you will be with me in Paradise

What follows is a little speculative. If Jesus is praying the prayer of the psalmist both in Psalm 22 and Psalm 31, there is an interesting verse in this second psalm.

Psalm 31:8 (NIV) *You have not handed me over to the enemy but have set my feet in a **spacious place.***

This phrase *"a spacious place"* only occurs three times in the NIV. The other two occurrences are as follows.

Job 36:15-16 (NIV) *But those who suffer he delivers in their suffering; he speaks to them in their affliction. He is wooing you from the jaws of distress to a **spacious place** free from restriction, to the comfort of your table laden with choice food.*

Psalm18:17-19 (NIV; also repeated in 2 Samuel 22:20) *He rescued me from my powerful enemy, from my foes, who were too strong for me. They confronted me in the day of my disaster, but the LORD was my support. He brought me out into a **spacious place**; he rescued me because he delighted in me.*

In all of these instances, God brings his people out of extreme suffering into a place of comfort where there is abundance and which is also free from restrictions. This could mean Paradise but I stress the word *"could"*. I am reminded of the words of Jesus.

John 14:1-3 (NIV) *Do not let your hearts be troubled. Trust in God; trust also in me. In my Father's house are many rooms; if it were not so, I would have told you. I am going there to prepare a place for you. And if I go and prepare a place for you, I will come back and take you to be with me that you also may be where I am.*

Jesus goes to prepare a place. There are many rooms. There is a lot of space. The garden of the house is paradise as we have discussed previously. The important word to focus on in these verses in John is the word *"trust"*. At the moment of death, we have to trust God to care for us and to bring us into this spacious place. This was also true for the thief on the cross, for the beggar Lazarus in Luke 16, and for the afflicted one in the psalms where the word *"trust"* features rather a lot.

Psalm 22:4-9 (NIV) *In you our fathers put their **trust**; they **trusted** and you delivered them. They cried to you and were saved; in you they **trusted** and were not disappointed. But I am a worm and not a man, scorned by men and despised by the people. All who see me mock me; they hurl insults, shaking their heads: "He **trusts** in the LORD; let the LORD rescue him. Let him deliver him, since he delights in him." Yet you brought me out of the womb; you made me **trust** in you even at my mother's breast.*

Psalm 31:6, 14-15 (NIV) *I **trust** in the LORD … But I **trust** in you, O LORD; I say, "You are my God." My times are in your hands …*

I think that in his humanity Jesus had no other option at the end of his suffering but to trust in his Father. And so he says, *"Father into your hands I commit my spirit"*.

Pay Back!

Psalm 31:23-24 *Love the LORD, all his saints! The LORD preserves the faithful, but the proud he **pays back in full**. Be strong and take heart, all you who hope in the LORD.*

Just by way of completion, Psalm 31 also includes the concept of pay back. Ultimately, the judge of all the earth will do right. And we will consider this in greater detail when we look at resurrection.

CHAPTER TEN

The Butterfly

In these next chapters, we turn our attention to the resurrection of the Jewish people out of the ashes of the Holocaust. The little child is hidden away in the womb of the crematorium but, through his suffering; the hand of the child penetrates through the door and clutches the ground. Throughout the ages the children have been the greatest victims of the persecution of the people of Israel.

The children of the ghetto

Jeremiah 31:15-17 (RSV) *Thus says the LORD: "A voice is heard in Ramah, lamentation and bitter weeping. Rachel is weeping for her children; she refuses to be comforted for her children, because they are not." Thus says the LORD: "Keep your voice from weeping, and your eyes from tears; for your work shall be rewarded, says the LORD, and they shall come back from the land of the enemy. There is hope for your future, says the LORD, and your children shall come back to their own country.*

These words were fulfilled in part at the time of the Babylonian destruction of Jerusalem. They were also fulfilled during the time of Herod.

Matthew 2:16-18 (RSV) *Then Herod, when he saw that he had been tricked by the wise men, was in a furious rage, and he sent and killed all the male children in Bethlehem and in all that region who were two years old or under, according to the time which he had ascertained from the wise men. Then was fulfilled what was spoken by the prophet Jeremiah: "A voice was heard in Ramah, wailing and loud lamentation, Rachel weeping for her children; she refused to be consoled, because they were no more."*

These words were also fulfilled at the time of the Roman destruction of Jerusalem. Listen to the terrible words of Jesus:

Luke 19:41-44 (NIV) *As he approached Jerusalem and saw the city, he wept over it and said, "If you, even you, had only known on this day what would bring you peace — but now it is hidden from your eyes. The days will come upon you when your enemies will build an embankment against you and encircle you and hem you in on every side. They will dash you to the ground, you **and the children within your walls.** They will not leave one stone on another, because you did not recognize the time of God's coming to you."*

Luke 21:20-24 (NIV) *When you see Jerusalem being surrounded by armies, you will know that its desolation is near. Then let those who are in Judea flee to the mountains, let those in the city get out, and let those in the country not enter the city for this is the time of punishment in fulfillment of all that has been written. How dreadful it will be in those days for **pregnant women and nursing mothers**! There will be great distress in the land and wrath against this people. They will fall by the sword and will be taken as prisoners to all the nations. Jerusalem will be trampled on by the Gentiles until the times of the Gentiles are fulfilled.*

A Nursing Mother in the Ghetto

But without question, the greatest fulfillment of these words, in my opinion, was during the Holocaust. If this is true then the words of Jesus are also totally fulfilled.

Matthew 24:21 (NIV) *For then there will be great distress, unequalled from the beginning of the world until now - and never to be equaled again.*

Jeremiah chapters 30 and 31 are the prophet's overview of the ultimate future and destiny of the people of Israel. In a sense it is a chronological sequence but as we will see the establishment of the New Covenant took place when Jesus shed his blood which was to be the seal of this promise. However, the ultimate result of the New Covenant is as follows:

Jeremiah 31:34 (NIV) *No longer will a man teach his neighbor, or a man his brother, saying, 'Know the LORD,' because they will all know me, from the least of them to the greatest," declares the LORD. "For I will forgive their wickedness and will remember their sins no more."*

It is important to realize that the New Covenant is made with the people of Israel and the people of Judah.[1] It is interesting to note that two peoples are mentioned. The reason for this is that, at the time of Jeremiah, the nation of Israel was divided into the Northern and Southern Kingdoms. The Bible predicts a reversal of this division but that is beyond the scope of this study. The context of these two chapters is given in the first three verses.

---

[1] Jeremiah 31:31 "The time is coming," declares the LORD, "when I will make a new covenant with the house of Israel and with the house of Judah.

Jeremiah 30:1-3 (NIV) *This is the word that came to Jeremiah from the LORD: "This is what the LORD, the God of Israel, says: 'Write in a book all the words I have spoken to you. The days are coming,' declares the LORD, 'when I will bring my people Israel and Judah back from captivity and restore them to the land I gave to their forefathers to possess,' says the LORD."*

Possessing the Land

Again, note that the words are spoken to two peoples. This sets the fulfillment into the distant future because the return from Babylon only involved the Southern Kingdom and the return of a remnant of Jewish people under the leadership of Zerubbabel, Ezra and Nehemiah. The final fulfillment has to involve the return of all 12 tribes to the Land. In other words, there will be no lost tribes! As we will see, only God can know the identity of Israel for he who scattered them will re-gather them to the Land he gave their forefathers. However, the next verses in Jeremiah chapter 30 come as a shock.

The Time of Jacob's Trouble

Jeremiah 30:4-7 (NIV) *These are the words the LORD spoke concerning Israel and Judah: "This is what the LORD says: "'Cries of fear are heard - terror, not peace. Ask and see: Can a man bear children? Then why do I see every strong man with his hands on his stomach like a woman in labor, every face turned deathly pale? How awful that day will be! None will be like it. It will be a time of trouble for Jacob, but he will be saved out of it.*

Every Face turned Deathly Pale

The question to consider is whether the Holocaust that occurred during World War 2 is the fullest and final expression of the period described in as *"the time of Jacob's trouble"*. Certainly Jewish people have suffered through millennia like no other people. However, there are some evangelical preachers and theologians who regard the Holocaust simply as a foretaste of something greater to come. I totally reject this position for several reasons.[2]

1. Israel will be saved out of it

But what do we mean by *"saved"*? The Christian position would emphasize the spiritual realities but the Hebraic mind does not separate the physical from the spiritual. The re-gathering of the people of Israel to their own land is as much a part (and is pre-requisite, in my opinion,) to the greater realities to come. This physical salvation is reflected in many places in these chapters.

Jeremiah 30:10-11 (NIV) *'So do not fear, O Jacob my servant; do not be dismayed, O Israel,' declares the LORD.* **'I will surely save you out of a distant place**, *your descendants from the land of their exile. Jacob will again have peace and security, and no-one will make him afraid.* **I am with you and will save you**,*' declares the LORD. 'Though I completely destroy all the nations among which I scatter you, I will not completely destroy you. I will discipline you but only with justice; I will not let you go entirely unpunished.'*

---

[2] I develop this theme in much greater detail in a separate booklet which is entitled "Is it Safe?" This is available on request. Please contact the author by email: gjrb2@aol.com

Jeremiah 31:7-8 (NIV) *This is what the LORD says. "Sing with joy for Jacob, shout for the foremost of the nations. Make your praises heard, and say,* **'O LORD, save your people, the remnant of Israel.'** *See, I will bring them from the land of the north and gather them from the ends of the earth. Among them will be the blind and the lame, expectant mothers and women in labor; a great throng will return. They will come with weeping; they will pray as I bring them back. I will lead them beside streams of water on a level path where they will not stumble, because I am Israel's father, and Ephraim is my firstborn son.*

"O Lord, save your People, the Remnant of Israel"

As we will see this encouragement to sing, shout and supplicate for the salvation of Israel will result in the Lord bringing his people back to the Land from the ends of the earth. I submit that this is exactly what has happened as a direct result of the Holocaust. Whatever, the future holds (and I accept that this may be difficult), Israel exits!

Jeremiah 31:10-11 (NIV) *Hear the word of the LORD, O nations; proclaim it in distant coastlands: 'He who scattered Israel will gather them and will watch over his flock like a shepherd.' For the LORD will ransom Jacob and redeem them from the hand of those stronger than they.*

2. The Remnant that Returns is the Remnant that is Saved

The encouragement to pray is that the Lord will save the remnant of Israel. The fact is only a remnant will return.

Isaiah 10:20-22 (RSV) *In that day the remnant of Israel and the survivors of the house of Jacob will no more lean upon him that smote them, but will lean upon the LORD, the Holy One of Israel, in truth. A remnant will return, the remnant of Jacob, to the mighty God. For though your people Israel be as the sand of the sea, only a remnant of them will return.*

This is quoted by the Apostle Paul in the letter to the Romans.

Romans 9:27 (RSV) *And Isaiah cries out concerning Israel: "Though the number of the sons of Israel be as the sand of the sea, only a remnant of them will be saved.*

Putting two and two together, the remnant that returns will be the remnant that is saved and it will eventually lead to this remnant returning to the Mighty God. We will consider this again. So what does this mean for Jewish people in the world? What does it mean for those Jewish people who have no desire to return to the Land? Will they be saved? Well, we just have to wait and see and continue to pray. The situation in the world is deteriorating and it may be that an increasing number will have the desire to flee for safety. Events may transpire in the Middle East that will be added encouragement to make Aliyah.

Whatever happens, God is committed to bringing back this remnant to the Land. *He who scattered Israel will gather them and watch over his flock like a shepherd* (Jeremiah 31:10). This is repeated in other places in the prophetic scriptures.

Micah 2:12-13 (RSV) *I will surely gather all of you, O Jacob, I will gather the remnant of Israel; I will set them together like sheep in a fold, like a flock in its pasture, a noisy multitude of men. He who opens the breach will go up before them; they will break through and pass the gate, going out by it. Their king will pass on before them, the LORD at their head.*

These words remind me of statements of Jesus in John's Gospel.

John 10:9-11 (NIV) *I am the gate; whoever enters through me will be saved. He will come in and go out, and find pasture. The thief comes only to steal and kill and destroy; I have come that they may have life, and have it to the full. "I am the good shepherd. The good shepherd lays down his life for the sheep.*

The King who is at their head is also the Good Shepherd. Of course, David is the archetype. The Son of David is the fulfillment. The Good Shepherd alludes to the passage in Ezekiel.

Ezekiel 34:12-15 (RSV) *As a shepherd seeks out his flock when some of his sheep have been scattered abroad, so will I seek out my sheep; and I will rescue them from all places where they have been scattered on a day of clouds and thick darkness. And I will bring them out from the peoples, and gather them from the countries, and will bring them into their own land; and I will feed them on the mountains of Israel, by the fountains, and in all the inhabited places of the country. I will feed them with good pasture, and upon the mountain heights of Israel shall be their pasture; there they shall lie down in good grazing land, and on fat pasture they shall feed on the mountains of Israel. I myself will be the shepherd of my sheep, and I will make them lie down, says the Lord GOD.*

The day of clouds and darkness is exemplified in the days of the Holocaust. It is out of the Holocaust that the Lord saves them. But it is only a remnant that is saved.

3. Salvation comes out of Holocaust

Jeremiah 30:8-11 (RSV) *And it shall come to pass in that day, says the LORD of hosts, that I will break the yoke from off their neck, and I will burst their bonds, and strangers shall no more make servants of them. But they shall serve the LORD their God and David their king, whom I will raise up for them. "Then fear not, O Jacob my servant, says the LORD, nor be dismayed, O Israel; for lo, I will save you from afar, and your offspring from the land of their captivity. Jacob shall return and have quiet and ease, and none shall make him afraid. For I am with you to save you, says the LORD; I will make a full end of all the nations among whom I scattered you, but of you I will not make a full end. I will chasten you in just measure, and I will by no means leave you unpunished.*

Unfortunately, one cannot escape the fact that God is sovereign over the suffering of his people as most certainly he was sovereign over the suffering of his son. It is the consistent testimony in the Tanach that the return of the remnant is out of a time of extreme suffering and that this is also judgment as God says *"I will not completely destroy you. I will discipline you but only with justice; I will not let you go entirely unpunished."* (Jeremiah 30:11).

This truth, no matter how unpalatable, is also seen in Isaiah.

Isaiah 42:24-25 (NIV) *Who handed Jacob over to become loot, and Israel to the plunderers? Was it not the LORD, against whom we have sinned? For they would not follow his ways; they did not obey his law. So he poured out on them his burning anger, the violence of war. It enveloped them in flames, yet they did not understand; it consumed them, but they did not take it to heart.*

It is a terrible truth to realize that the Lord *"poured out on them his burning anger"*. This anger was expressed in the violence of war and enveloping flames. If this is not a description of the Holocaust (and the crematoria in particular) then I do not know what is. *"But now this is what the Lord says ..."* The people of Israel will be saved through this ordeal. They will go through the water and through the flames but they will come out of it into a new place. This is how Jeremiah expresses the return of the Remnant, *"Oh Lord, save your people, the remnant of Israel. See I will bring them to the Land of the North"* (Jeremiah 31:7-8). Isaiah puts it like this:

Isaiah 43:5-6 (NIV) *Do not be afraid, for I am with you; I will bring your children from the east and gather you from the west. I will say to the north, 'Give them up!' and to the south, 'Do not hold them back.' Bring my sons from afar and my daughters from the ends of the earth.*

The Valley of the Dry Bones

A Mass Grave in Bergen Belsen

The prophet Ezekiel has a vision of a valley filled with the bones of the slaughtered. I have no doubt that his vision was fulfilled by the atrocities committed against the Jewish People either in the death camps or in places such as Babi Yar on the outskirts of Kiev.

We shall have occasion to look in greater detail at this passage in the next chapter but it is sufficient to see that salvation (involving the return to the land) is consistently described in the Tanach as taking place out of Holocaust.

Ezekiel 37:11-13 (NIV) *Then he said to me: "Son of man, these bones are the whole house of Israel. They say, 'Our bones are dried up and our hope is gone; we are cut off.' Therefore prophesy and say to them: 'this is what the Sovereign LORD says: O my people, I am going to open your graves and bring you up from them; I will bring you back to the land of Israel. Then you, my people, will know that I am the LORD, when I open your graves and bring you up from them.'*

Consequently, I am convinced that the final and most complete fulfillment of *"the time of Jacob's trouble"* was the Holocaust. The nation of Israel has been re-established. It is a fact of history. Although the nations of the world are trying to reverse this fact through the delegitimizing of the nation, I believe that Israel is here to stay and that this Land is now the only place of safety for the Jewish people. I recognize that humanly speaking this is totally counter-intuitive but I believe we will live to see it. Furthermore, the preservation of this nation against insuperable odds will reflect what took place in the War of Independence in 1948 - only more so.

Jeremiah 31:27-28 (NIV) *"The days are coming," declares the LORD, "when I will plant the house of Israel and the house of Judah with the offspring of men and of animals. Just as I watched over them to uproot and tear down, and to overthrow, destroy and bring disaster, so I will watch over them to build and to plant," declares the LORD.*

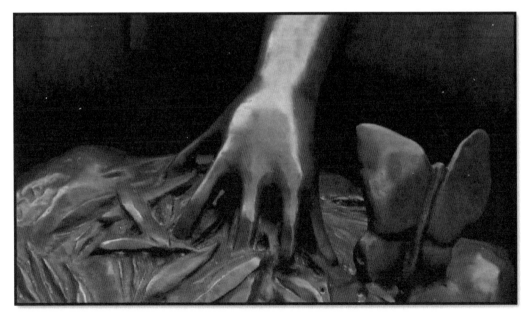

The Ground represents the Land of Israel

The prophet Amos agrees and states categorically:

Amos 9:15 (NIV) *I will plant Israel in their own land, never again to be uprooted from the land I have given them," says the LORD your God.*

These words were not fulfilled in the return from Babylon. The exile of the Jewish people that began at the time of the Roman destruction led to their dispersion to the ends of the earth. We have seen, in our day, the return of the Jewish people to their land from the ends of the earth. The Lord said that he would do this.

Isaiah 11:11-12 (RSV) *In that day the Lord will extend his hand yet a second time to recover the remnant which is left of his people, from Assyria, from Egypt, from Pathros, from Ethiopia, from Elam, from Shinar, from Hamath, and from the coastlands of the sea. He will raise an ensign for the nations, and will assemble the outcasts of Israel, and gather the dispersed of Judah from the four corners of the earth.*

The return from Babylon does not fulfill this prophecy. If, as I believe, we have lived to see this prophecy fulfilled in our day then, according to Amos, the nation will never be uprooted again. Israel becomes the only safe place on earth for the people of Israel. Their return to the Land ensures their salvation in every respect. The resurrection of the Nation is also seen in the prophecy of Hosea.

Hosea 6:1-2 (NIV) *Come let us return to the LORD. He has torn us to pieces but he will heal us; he has injured us but he will bind up our wounds. After two days he will revive us;* **on the third day** *he will restore us that we may live in his presence.*

It is probable that this is the passage of Scripture where there is the closest identification of the resurrection of the people of Israel with the resurrection of Jesus. The very next mention of *"the third day"* in the entire Bible is this.

Matthew 16:21 (NIV) *From that time on Jesus began to explain to his disciples that he must go to Jerusalem and suffer many things at the hands of the elders, chief priests and teachers of the law, and that he must be killed and on the third day be raised to life.*

Jesus was raised to life on the third day. After three days, the people of Israel will be restored and will live in his presence. But the prophet Hosea emphasizes the following:

"He will bind up our wounds" [3]

Hosea 6:1 (NIV) *He has torn us to pieces but he will heal us; he has injured us but he will bind up our wounds.*

God is described as the instrument of their wounding as he was the instrument of the wounding of Jesus (see Isaiah 53[4]). Moreover, he is the one who injured them.

Auschwitz

---

[3] Photograph taken after the liberation of Bergen Belsen in 1945

[4] Isaiah 53:5-6 But he was pierced for our transgressions, he was crushed for our iniquities; the punishment that brought us peace was upon him, and by his wounds we are healed. We all, like sheep, have gone astray, each of us has turned to his own way; and the LORD has laid on him the iniquity of us all.

4. The Holocaust is the Open Wound

Jeremiah 30:12-14 (RSV) *For thus says the LORD: Your hurt is incurable, and your wound is grievous. There is none to uphold your cause, no medicine for your wound, no healing for you. All your lovers have forgotten you; they care nothing for you; for I have dealt you the blow of an enemy, the punishment of a merciless foe, because your guilt is great, because your sins are flagrant.*

While Israel waits in a period of transition, it is inevitable that they perceive the Holocaust as an open wound and a festering sore. We sometimes say there are no answers to this question although the Bible is rather explicit. This wound is also referred to in chapter eight in the prophecy of Jeremiah.

Jeremiah 8:11, 15 (NIV) *They dress the wound of my people as though it were not serious. "Peace, peace," they say, when there is no peace … We hoped for peace but no good has come, for a time of healing but there was only terror …*

and

Jeremiah 8:18-22 (NIV) *O my Comforter in sorrow, my heart is faint within me. Listen to the cry of my people from a land far away: "Is the LORD not in Zion? Is her King no longer there?" "Why have they provoked me to anger with their images, with their worthless foreign idols?" "The harvest is past, the summer has ended, and we are not saved." Since my people are crushed, I am crushed; I mourn, and horror grips me. Is there no balm in Gilead? Is there no physician there?* **Why then is there no healing for the wound of my people?**

As we have seen, this is the actual context for the **very next** verse.

Jeremiah 9:1 (NIV; but in some European Bibles Jeremiah 8:23) *Oh, that my head were a spring of water and my eyes a fountain of tears that I would weep day and night for the slain of my people.*

I believe that this may be the main reason for the building of the Fountain of Tears. I believe that the Holocaust IS the open wound that is described in the prophecy of Jeremiah. Why did God allow it? Why did he appear to abandon them to the Nazis? Why did the people go like lambs to the slaughter and not, for the most part, resist?

God, however, hears the intercession of the prophet (and the Fountain). He is also the one (and I would suggest the only one) who can bring healing to this fatal wound.

5. The Healing of the Open Wound

Hosea puts it this way: *"he will bind up our wounds"*. The prophet Jeremiah says:

Jeremiah 30:15-17 (RSV) *Why do you cry out over your hurt? Your pain is incurable. Because your guilt is great, because your sins are flagrant, I have done these things to you. Therefore all who devour you shall be devoured, and all your foes, every one of them, shall go into captivity; those who despoil you shall become a spoil, and all who prey on you I will make a prey. For I will restore health to you, and your wounds I will heal, says the LORD, because they have called you an outcast: 'It is Zion, for whom no one cares!'*

This is also repeated in

Jeremiah 33:6-7 (NIV) *Nevertheless, I will bring health and healing to it; I will heal my people and will let them enjoy abundant peace and security. I will bring Judah and Israel back from captivity and will rebuild them as they were before.*

One has to except that the unbelievable suffering of the Jewish people was a judgment. God is sovereign over the suffering of his people and of his son. Although it may be extremely politically incorrect to say this, their greatest mistake was to reject God's salvation plan and to call down this terrible curse.

Matthew 27:25 (NIV) *All the people answered, "Let his blood be on us and on our children!"*

However, in this, the mystery of God's purposes for the entire world is revealed as Paul says in the letter to the Romans.

Romans 11:25-27 (KJV) *For I would not, brethren, that ye should be ignorant of this mystery, lest ye should be wise in your own conceits; that blindness in part is happened to Israel, until the fullness of the Gentiles be come in. And so all Israel shall be saved: as it is written, There shall come out of Sion the Deliverer, and shall turn away ungodliness from Jacob: For this is my covenant unto them, when I shall take away their sins.*

6. Pay Back!

Jeremiah 30:18-19 (NIV) *This is what the LORD says: "'I will restore the fortunes of Jacob's tents and have compassion on his dwellings; the city will be rebuilt on her ruins, and the palace will stand in its proper place. From them will come songs of thanksgiving and the sound of rejoicing. I will add to their numbers, and they will not be decreased; I will bring them honor, and they will not be disdained.*

In this passage we see something of the pay back that God promises his people. This might be most wonderfully expressed in the prophecy of Joel.

Joel 2:25-27 (RSV) *I will restore to you the years which the swarming locust has eaten, the hopper, the destroyer, and the cutter, my great army, which I sent among you. "You shall eat in plenty and be satisfied, and praise the name of the LORD your God, who has dealt wondrously with you. And my people shall never again be put to shame. You shall know that I am in the midst of Israel, and that I, the LORD, am your God and there is none else. And my people shall never again be put to shame. And it shall come to pass afterward, that I will pour out my spirit on all flesh ….*

This is an important passage because it sets the context of the sermon that Peter preached on the day of Pentecost. It is obvious from these verses in Joel that the outpouring of the Spirit will occur after God restores the years that the locusts have eaten at a time when it will be rightly said that *"never again will [his] people be shamed"*. The future fulfillment of these words is also emphasized by the facts that this final outpouring will be accompanied by cosmic signs that presumably did not happen in anything like the fullest sense on the day of Pentecost.

Joel 2:30-32 (RSV) *I will give portents in the heavens and on the earth, blood and fire and columns of smoke. The sun shall be turned to darkness, and the moon to blood, before the great and terrible day of the LORD comes. And it shall come to pass that all who call upon the name of the LORD shall be delivered; for in Mount Zion and in Jerusalem there shall be those who escape, as the LORD has said, and among the survivors shall be those whom the LORD calls.*

This is also confirmed by the words of Jesus.

Mark 13:24-26 (NIV) *But in those days, following that distress, "'the sun will be darkened, and the moon will not give its light; the stars will fall from the sky, and the heavenly bodies will be shaken.' "At that time men will see the Son of Man coming in clouds with great power and glory."*

Thus the events on the Day of Pentecost are but a foretaste of what will transpire in the days to come. We will consider this in greater detail in the next chapter. The greatest emphasis, however, regarding pay back is towards the enemies of the people of Israel.

Psalm 31:23-24 (NIV) *Love the LORD, all his saints! The LORD preserves the faithful, but the proud he **pays back in full.** Be strong and take heart, all you who hope in the LORD.*

It is a consistent pattern in Scripture that God uses invading nations as an instrument of judgment on the people of God but eventually the instruments of judgment fall under judgment themselves.

Jeremiah 30:16 (NIV) *But all who devour you will be devoured; all your enemies will go into exile. Those who plunder you will be plundered; all who make spoil of you I will despoil.*

7. First for the Jew then for the Gentile

Another reason why I do not believe that *"the time of Jacob's trouble"* for the people of Israel is still future, is the principle that was established by the Apostle Paul. We are familiar with the declaration of Paul in chapter 1 of the letter to the Romans.

Romans 1:16 (NIV) *I am not ashamed of the gospel, because it is the power of God for the salvation of everyone who believes: first for the Jew, then for the Gentile.*

But this familiar passage is only one of three *"first for the Jew and then for the Gentile"* statements. The second one is to do with wrath.

Romans 2:9 (NIV) *There will be trouble and distress for every human being who does evil: first for the Jew, then for the Gentile …*

If the Holocaust was *"the time of Jacob's trouble"* for the people of Israel then what is ahead will be catastrophic for the world as a whole. As Jesus said:

Luke 21:26 (NIV) *Men will faint from terror, apprehensive of what is coming on the world, for the heavenly bodies will be shaken.*

Romans 2:10 (NIV) *Glory, honor and peace for everyone who does good: first for the Jew, then for the Gentile.*

Following the time of wrath, there is the promise of glory, peace and honor. This I believe is the destiny of the people of Israel.

Jeremiah 30:20-22 (RSV) *Their children shall be as they were of old, and their congregation shall be established before me; and I will punish all who oppress them. Their prince shall be one of themselves, their ruler shall come forth from their midst; I will make him draw near, and he shall approach me, for who would dare of himself to approach me? says the LORD. And you shall be my people, and I will be your God."*

8. A Summary

Jeremiah 30:23-24 (RSV) *Behold the storm of the LORD! Wrath has gone forth, a whirling tempest; it will burst upon the head of the wicked. The fierce anger of the LORD will not turn back until he has executed and accomplished the intents of his mind. In the latter days you will understand this.*

God's ways are not our ways. The return to the Land is pre-requisite to an event which is destined to change the face of history and the Middle East in particular. We shall consider this in the next chapter when we understand the significance of the empty cup.

CHAPTER ELEVEN

The Empty Cup

Peace at Last

We have seen in a previous chapter that Jeremiah chapters 30 and 31 are a chronological sequence of events. The prophet anticipates that a day would come when, out of Holocaust, the people of Israel and Judah would return to the Land. But this is only the beginning of their resurrection. Once they are back in the Land, events will transpire that would bring the people into an even closer relationship with God. This is the consistent expectation in the Tanach. We see it clearly expressed in the Torah.

Deuteronomy 30:4-6 (RSV) *If your outcasts are in the uttermost parts of heaven, from there the LORD your God will gather you, and from there he will fetch you; and the LORD your God will bring you into the land which your fathers possessed, that you may possess it; and he will make you more prosperous and numerous than your fathers. And the LORD your God will circumcise your heart and the heart of your offspring, so that you will love the LORD your God with all your heart and with all your soul, that you may live.*

Within these three verses we see a number of things. Firstly, the verses clearly state that the people of Israel would be banished to the most distant lands imaginable. This, without doubt, is looking beyond Assyria (northern Kingdom) and Babylon (southern Kingdom) to a dispersion that would last nearly 2000 years. But as we have already considered in Jeremiah 31:10 *"He who scattered Israel will gather them".*

The Declaration of the State of Israel in May 1948

Secondly, upon their return to the Land, they will be more prosperous (and numerous) than ever before. Again, without doubt, this sets this prophecy into the modern day. Never in history can it be said that they returned to the Land in such a condition. Thirdly, it is within the Land that God will take an initiative (as he always does) to do something to the hearts of the returnees and their descendants that would cause them to love him with all their heart and soul. This will be the fulfillment of the Shema.

Deuteronomy 6:4-6 (NIV) *Hear, O Israel: The LORD our God, the LORD is one. Love the LORD your God with all your heart and with all your soul and with all your strength.* ***These commandments that I give you today are to be upon your hearts.***

God original intention was not to keep the Law written on tablets of stone or written with ink on scrolls hidden away in a Holy Ark found in every synagogue. His original intention is that the Law would be written on the hearts of his people. The apostle Paul agrees.

2 Corinthians 3:3 (NIV) *… written not with ink but with the Spirit of the living God, not on tablets of stone but on tablets of human hearts.*

However, it is my opinion that the return to the Land is pre-requisite to this renewal taking place within the lives of the people of Israel.

As the prophet Ezekiel consistently declares:

Ezekiel 11:17-20 (RSV) *Therefore say, 'Thus says the Lord GOD: I will gather you from the peoples, and assemble you out of the countries where you have been scattered, and I will give you the land of Israel.' And when they come there, they will remove from it all its detestable things and all its abominations. And I will give them one heart, and put a new spirit within them; I will take the stony heart out of their flesh and give them a heart of flesh, that they may walk in my statutes and keep my ordinances and obey them; and they shall be my people, and I will be their God.*

and

Ezekiel 37:12-14 (NIV) *Therefore prophesy and say to them: 'This is what the Sovereign LORD says: O my people, I am going to open your graves and bring you up from them; I will bring you back to the land of Israel. Then you, my people, will know that I am the LORD, when I open your graves and bring you up from them.* **I will put my Spirit in you and you will live***, and I will settle you in your own land. Then you will know that I the LORD have spoken, and I have done it, declares the LORD.*

Heart and Stone

The Law was given to the people of Israel at Sinai. It was given at Shavuot (the Feast of Weeks also known as Pentecost). The blood of the Passover lamb had been shed and applied to the doorposts by the people in Egypt. The people were free to leave and passed through the Red Sea after three days and three nights. After 50 days, they were camped at Mount Sinai. And when the Day of Pentecost was come they were all gathered in one place. At Sinai, God met Moses ...

Exodus 19:1 (NIV)   *In the third month after the Israelites left Egypt -* **on the very day** *- they came to the Desert of Sinai.*

God entered into a covenant with his people[1] and gave the Law written on stone. It is therefore not really that surprising that the Law would be written on the hearts, beginning at another Pentecost.

---

[1] The Mosaic Covenant

Acts 2:1-4 (RSV) *When the day of Pentecost had come, they were all together in one place. And suddenly a sound came from heaven like the rush of a mighty wind, and it filled all the house where they were sitting. And there appeared to them tongues as of fire, distributed and resting on each one of them. And they were all filled with the Holy Spirit and began to speak in other tongues, as the Spirit gave them utterance.*

Shavuot is also known as the Feast of Firstfruits. What took place in Jerusalem two thousand years ago, anticipates a much greater final harvest at the end of history. As we will see, this foretaste of the New Covenant would lead to the Gospel being taken to the ends of the earth.

John 3:16 (RSV) *For God so loved the world that he gave his only Son, that whoever believes in him should not perish but have eternal life.*

Outward Circumcision is the Seal of the Abrahamic Covenant

Genesis 17:7-11 (RSV) *And I will establish my covenant between me and you and your descendants after you throughout their generations for an everlasting covenant, to be God to you and to your descendants after you. And I will give to you, and to your descendants after you, the land of your sojournings, all the land of Canaan, for an everlasting possession; and I will be their God." And God said to Abraham, "As for you, you shall keep my covenant, you and your descendants after you throughout their generations. This is my covenant, which you shall keep, between me and you and your descendants after you: Every male among you shall be circumcised. You shall be circumcised in the flesh of your foreskins, and it shall be a sign of the covenant between me and you.*

Romans 4:11 (NIV) *And he received the sign of circumcision, a seal of the righteousness that he had by faith while he was still uncircumcised.*

Gentiles have no need of physical circumcision. They are not part of that aspect of the covenant that God made with Abraham over the possession of the Land. As we know, this became a heated controversy in the early church and it was only resolved after the Council of Jerusalem that we read about in Acts chapter 15. On the other hand, the early apostles were astonished.

Acts 10:45 (NIV) *The circumcised believers who had come with Peter were astonished that the gift of the Holy Spirit had been poured out **even on the Gentiles.***

This was just not anticipated. The Gentiles had not been given the Law, so how come that the Holy Spirit would now begin to write Law on their hearts? However, if we can step back for a minute and think about this. God loves the world. He wants everyone to have the opportunity to know him. We can only know him through the administration of the Holy Spirit in the heart. This is for Jew and Gentile alike. It has nothing to do with religion, gender or geography.

Inward Circumcision is the Seal of the New Covenant

Ephesians 4:30 (NIV) *And do not grieve the Holy Spirit of God, with whom you were sealed for the day of redemption.*

2 Corinthians 1:21-22 (NIV) *Now it is God who makes both us and you stand firm in Christ. He anointed us, set his seal of ownership on us, and put his Spirit in our hearts as a deposit, guaranteeing what is to come.*

Although physical circumcision has no meaning or benefit (apart for some possible health benefit) for Gentiles, the circumcision of the heart is quite different. We have come to understand that this circumcision facilitates the writing of God's Law on the human heart and it is through this that we can know him and love him. It is all to do with relationship. It has very little to do with religion and God forbid that it would be said of us.

Isaiah 29:13 (NIV) *The Lord says: "These people come near to me with their mouth and honor me with their lips, but their hearts are far from me. Their worship of me is made up only of rules taught by men.*

This is probably the best definition of religion that there is. Rules taught by men. God is looking for relationship and the adoration of man's heart. And for this to happen, the heart of man (which is desperately wicked[2]) has to be circumcised and here there is no difference between Jew and Gentile.

Romans 10:12-13 (RSV) *For there is no distinction between Jew and Greek; the same Lord is Lord of all and bestows his riches upon all who call upon him. For, "every one who calls upon the name of the Lord will be saved."*

It is very interesting that Paul quotes the prophecy of Joel which we have already considered.

---

[2] Jeremiah 17:9

Inward Circumcision is the Baptism in the Holy Spirit

Mark 1:8 (NIV) *I baptize you with water, but he will baptize you with the Holy Spirit*

Acts 1:4-8 (RSV) *And while staying with them he charged them not to depart from Jerusalem, but to wait for the promise of the Father, which, he said, "you heard from me, for John baptized with water, but before many days you shall be baptized with the Holy Spirit." So when they had come together, they asked him, "Lord, will you at this time restore the kingdom to Israel?" He said to them, "It is not for you to know times or seasons which the Father has fixed by his own authority. But you shall receive power when the Holy Spirit has come upon you; and you shall be my witnesses in Jerusalem and in all Judea and Samaria and to the end of the earth.*

This is an amazing passage in the book of Acts. The resurrected Jesus had spent approximately 40 days teaching his disciples. It must have been the most incredible time. And yet, when the disciples come to him they are extremely perplexed. Their primary concern is for the destiny of Israel. *"Lord, are you **at this time** going to restore the kingdom to Israel?"* They knew he was going to leave them. They had no idea that the next stage in the redemption of the world would take them ultimately to the ends of the earth.

However, to be effective witnesses they **had** to be baptized in the Holy Spirit. They were to be the firstfruits of the ultimate harvest of souls that would be both Jew and Gentile. This firstfruits experience of the Holy Spirit at Pentecost does not obviate the final fulfillment and objective of the New Covenant that is made with the House of Israel.

Jeremiah 31:33-34 (NIV) *This is the covenant that I will make with the house of Israel after that time," declares the LORD. "I will put my law in their minds and write it on their hearts. I will be their God, and they will be my people ... because they will all know me, from the least of them to the greatest," declares the LORD. "For I will forgive their wickedness and will remember their sins no more."*

The message would be taken to the ends of the earth. This would take a long time. In fact, it has taken 2000 years. But it is from the ends of the earth that the Lord promises to bring his people back to their land to meet with them there.

Ezekiel 36:24-28 (RSV) *For I will take you from the nations, and gather you from all the countries, and bring you into your own land. I will sprinkle clean water upon you, and you shall be clean from all your uncleanness, and from all your idols I will cleanse you. A new heart I will give you, and a new spirit I will put within you; and I will take out of your flesh the heart of stone and give you a heart of flesh. And I will put my spirit within you, and cause you to walk in my statutes and be careful to observe my ordinances. You shall dwell in the land which I gave to your fathers; and you shall be my people, and I will be your God.*

A New Heart is Required

Out of Holocaust, the Lord brings his people back to the Land and it will begin to prosper.

Joel 2:21-24 (RSV) *"Fear not, O land; be glad and rejoice, for the LORD has done great things! Fear not, you beasts of the field, for the pastures of the wilderness are green; the tree bears its fruit, the fig tree and vine give their full yield. "Be glad, O sons of Zion, and rejoice in the LORD, your God; for he has given the early rain for your vindication, he has poured down for you abundant rain, the early and the latter rain, as before. "The threshing floors shall be full of grain, the vats shall overflow with wine and oil.*

This is also described in the Prophecy of Ezekiel.

Ezekiel 36:28-31 (RSV) *You shall dwell in the land which I gave to your fathers; and you shall be my people, and I will be your God. And I will deliver you from all your uncleanness; and I will summon the grain and make it abundant and lay no famine upon you. I will make the fruit of the tree and the increase of the field abundant, that you may never again suffer the disgrace of famine among the nations. Then you will remember your evil ways, and your deeds that were not good; and you will loathe yourselves for your iniquities and your abominable deeds ...*

Ezekiel 36:37-38 (RSV) *Thus says the Lord GOD: This also I will let the house of Israel ask me to do for them: to increase their men like a flock. Like the flock for sacrifices, like the flock at Jerusalem during her appointed feasts, so shall the waste cities be filled with flocks of men. Then they will know that I am the LORD.*

So, God will restore the years that the locust has eaten.

Joel 2:25-27 (NIV) *I will repay you for the years the locusts have eaten, the great locust and the young locust, the other locusts and the locust swarm, my great army that I sent among you. You will have plenty to eat, until you are full, and you will praise the name of the LORD your God, who has worked wonders for you; never again will my people be shamed. Then you will know that I am in Israel, that I am the LORD your God, and that there is no other; never again will my people be shamed.*

And now at the end of history, God pours out his Spirit within the Land:

Joel 2:28-32 (NIV) *And afterwards, I will pour out my Spirit on all people. Your sons and daughters will prophesy, your old men will dream dreams, your young men will see visions. Even on my servants, both men and women, I will pour out my Spirit in those days. I will show wonders in the heavens and on the earth, blood and fire and billows of smoke. The sun will be turned to darkness and the moon to blood before the coming of the great and dreadful day of the LORD. And everyone who calls on the name of the LORD will be saved; for on Mount Zion and in Jerusalem there will be deliverance, as the LORD has said, among the survivors whom the LORD calls.*

Living Water is Poured out on the Land

It is interesting to compare this rendition with the one that the Apostle Paul gives and which we referred to earlier.

Romans 10:12-13 (NIV) *For there is no difference between Jew and Gentile, the same Lord is Lord of all and richly blesses all who call on him, for, "Everyone who calls on the name of the Lord will be saved."*

Paul does not quote the second part of the verse in Joel chapter 2, namely:

Joel 2:32 (NIV) *And everyone who calls on the name of the LORD will be saved; for on Mount Zion and in Jerusalem there will be deliverance, as the LORD has said, among the survivors whom the LORD calls.*

The final fulfillment of these words will be in Jerusalem. And this is in Paul's mind when he writes the following in Romans chapter 11.

Romans 11:25-27 (NIV) *I do not want you to be ignorant of this mystery, brothers, so that you may not be conceited: Israel has experienced a hardening in part until the full number of the Gentiles has come in. And so all Israel will be saved, as it is written: "The deliverer will come from Zion; he will turn godlessness away from Jacob. And this is my covenant with them when I take away their sins."*

"The Deliverer will come from Zion"

The Deliverer will come from Zion because there will be deliverance on Mount Zion and in Jerusalem. Paul combines the prophecies of Isaiah and Jeremiah.

Isaiah 59:20-21 (NIV) *"The Redeemer will come to Zion, to those in Jacob who repent of their sins," declares the LORD. "As for me, this is my covenant with them," says the LORD. "My Spirit, who is on you, and my words that I have put in your mouth will not depart from your mouth or from the mouths of your children, or from the mouths of their descendants from this time on and forever," says the LORD.*

When will this Event happen?

I believe the Tanach is also totally consistent in describing the events that will lead to an outpouring of the Holy Spirit in the land of Israel. It occurs during a time of increasing conflict with the surrounding nations.

Zechariah 12:1-3 (NIV) *This is the word of the LORD concerning Israel. The LORD, who stretches out the heavens, who lays the foundation of the earth, and who forms the spirit of man within him, declares: "I am going to make Jerusalem a cup that sends all the surrounding peoples reeling. Judah will be besieged as well as Jerusalem. On that day, when all the nations of the earth are gathered against her, I will make Jerusalem an immovable rock for all the nations. All who try to move it will injure themselves.*

Jerusalem - an Immovable Rock

Israel is becoming increasingly isolated in the world and, in particular, all the surrounding peoples are gathering momentum in their antipathy towards them. Eventually, and inevitably, this will lead to war. However, inexplicably, the nation will come through this conflict largely unscathed.

Zechariah 12:6-9 (RSV)   *"On that day I will make the clans of Judah like a blazing pot in the midst of wood, like a flaming torch among sheaves; and they shall devour to the right and to the left all the peoples round about, while Jerusalem shall still be inhabited in its place, in Jerusalem. "And the LORD will give victory to the tents of Judah first, that the glory of the house of David and the glory of the inhabitants of Jerusalem may not be exalted over that of Judah. On that day the LORD will put a shield about the inhabitants of Jerusalem so that the feeblest among them on that day shall be like David, and the house of David shall be like God, like the angel of the LORD, at their head. And on that day I will seek to destroy all the nations that come against Jerusalem.*

What can we say about this situation? Firstly, Israel exists. Secondly, the status of Jerusalem is controversial to say the very least. It is like a poisoned chalice that sends the surrounding nations into frenzy. Thirdly, whatever the warfare will be like, Israel will more than survive and Jerusalem will remain *intact in her place* (see NIV) and expressed as *"shall still be inhabited in its place"* (RSV as shown above). Fourthly, God himself acts on behalf of his people both to shield them and to destroy the attacking forces. It is then that the following will take place.

Zechariah 12:10 (NIV) ***And I will pour out on the house of David and the inhabitants of Jerusalem a spirit of grace and supplication.*** *They will look on me, the one they have pierced, and they will mourn for him as one mourns for an only child, and grieve bitterly for him as one grieves for a firstborn son.*

This leads to an extended period of mourning and lamentation which seems somewhat counter-intuitive since Israel has inexplicably survived the onslaught of the surrounding nations. Why this period of mourning? If has to be the realization that the one that they have rejected over 2000 years is actually their King. However, this period leads them to deep repentance and to cleansing through the same administration of the Holy Spirit.

Zechariah 13:1 (NIV) *On that day a fountain will be opened to the house of David and the inhabitants of Jerusalem, to cleanse them from sin and impurity.*

A Fountain of Grace [2]

It is this writer's opinion that the event described in Zechariah chapter 12 is not the same event as that described in Zechariah 14.[3] The outworking of this primary conflict is the salvation of Israel. It cannot be at the end of the Age.

The event described in Zechariah chapter 12 may also be described in chapters 38 and 39 of Ezekiel. In particular, chapter 38 describes a conflict that involves surrounding nations. God intervenes both to shield and to destroy the invading armies. The outworking of this conflict is the salvation of Israel and the recognition among the nations that the living God is, and has always been, the God of Israel. A summary of all these things is given in the concluding verses of Ezekiel chapter 39.

---

[2] *Fountain Of Grace* is a photograph by Donna Blackhall uploaded on November 22nd, 2010. To see and to order this photograph in color, visit: http://fineartamerica.com/featured/fountain-of-grace-donna-blackhall.html

[3] I develop this theme in much greater detail in the booklet "Is it Safe?" which is available on request. Please contact the author by email on: gjrb2@aol.com

Ezekiel 39:25-29 (RSV) *Thus says the Lord GOD: Now I will restore the fortunes of Jacob, and have mercy upon the whole house of Israel; and I will be jealous for my holy name. They shall forget their shame, and all the treachery they have practiced against me, when they dwell securely in their land with none to make them afraid, when I have brought them back from the peoples and gathered them from their enemies' lands, and through them have vindicated my holiness in the sight of many nations. Then they shall know that I am the LORD their God because I sent them into exile among the nations, and then gathered them into their own land. I will leave none of them remaining among the nations any more; and I will not hide my face any more from them,* **when I pour out my Spirit upon the house of Israel***.*

Isaiah 44:2-3 (NIV) *This is what the LORD says — he who made you, who formed you in the womb, and who will help you: Do not be afraid, O Jacob, my servant, Jeshurun, whom I have chosen. For I will pour water on the thirsty land, and streams on the dry ground;* **I will pour out my Spirit on your offspring, and my blessing on your descendants.**

I do not believe that the events described Ezekiel 38 and 39 as well as in Zechariah 12 are the end of the Age. For example, a period of seven years (Ezekiel 39:9) and seven months (Ezekiel 39:12) is described during which the Land is being cleansed. Quite what this means is unclear because it is written in somewhat archaic language.

Eventually, and in the midst of subsequent conflict which may be at least seven years later, Jesus returns to planet Earth. This was clearly stated on the Mount of Olives when Jesus ascended into Heaven.

Acts 1:11-12 (NIV) *"Men of Galilee," they said, "why do you stand here looking into the sky? This same Jesus, who has been taken from you into heaven, will come back in the same way you have seen him go into heaven." Then they returned to Jerusalem from the hill called the Mount of Olives, a Sabbath day's walk from the city.*

So he has to return to the Mount of Olives and this, in my opinion, is why East Jerusalem is the most contested geographical area on the planet. He will return in the events clearly described in Zechariah.

Zechariah 14:2-4 (NIV) *I will gather all the nations to Jerusalem to fight against it; the city will be captured, the houses ransacked, and the women raped. Half of the city will go into exile, but the rest of the people will not be taken from the city. Then the LORD will go out and fight against those nations, as he fights in the day of battle. On that day his feet will stand on the Mount of Olives, east of Jerusalem …*

These words describe a conflict which cannot be the same as that described in Zechariah chapter 12. The city of Jerusalem begins to fall (rather than remaining intact in her place) and many of the inhabitants flee through a valley that is created by a geological phenomenon that has definitely not taken place yet.[4] However, at the last, God intervenes and the Kingdom is restored to Israel simply because the King has come.

Zechariah 14:6-9 (NIV) *On that day there will be no light, no cold or frost. It will be a unique day, without daytime or night-time - a day known to the LORD. When evening comes, there will be light. On that day living water will flow out from Jerusalem, half to the eastern sea and half to the western sea, in summer and in winter. The LORD will be king over the whole earth. On that day there will be one LORD, and his name the only name.*

And on that day the Cup of Salvation will again be lifted high ..,

Psalm 116:12-19 (NIV) *How can I repay the LORD for all his goodness to me? I will lift up the cup of salvation and call on the name of the LORD. I will fulfill my vows to the LORD in the presence of all his people. Precious in the sight of the LORD is the death of his saints. O LORD, truly I am your servant; I am your servant, the son of your maidservant; you have freed me from my chains. I will sacrifice a thank-offering to you and call on the name of the LORD. I will fulfill my vows to the LORD in the presence of all his people, in the courts of the house of the LORD - in your midst, O Jerusalem. Praise the LORD.*

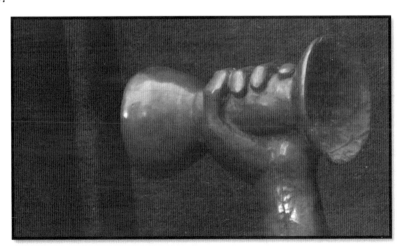

The Cup was once Full but now the Cup is Empty.

---

[4] **Zechariah 14:4-5 (NIV)** The Mount of Olives will be split in two from east to west, forming a great valley, with half of the mountain moving north and half moving south. You will flee by my mountain valley, for it will extend to Azel. You will flee as you fled from the earthquake in the days of Uzziah king of Judah. Then the LORD my God will come, and all the holy ones with him.

One of the lasting final images seen at the Fountain of Tears is the raising of an empty cup. This is the cup of Salvation but it is also the cup of God's wrath. It is not raised in triumph but its shadow falls over the Holocaust Survivor and Jesus. We declare that this cup has been drunk by them both. As mentioned in the second chapter of this book, Jesus understood the significance of this cup and that is why he struggled.

"Take this Cup from Me"

The fact is this: Jesus and the People of Israel have drunk from this cup to the full.

Isaiah 51:17 (RSV) *Rouse yourself, rouse yourself, stand up, O Jerusalem, you who have drunk at the hand of the LORD the cup of his wrath, who have drunk to the dregs the bowl of staggering.*

But the fact is also this: the cup has been taken from their hands and it is now in the hands of the nations that have abused them.

Isaiah 51:22-23 (RSV) *Thus says your Lord, the LORD, your God who pleads the cause of his people: "Behold, I have taken from your hand the cup of staggering; the bowl of my wrath **you shall drink no more**; and I will put it into the hand of your tormentors.*

The Prophet Isaiah goes on:

Isa 54:4-8 (RSV) *Fear not, for you will not be ashamed; be not confounded, for you will not be put to shame; for you will forget the shame of your youth, and the reproach of your widowhood you will remember no more. For your Maker is your husband, the LORD of hosts is his name; and the Holy One of Israel is your Redeemer, the God of the whole earth he is called. For the LORD has called you like a wife forsaken and grieved in spirit, like a wife of youth when she is cast off, says your God. For a brief moment I forsook you, but with great compassion I will gather you. In overflowing wrath for a moment I hid my face from you, but with everlasting love I will have compassion on you, says the LORD, your Redeemer.*

"Arise My Love and Come with Me" [5]

The winter is over and past and the time of singing will come.

---

[5] Sculpture by Rick Wienecke. This was a special gift to Geoff and Caryl on the occasion of their wedding in 1988. It is based on the verse in Song of Solomon, namely, **Song 2:10-12 (RSV)** My beloved speaks and says to me: "Arise, my love, my fair one, and come away; for lo, the winter is past, the rain is over and gone. The flowers appear on the earth, the time of singing has come, and the voice of the turtledove is heard in our land. "

The Lord will Comfort Zion

There are so many verses that could be listed which clearly speak of a time when the people of Israel and the city of Jerusalem, in particular, will be comforted.

Isaiah 49:13 (RSV) *Sing for joy, O heavens, and exult, O earth; break forth, O mountains, into singing! For the LORD has comforted his people, and will have compassion on his afflicted.*

It is interesting to note this verse because the verses immediately following are ones that we have already considered in earlier chapters.

Isaiah 49:14-16 (RSV) *But Zion said, "The LORD has forsaken me, my Lord has forgotten me." "Can a woman forget her sucking child, that she should have no compassion on the son of her womb? Even these may forget, yet I will not forget you. Behold, I have graven you on the palms of my hands; your walls are continually before me.*

The Lord will Comfort Zion

I am reminded of a passage in Luke's Gospel, when Jesus arrives at the Synagogue in his home town of Nazareth.

Luke 4:16-21 (RSV) *And he came to Nazareth, where he had been brought up; and he went to the synagogue, as his custom was, on the Sabbath day. And he stood up to read; and there was given to him the book of the prophet Isaiah. He opened the book and found the place where it was written, "The Spirit of the Lord is upon me, because he has anointed me to preach good news to the poor. He has sent me to proclaim release to the captives and recovering of sight to the blind, to set at liberty those who are oppressed, to proclaim the acceptable year of the Lord." And he closed the book, and gave it back to the attendant, and sat down; and the eyes of all in the synagogue were fixed on him. And he began to say to them, "Today this scripture has been fulfilled in your hearing."*

This is such a fascinating narrative and there is so much that could be said that is outside the scope of this study. Suffice to say at this stage is that Jesus only read part of the passage in Isaiah before he sat down. No wonder the eyes of everyone in the synagogue were fixed on him. Let us remind ourselves of the relevant passage in Isaiah chapter 61.

Isaiah 61:1-3 (NIV) *The Spirit of the Sovereign LORD is on me, because the LORD has anointed me to preach good news to the poor. He has sent me to bind up the brokenhearted, to proclaim freedom for the captives and release from darkness for the prisoners, to proclaim the year of the LORD's favor and the day of vengeance of our God, to comfort all who mourn, and provide for those who grieve in Zion—to bestow on them a crown of beauty instead of ashes, the oil of gladness instead of mourning, and a garment of praise instead of a spirit of despair. They will be called oaks of righteousness, a planting of the LORD for the display of his splendor.*

There are some subtle differences between the passage in Isaiah and what is recorded in Luke's account of the words of Jesus in the synagogue. It is as though the ministry of Jesus is in two parts. He could only declare in that synagogue those things that God had anointed him to do at that time.[6] In brief, the ministry that Jesus undertook at that time was five-fold, namely: (i) preaching good news to the poor; (ii) proclaiming release to the prisoners; (iii) healing the blind; (iv) to give freedom to the oppressed; (v) to proclaim the year of the Lord's favor.

He stopped mid-sentence. Why?

---

[6] I am perfectly aware that there is variation in what is recorded in Luke's Gospel between the KJV and almost every other modern translation of the Bible in English. This is beyond the scope of this study but the author has made a presentation entitled "Beauty for Ashes" which is available on request. Please contact the author by email: gjrb2@aol.com

I believe that it is simply because the time was not right for Jesus to effect all the other aspects of Messiah's ministry. The second part of the ministry of the anointed one, who is the Messiah is as follows:

1. To Proclaim the Day of Vengeance of Our God

Isaiah 34:8 (RSV) *For the LORD has a day of vengeance, a year of recompense for the cause of Zion.*

When Jesus spoke in Nazareth, the day of vengeance to uphold Zion's cause was in the distant future. Jesus knew that *"Jerusalem will be trodden down by the Gentiles"* but only *"until the times of the Gentiles be fulfilled"* (Luke 21:24). If the times of the Gentiles were fulfilled in 1967 (and I am not being dogmatic) , when the IDF recovered the Old City of Jerusalem, then it is only after then (and perhaps much later still) that the day of vengeance can be proclaimed.

2. To Comfort those that Mourn

Isaiah 52:9-10 (RSV) *Break forth together into singing, you waste places of Jerusalem; for the LORD has comforted his people, he has redeemed Jerusalem. The LORD has bared his holy arm before the eyes of all the nations; and all the ends of the earth shall see the salvation of our God.*

This inevitably follows the proclamation (and the outworking) of the day of vengeance to uphold Zion's cause.

3. To Provide for those who Grieve in Zion

Jeremiah 33:9 (RSV) *And this city shall be to me a name of joy, a praise and a glory before all the nations of the earth who shall hear of all the good that I do for them; they shall fear and tremble because of all the good and all the prosperity I provide for it.*

Prosperity is the sign of God's blessing. We have considered many passages that speak of Israel's current and future prosperity. At the end of this age, this is perhaps the main factor that will draw the armies of Antichrist to Jerusalem for the final conflict.

4. To Bestow Beauty for Ashes

Out of the ashes of the Holocaust, the nation has been established.

**One of Many Piles of Ash and Bones found at
the Buchenwald Concentration Camp**

5. To Give the Oil of Gladness instead of Mourning

Jeremiah 31:13 (NIV) *Then maidens will dance and be glad, young men and old as well. I will turn their mourning into gladness; I will give them comfort and joy instead of sorrow.*

6. To Provide a Garment of Praise instead of a Spirit of Despair

We have discussed at length the significance of Psalm 22. It is the clearest depiction of the suffering of Jesus (in his crucifixion) and the suffering of the people of Israel over millennia. In the early part of this psalm, the afflicted one is in despair. He perceives that God has forsaken him and he is surrounded by violent men and animals.

It would be a profound mistake, however, not to consider the second half of the psalm. Like the passage in Isaiah chapter 61, the ministry of the Messiah (and his people) is in two parts. I believe that this is also expressed in the wrapping of the afikomen in the Passover Seder. This is the broken second motzah that is wrapped in a white cloth and hidden away from sight until the end of the story.

Psalm 22:22-24 (RSV) *I will tell of thy name to my brethren; in the midst of the congregation I will praise thee: You who fear the LORD, praise him! all you sons of Jacob, glorify him, and stand in awe of him, all you sons of Israel! For he has not despised or abhorred the affliction of the afflicted; and he has not hid his face from him, but has heard, when he cried to him.*

The one who is speaking is going to be restored to his people who are the sons of Jacob. He re-assures them that their suffering has not been despised or abhorred. This is part of the garment of praise

Psalm 22:25-26 (RSV) *From thee comes my praise in the great congregation; my vows I will pay before those who fear him. The afflicted shall eat and be satisfied; those who seek him shall praise the LORD! May your hearts live for ever!*

Those who were afflicted with rejoice in the bounty and provision of the Lord.

Psalm 22:27-28 (RSV) *All the ends of the earth shall remember and turn to the LORD; and all the families of the nations shall worship before him. For dominion belongs to the LORD, and he rules over the nations.*

A day is coming when Jesus will be king over the entire earth. He will rule the nations with a rod of iron but they will also come to Jerusalem to worship him.

Psalm 22:29 (RSV) *Yea, to him shall all the proud of the earth bow down; before him shall bow all who go down to the dust, and he who cannot keep himself alive.*

This remarkable verse speaks of resurrection. All who go down to the dust and who cannot keep themselves alive will bow down before him. I think we will be surprised as to all those who will have called out to the Lord, like that thief of old *"Lord, remember me when you come into your kingdom".*

Psalm 22:30-31 (RSV) *Posterity shall serve him; men shall tell of the Lord to the coming generation, and proclaim his deliverance to a people yet unborn, that he has wrought it.*

A day will come when all will be fulfilled. We look forward and hasten the day when this will happen. In the meantime, we reach out with words of comfort to the people of Israel. We are his representatives who also depend on the Spirit of the Sovereign Lord. In the final chapter of this book, we will consider in some depth the meaning of the words that open the fortieth chapter in the prophecy of Isaiah.

CHAPTER TWELVE

Comfort, Comfort My People

An In-Depth Study of Isaiah Chapter 40 Verses 1 and 2

Isaiah 40:1-2 (NIV) *Comfort, comfort my people, says your God. Speak tenderly to Jerusalem, and proclaim to her that her hard service has been completed, that her sin has been paid for, that she has received from the LORD's hand double for all her sins.*

Isaiah 40:1-2 (KJV) *Comfort ye, comfort ye my people, saith your God. Speak ye comfortably to Jerusalem, and cry unto her, that her warfare is accomplished, that her iniquity is pardoned: for she hath received of the LORD's hand double for all her sins.*

Comfort, comfort my people says your God

Hebrew Text: נַחֲמוּ נַחֲמוּ עַמִּי יֹאמַר אֱלֹהֵיכֶם

Transliteration: Nachamoo, Nachamoo ami yomar elo-haychem

There is a double imperative to comfort but to whom is the Lord speaking? It is not a single person because the verb is plural. Some have suggested the prophets. The Septuagint version even includes the words *"priests"*. Others have suggested a heavenly council. All of this is conjecture. What we can say with confidence is that the imperative to comfort is given by the one who is designated "your God". Therefore, the response can only come from those in intimate relationship with him (i.e. listening to his voice) <u>and</u> with his people. It is simply not possible to comfort anyone that you do not know and interact with in any way.

Speak tenderly (comfortably) to Jerusalem, and proclaim (cry) to her …

Hebrew Text: דַּבְּרוּ עַל־לֵב יְרוּשָׁלַם וְקִרְאוּ אֵלֶיהָ

Transliteration: Dabroo al-lev yerushalayim v'kiroo elay-hah

This double imperative to comfort is followed by two other commands, namely, to speak [דַּבְּרוּ; dabroo] and then to cry (or proclaim) [קִרְאוּ; kiroo]. Again, there has to be a relationship between the comforter and the comforted in order to fulfill this calling. In particular, if one is to speak, this can only take place where there is close proximity. You have to be with (or among) his people in order to speak to them. But how does anyone speak to the heart [עַל־לֵב; al-lev] of a city, even the city of Jerusalem? Can you use words? Does the heart of a city respond to words?

HEART TO HEART

It is interesting to note that the Hebrew phrase literally *"to the heart"* [עַל־לֵב; al-lev] is used several times in Scripture. In most cases, it is translated *"comfortably"* in the KJV. In the NIV, it is translated *"tenderly"*. A classic example is in Hosea.

Hosea 2:14 (KJV) *Therefore, behold; I will allure her, and bring her into the wilderness, and speak* **comfortably** *unto her.*

Hosea 2:14 (NIV) *Therefore I am now going to allure her; I will lead her into the desert and speak* **tenderly** *to her.*

In this verse, the literal meaning is *"and speak to her heart"* [עַל־לִבָּהּ וְדִבַּרְתִּי ; v'dibarti al-livaah]. There is a maternal gentleness about this phrase. You get the impression that there is an embrace between the Lord and his people.

The Empty Cup [1]

---

[1] This is a small version of the final piece of the Fountain of Tears created by Rick Wienecke.

The significant aspect of this verse in Hosea is that it is the Lord himself who is doing the comforting. I am also reminded of a later verse in Isaiah 40.

Isaiah 40:11 (NIV) *He tends his flock like a shepherd: He gathers the lambs in his arms and carries them close to his heart; he gently leads those that have young.*

Strictly speaking, the word *"heart"* is not mentioned in this verse. He is carrying the lambs close to his *"bosom"*. But the sense here is of a motherly embrace and in this embrace they are comforted.

The Good Shepherd [2]

I am reminded of the words of Jesus when he spoke to the heart of Jerusalem.

Matthew 23:37-39 (NIV) *O Jerusalem, Jerusalem, you who kill the prophets and stone those sent to you, how often I have longed to gather your children together, as a hen gathers her chicks under her wings, but you were not willing. Look, your house is left to you desolate. For I tell you, you will not see me again until you say, 'Blessed is he who comes in the name of the Lord'.*

---

[2] https://ambirkelo.wordpress.com/2013/05/28/being-sick-in-my-luxurious-little-world/

This is a very poignant passage. The maternal embrace was rejected by Jerusalem and this was to have inevitable consequences. The city and its Temple were to be destroyed following the Jewish-Roman wars in the first and second centuries. The people would be sent into exile but, even here, Jesus makes it perfectly clear that it is only *"until"*. In the far distant future, Jesus recognizes that a time will come when the city will welcome him with open arms.

As previously mentioned in this study, this maternal relationship between the Lord and his people is perhaps most beautifully expressed in Isaiah 49.

Isaiah 49:13-16 (NIV) *Shout for joy, O heavens; rejoice O earth; burst into song, O mountains! For the LORD comforts [נחם] his people and will have compassion [ירחם] on his afflicted ones. But Zion said, "The LORD has forsaken me, the Lord has forgotten me." "Can a mother forget the baby at her breast and have no compassion [ירחם] on the child she has borne? Though she may forget, I will not forget you! See, I have engraved you on the palms of my hands; your walls are ever before me."*

"My God, My God, Why Have You Forsaken Me?" [3]

[3] Sculpture by Rick Wienecke – Panel 4 at "The Fountain of Tears" – Photo by Vij Sodera

In the passage in Isaiah chapter 49, the three letters highlighted are the Hebrew root נָחַם (nacham) from which we get all the words associated with comfort (including those in Isaiah 40:1).[4] Some have suggested that there might even be a linguistic connection between נחם (nacham) and רחם (racham) which is often translated compassion (or tender mercy) and is, remarkably, the word used for the mother's womb.

In this passage, it is important to recognize that Zion (a.k.a. Jerusalem) initially finds it very difficult to accept that the Lord has comforted his people. They feel forsaken, forgotten and very discouraged. Nevertheless, in a later verse in the same chapter, the city is encouraged to look up.

Isaiah 49:18 (NIV) *Lift up your eyes and look around; all your sons gather and come to you.*

The return of the Jewish people to the land (and to Jerusalem in particular) is that which ultimately brings them comfort.[5] It has often been said that Jesus has no hands (or arms) but our hands (or arms). It is no surprise, therefore, that we read, in the same chapter, God's commission to the Gentiles to carry his people back to the land.

Isaiah 49:22-23 (NIV) *See, I will beckon to the Gentiles, I will lift up my banner to the peoples; they will bring your sons in their arms and carry your daughters on their shoulders. Kings will be your foster fathers, and their queens **your nursing mothers**.*

A nursing mother is literally holding the sons and daughters to their bosom which is close to their heart. Thus, in summary, it is only those who have that intimate relationship both with the Lord and with his people who will be able to comfort them. In particular, since it is the return of the Jewish people to the land (and to the city) that will ultimately bring comfort, there is an obvious obligation and urgency, on behalf of believers, to expedite this aliyah. Furthermore, speaking to the heart of Jerusalem is pre-requisite for any subsequent cry [קְראוּ; kiroo] to take place.

There are essentially three elements to this proclamation.

---

[4] נַחֲמוּ נַחֲמוּ עַמִּי יאמַר אֱלֹהֵיכֶם (Nachamoo, Nachamoo ami yomar elo-haychem)

[5] See also **Isaiah 66:13 (NIV)** As a mother comforts her child, so will I comfort you; and you will be comforted over Jerusalem.

1. That her hard service (warfare) has been completed (accomplished)

Hebrew Text: כִּי מָלְאָה צְבָאָהּ

Transliteration: Ki malaah tzev-a-ah

If there is to be real comfort for his people, then it is necessary for something to be at an end. The NIV calls it *"hard service"* The KJV calls it *"warfare".* What is more straightforward is the fact that the Hebrew verb *"to fill"* or *"to be full"* is based on the root מלא (malah) as in the above. It also has the meaning *"to fulfill"* or *"to be fulfilled".* In other words, something has to be fulfilled and this is rendered *"completed"* in the NIV and *"accomplished"* in the KJV. However, in my opinion, I believe that the word *"fulfilled"* is much more relevant taking into account other elements of the proclamation. But this suggestion does not answer the question as to what has been fulfilled.

The Hebrew word צְבָאָהּ (tzev-a-ah) ends with the letter hay [ה] which provides the feminine gender. It is feminine because the proclamation is given to the city of Jerusalem, and all cities, in the Hebrew language, are feminine. In other words, something related to Jerusalem is fulfilled, completed and/or accomplished.

It is interesting to note that the modern Hebrew word for *"army"* is צבא (tza-va). Thus, the simplest rendering of the phrase would be *"that her army has been completed",* although this, at first glance, does not make obvious sense. The three letter root (צבא) is used in several other verses in the Bible. In many of these instances, the word is translated *"host".*

For example, **2 Chronicles 18:18 (NIV)** *Hear the word of the LORD: I saw the LORD sitting on his throne with all the host of heaven standing on his right and on his left.*

"And all the host of heaven" is a translation of וְכָל-צְבָא הַשָּׁמַיִם (v'col tze-vah ha-shamayim). And in another place:

Psalm 24:10 (KJV) *The LORD of hosts, he is the King of glory.*

The Lord of Hosts is יְהוָה צְבָאוֹת (Adonai[6] Tze-vah-ot). In other words, he is the Lord of the heavenly armies. There are, however, other places in Scripture when the word צבא is translated *"war"* or *"warfare".*

---

[6] "Adonai" is used to avoid the vocalization of the Tetragrammaton [יְהוָה] which is the Name of God

For example, **1 Samuel 28:1 (KJV)** *And it came to pass in those days, that the Philistines gathered their armies* [lit. encampments] *together **for warfare** [לַצָּבָא; la-tzah-vah], to fight with Israel.*

and

Numbers 1:3 (KJV) *From twenty years old and upward, all that are able to go forth to **war** [צָבָא; tzah-vah] in Israel: thou and Aaron shall number them **by their armies** [לְצִבְאֹתָם; la-tziv-otam].*

Thus, the word has the meaning of warfare and of the armies preparing for war. So why does the NIV translate the word as *"hard service"*? It is worth noting that, very occasionally, the three letter root (צבא) is used for *"service"* particularly service within the Tabernacle.

For example: **Numbers 4:23 (KJV)** *From thirty years old and upward until fifty years old shalt thou number them; all that enter in to perform the **service** [צָבָא; tzah-vah], to do the work in the tabernacle of the congregation.*

Numbers 4:23 (NIV) *Count all the men from thirty to fifty years of age who come to serve in the work at the Tent of Meeting.*

The normal Hebrew word for *"service"* is עֲבֹדָה (ah-vod-ah) which most often means *"work"*. However, when the context of the verse is entering (or coming) into service then, invariably, the word צָבָא (tzah-vah) is used. In addition, there is a specified period of service implicit in the use of this word. With respect to the Tabernacle, the upper age limit was 50 years old.

In this regard, there is an obvious connection with the army which, in English idiom, is sometimes described as one of the *"services"*. Enlisting in the army is usually for a specified period. Furthermore, in the NIV translation, the word צבא (tzah-vah) is also used in the book of Job to indicate service – perhaps even hard service. Here are some examples:

Job 7:1 (NIV) *Does not man have **hard service** [צָבָא; tzah-vah] on earth? Are not his days like those of a hired man?*

The KJV, however, translates this somewhat differently.

Job 7:1 (KJV) *Is there not **an appointed time** [צָבָא; tzah-vah] to man upon earth? Are not his days also like the days of an hireling?*

Consistent with respect to service in the Tabernacle, the KJV translates צָבָא [tzah-vah] as a specified period – even an appointed time. We see this distinction in another verse in the book of Job.

Job 14:14 (NIV) *If a man dies, will he live again? All the days of **my hard service** [צְבָאִי; tze-vah-i] I will wait for my renewal to come.*

Again the KJV translates this passage as:

Job 14:14 (KJV) *If a man dies, shall he live again? All the days of **my appointed time** [צְבָאִי; tze-vah-i] will I wait, till my change come.*

It is not clear why the NIV wishes to use the words *"hard service"*. I would think that this should be indicated by the addition of the adjective "hard" which in Hebrew is קָשָׁה (kah-shah). An example of its use is:

Exodus 1:14 (NIV) *And they made their lives bitter with **hard bondage*** [עֲבֹדָה קָשָׁה; ah-vodah kah-shah; literally *"hard work"*].

It is interesting to note, however, that the Young's Literal Translation (YLT) of the two verses in Job shown above still translate the word צבא as *"warfare"*.

For example: **Job 14:14 (YLT**) *If a man dieth - doth he revive? All days of **my warfare** [צְבָאִי; tze-vah-i] I wait, till my change come.*

So, the other question for us now to consider is whether Jerusalem's warfare has actually been accomplished. This is problematic since the prophetic expectation is that there are several more battles involving Jerusalem still to come. For example, as we have mentioned in earlier chapters,

Zechariah 12:3 (NIV) *On that day, when all the nations of the earth are gathered against her, I will make Jerusalem an immovable rock for all the nations. All who try to move it will injure themselves.*

In other words, can we actually comfort God's people by suggesting that their warfare is fulfilled? Maybe we can. If, for example, the status of Jerusalem is now inviolate as Zechariah chapter 12 seems to suggest, then whatever happens in the immediate future will result in victory for the Israel Defence Forces (IDF) as her army is now complete!

Zechariah 12:5-6 (NIV) *Then the leaders of Judah will say in their hearts, 'The people of Jerusalem are strong, because the LORD Almighty is their God.' "On that day I will make the leaders of Judah like a firepot in a woodpile, like a flaming torch among sheaves. They will consume right and left all the surrounding peoples, **but Jerusalem will remain intact in her place**.*

As we will see, the violence of war as described, for example, in Isaiah 42:25 has accomplished everything that the Lord intended. Out of the ashes of the Holocaust, the nation of Israel has been re-established - and as Jesus said:

Luke 21:24 (NIV) *They will fall by the sword and will be taken as prisoners to all the nations. Jerusalem will be trampled on by the Gentiles **until the times of the Gentiles are fulfilled**.*

In the modern Hebrew New Testament, the phrase *"the times of the Gentiles are fulfilled"* is translated as **ימלאו עתות הגוים** [yi-mal-oo otot ha-goyim].[7]

If the times of the Gentiles are now actually fulfilled, Jerusalem's warfare (or even "hard" service) is actually accomplished. All that is left is but minor skirmish. Of course, we still have to experience the events of Zechariah 14.

Zechariah 14:2-4 (NIV) *I will gather all the nations to Jerusalem to fight against it; the city will be captured, the houses ransacked, and the women raped. Half of the city will go into exile, but the rest of the people will not be taken from the city. Then the LORD will go out and fight against those nations, as he fights in the day of battle.*

Paul describes this event as follows:

2 Thessalonians 1:7 (NIV) *This will happen when the Lord Jesus is revealed from heaven in blazing fire with his powerful angels.*

Jesus is **יְהוָה צְבָאוֹת**. He is the Lord of the heavenly armies. Their number is most certainly complete and all we await is the time for their revealing.

The psalmist also describes this event:

Psalm 21:8-9 (NIV) *Your hand will lay hold on all your enemies; your right hand will seize your foes. At the time of your appearing, you will make them like a fiery furnace. In his wrath, the LORD [יְהוָה] will swallow them up, and his fire will consume them.*

By the way, the LORD [יְהוָה] has two hands **and** two feet.

Zechariah 14:3-4 (NIV) *Then the LORD [יְהוָה] will go out and fight against those nations, as he fights in the day of battle. On that day **his feet** will stand on the Mount of Olives, east of Jerusalem, and the Mount of Olives will be split in two from east to west, forming a great valley, with half of the mountain moving north and half moving south.*

---

[7] Note the use of the root **מלא** [mala] to fulfil or be fulfilled

2. That her sin (iniquity) has been paid for (Is pardoned)

Hebrew Text: כִּי נִרְצָה עֲוֹנָה

Transliteration: Ki nir-tzah ah-vown-ah

The root of the specific verb is רצה which forms the basis of Modern Hebrew verb *"to want"*. However, the actual form of the verb in Isaiah 40:2 is nifal and is simple, passive, masculine and perfect. In other words, as far as biblical Hebrew is concerned, it is a completed action. The root is used to mean to be pleased with, be favorable to, or to accept favorably. Significantly, the actual form of the verb in Isaiah 40:2 is also used in the book of Leviticus.

Leviticus 1:4 (NIV) *He is to lay his hand on the head of the burnt offering, and **it will be accepted** [וְנִרְצָה; v'nir-tzah] on his behalf to make atonement for him.*

The addition of the letter vav (וֹ; and) in this particular verse has the effect of changing the tense of the verb to the future (i.e. it will be accepted). The Hebrew word ah-vown-ah [עֲוֹנָה] has a feminine ending and can mean her iniquity. It is used, as such, in several verses. An example is:

Numbers 5:31 (NIV) *The man shall be free from [his] iniquity [מֵעָוֹן; meh-ah-von], but the woman shall bear her iniquity [אֶת־עֲוֹנָה; et-ah-vown-ah].*

However, the word can be (and perhaps more appropriately) translated *"punishment."* An example is in Genesis:

Genesis 4:13 (NIV) *Cain said to the LORD, "My punishment [עֲוֹנִי; ah-vown-i] is more than I can bear.*

Another interesting (and perhaps very important) example is:

Leviticus 26:41 (KJV) *I also have walked contrary unto them, and have brought them into the land of their enemies; if then their uncircumcised hearts be humbled, **and they then accept of the punishment of their iniquity** [וְנָם אָז יִרְצוּ אֶת־עֲ; az yir-tzoo et-ah-vo-nahm].*

The seven English words *"they accept the punishment of their iniquity"* is the translation of the two or perhaps three Hebrew words [יִרְצוּ אֶת־עֲוֹנָם] which brings together the concept of acceptance (Hebrew root רצה) with punishment for iniquity.

It is worth noticing the result of **their** *"acceptance"* of punishment which is given to us in the following verse:

Leviticus 26:42 (KJV) *Then will I remember my covenant with Jacob, and also my covenant with Isaac, and also my covenant with Abraham will I remember; and I will remember the land.*

So how do we really translate כִּי נִרְצָה עֲוֹנָהּ?

In my opinion, it has to mean *"because her punishment is accepted"*. But exactly who is doing the accepting in Isaiah 40, verse 2? It has to be the Lord as the form of the verb [נִרְצָה; nir-tzah] is third person masculine singular. And, as such, it cannot be separated from the next phrase.

3. That [because] she has received [taken] from the Lord's hand double for all her sins.

This third proclamation can be divided into three parts.

3.1 That [because] she has received [taken] …

Hebrew Text: כִּי לָקְחָה

Transliteration: Ki lahk-chah …

This form of the verb [i.e. לָקְחָה; lahk-chah] in modern Hebrew simply means *"she took"* or possibly *"she has taken"*. It seems, at first glance, that it is appropriate to translate the Hebrew as *"she has received"* although, in my opinion, *"she has taken"* has a different emphasis.[8]

In this form (i.e. third person feminine – perfect, completed action), the word only appears in one other place in the Tanach. Interestingly, the Lord is also speaking to the city of Jerusalem.

Zephaniah 3:1-2 (NIV) *Woe to the city of oppressors, rebellious and defiled! She obeys no one, she accepts [לָקְחָה; lahk-chah] no correction. She does not trust in the LORD, she does not draw near to her God.*

Strictly speaking, this is a rather poor translation. All the verbs are perfect which implies completed action. Accordingly, the KJV translates verse 2 as follows:

---

[8] "To receive" is more passive than "to take". The emphasis implicit in the verb "to receive" is on the one who gives. On the other hand "to take" gives greater emphasis to the one who takes (accepts or receives). I will refer to this again when considering Isaiah 51:22.

Zephaniah 3:2 (KJV) *She obeyed not the voice; she received [לָקְחָה; lahk-chah] not correction; she trusted not in the LORD; she drew not near to her God.*

Young's Literal Translation (YLT) is as follows:

Zephaniah 3:2 (YLT) *She hath not hearkened to the voice, She hath not accepted [לָקְחָה; lahk-chah] instruction, In Jehovah she hath not trusted, unto her God she hath not drawn near.*

A little later in Zephaniah chapter 3, we read in **Zephaniah 3:7a (NIV)** *I said to the city, 'Surely you will fear me and accept correction!'*

The form of the verb *"accept"* which can also mean *"take"* is תִּקְחִי [tik-chi] which based on the same root לקח but is 2nd person feminine and imperfect. In other words, in this verse, we see that the Lord's desire is that the city of Jerusalem would accept (take or receive) instruction (discipline). If they were to do this, the following would result.

Zephaniah 3:7b (NIV) *Then her dwelling would not be cut off, nor all my punishments come upon her.*

In the Young's Literal Translation (YLT) this is:

Zephaniah 3:7b (YLT) *And her habitation is not cut off, all that I have appointed for her.*

However, there was a "but"; perhaps the saddest "but" in history.

Zephaniah 3:7c (NIV) *But they were still eager to act corruptly in all they did.*

I am reminded again of Jesus' words to the city of Jerusalem.

Matthew 23:37-38 (NIV) *O Jerusalem, Jerusalem, you who kill the prophets and stone those sent to you, how often I have longed to gather your children together, as a hen gathers her chicks under her wings, but you were not willing. Look, your house is left to you desolate.*

and

Luke 19:41-44 (NIV) *As he approached Jerusalem and saw the city, he wept over it and said, "If you, even you, had only known on this day what would bring you peace - but now it is hidden from your eyes. The days will come upon you when your enemies will build an embankment against you and encircle you and hem you in on every side. They will dash you to the ground, you and the children within your walls. They will not leave one stone on another, because you did not recognize the time of God's coming to you."*

The inevitable consequence of Jerusalem's lack of recognition of *"God's coming"* was that her dwelling [habitation or even land] would be cut off (Zephaniah 3:7). This is paralleled by Jesus' words *"your house is left to you desolate"* not leaving *"one stone on another"*.

Furthermore, many would lose their lives. As Jesus said:

Luke 21:20-24 (NIV) *When you see Jerusalem being surrounded by armies, you will know that its desolation is near. Then let those who are in Judea flee to the mountains, let those in the city get out, and let those in the country not enter the city* **for this is the time of punishment in fulfillment of all that has been written.** *How dreadful it will be in those days for pregnant women and nursing mothers! There will be great distress in the land and wrath against this people. They will fall by the sword and will be taken as prisoners to all the nations. Jerusalem will be trampled on by the Gentiles until the times of the Gentiles are fulfilled.*

Isn't it interesting (even ironic) that the only other passage (apart from the Gospels) that speaks of *"nursing mothers"* is Isaiah 49:23 which we have referred to previously?[9]

The Destruction of Jerusalem in 70 CE [10]

---

[9] **Isaiah 49:22-23 (NIV)** This is what the Sovereign LORD says: "See, I will beckon to the Gentiles, I will lift up my banner to the peoples; they will bring your sons in their arms and carry your daughters on their shoulders. Kings will be your foster fathers, and their queens your **nursing mothers.** They will bow down before you with their faces to the ground; they will lick the dust at your feet.
[10] The Destruction of the Temple in Jerusalem (1867) by Francesco Hayez, Galleria d'Arte Moderna, Venice

3.2 From the Lord's Hand …

Hebrew Text: מִיַּד יְהוָה

Transliteration: mi-yad Adonai …

The significance of the words *"from the Lord's hand"* [מִיַּד יְהוָה; mi-yad Adonai] cannot be overstated. At the very least, the Lord allowed the Holocaust but perhaps even this is lessening the impact of the actual words.

There are other significant verses in the Tanach that include the exact words *"from the Lord's hand"* [מִיַּד יְהוָה; mi-yad Adonai]. Perhaps the most poignant for our study is found in Isaiah chapter 51.

Isaiah 51:17-19 (NIV) *Awake, awake! Rise up, O Jerusalem, you who have drunk **from the hand of the LORD** [מִיַּד יְהוָה] the cup of his wrath, you who have drained to its dregs the goblet that makes men stagger. Of all the sons she bore, there was none to guide her; of all the sons she reared, there was none to take her by the hand. These double calamities have come upon you who can comfort you? - ruin and destruction, famine and sword - who can console you?*

Again, Jerusalem is being addressed by the Lord. The cup of his wrath (anger) has been taken by her and she has drunk it to the dregs. Double calamity has come to her and who is there to bring comfort by speaking to her heart? The problem with the NIV here is that an incredible truth is missed by poor translation.

The KJV translates verse 19 as:

Isaiah 51:19 (KJV) *These two things are come unto thee; who shall be sorry for thee? desolation, and destruction, and the famine, and the sword: **by whom shall I comfort thee?***

The words *"by whom shall I comfort thee"* in a translation of the Hebrew חֲמֵךְ מִי אֲנַ [mi a-na-cha-meh-cha]. Again the root is nacham [נחם]. The words literally mean *"who [perhaps with a question mark] - I will comfort you"* and this comes through, to a certain extent, in the Young's Literal Translation (YLT).

Isaiah 51:19 (YLT) *These two are meeting thee, who is moved for thee? Spoiling and destruction - famine and sword, who - I comfort thee?*

Ultimately it is the Lord who is going to comfort his people. A little later in Isaiah, we read these beautiful words:

Isaiah 52:9-10 (NIV) *Burst into songs of joy together, you ruins of Jerusalem, for the LORD has comforted* [נחם; nacham] *his people, he has redeemed Jerusalem. The LORD **will lay bare his holy arm** in the sight of all the nations, and all the ends of the earth will see the salvation of our God.*

Here again we see that the Lord has an arm - even a holy arm – which will be seen by all nations. This salvation has several meanings. It speaks of the Gospel going to the ends of the earth. It also speaks of all that the Lord is doing and will do for his own people in the days to come. And as we will see, he has taken back the cup of his wrath from the hands of his people. He will give it to others to drink.

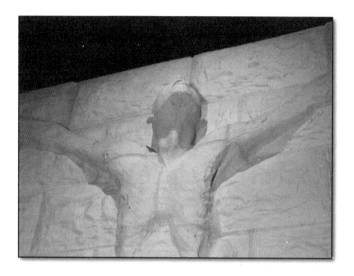

"The LORD Will Lay Bare His Holy Arm" [11]

Isaiah 51:22 (KJV) *Thus saith thy Lord the LORD, and thy God that pleadeth the cause of his people, Behold, I have taken out of thine hand the cup of trembling, even the dregs of the cup of my fury; **thou shalt no more drink it again.***

It is very important for us to recognize that the Hebrew word that is translated *"I have taken"* in the above verse is לָקַחְתִּי [la-kachti] which literally means *"I took"*. Please note that it does not mean *"I received"*. Thus the emphasis is on the Lord who **actively** takes the cup of his wrath from the hands of Jerusalem although they have drunk from it down to the dregs.

---

11 Sculpture by Rick Wienecke – Panel 4 at "The Fountain of Tears" – Photo by Vij Sodera

Gethsemane, the Cup of God's Wrath and the People of Israel

I have already written about the significance of the cup that Jesus is struggling with in the Garden of Gethsemane.

The Cup in the Hand of the Lord

Mark 14:35-36 (NIV) *"Abba, Father," he said, "everything is possible for you. Take this cup from me. Yet not what I will, but what you will."*

These words are incredibly profound. Did Jesus have a physical cup in his hand in the Garden of Gethsemane? Obviously not. Here perhaps more than anywhere else you see Jesus taking the place of his people. Even though it may be lost on us, the significance of the cup is not lost on Jesus. He is struggling with the cup of God's wrath which is now in his hands. **In other words, the cup is literally in the hand of the Lord.**

Isaiah 53:6 (KJV) *All we like sheep have gone astray; we have turned everyone to his own way; and the LORD hath laid on him the iniquity of us all.*

So the question before us is simply this: Did the people of Israel HAVE to drink from this cup? The fact is this: to reject this offer of forgiveness has had terrible consequences. All the people of Jerusalem cried out:

Matthew 27:25 (NIV) *"Let his blood be on us and on our children!"*

This is perhaps the most dreadful cry in history. What is effectively happening here is that the people are figuratively *"taking"* the cup of God's wrath from the hand of the Lord. And all that was left for the people of Jerusalem was for them to drink from this cup – even to the dregs. This has been their tragic experience over 2000 years. But the cup is now empty. The punishment is accepted. The cup is once again in the hand of the Lord and is being given to the nations to drink.

Isaiah 51:23 (KJV) *But I will put it [the cup] into the hand of them that afflict thee; which have said to thy soul, bow down, that we may go over: and thou hast laid thy body as the ground, and as the street, to them that went over.*

A Jewish Mass Grave [12]

I am reminded again of the words also to be found in the book of Isaiah.

Isaiah 42:23-25 (NIV) *Which of you will listen to this or pay close attention in time to come? Who handed Jacob over to become loot and Israel to the plunderers? Was it not the LORD, against whom we have sinned? For they would not follow his ways; they did not obey his law. So he poured out on them his burning anger, the violence of war. It enveloped them in flames, yet they did not understand; it consumed them,* **but they did not take it to heart [עַל־לֵב].**

By taking the cup from the hand of the Lord, the people of Israel have paid double for all their sins.

---

[12] A Jewish mass grave found near Zolochiv, West Ukraine (in Nazi occupied USSR). Photo was discovered by Soviets at former Gestapo headquarters in Zolochiv. Taken from: https://en.wikipedia.org/wiki/The_Holocaust

3.3 Double for all her sins

Hebrew Text: כִּפְלַיִם בְּכָל־חַטֹּאתֶיהָ

Transliteration: Cif-lie-im b'kol cha-tow-tay-yah

The Hebrew word used here for double is unusual and is כִּפְלַיִם (cif-lie-im). It is only used in one other place in Scripture in this actual form. It is on the lips of Zopher who, ironically, is one of Job's *"comforters"*. Interestingly, he is speaking of Job's guilt.

Job 11:5-6 (KJV) *But oh that God would speak, and open his lips against thee; and that he would shew thee the secrets of wisdom, that they are double [כִּפְלַיִם] to that which is! Know therefore that God exacteth of thee less than thine iniquity deserveth.*

These verses are translated in the NIV as follows:

Job 11:5-6 (NIV) *Oh, how I wish that God would speak, that he would open his lips against you and disclose to you the secrets of wisdom, for true wisdom has two sides [כִּפְלַיִם]. Know this: God has even forgotten some of your sin.*

This is an extremely obscure passage but there must be some connection with Isaiah 40:2 since the very same word [כִּפְלַיִם].is used in both passages and nowhere else.

Young's Literal translation (YLT) has this: **Job 11:6 (YLT)** *And declare to thee secrets of wisdom, for counsel hath **foldings** [כִּפְלַיִם]. And know thou that God forgetteth for thee, some of thine iniquity.*

It is interesting to note that the modern Hebrew verb *"to fold"* (or *"to tuck"*) is לְקַפֵּל [Le-ka-pel] which, linguistically, is virtually indistinguishable from the modern Hebrew verb *"to double"* לְכַפֵּל [Le-cha-fel].

Other modern Hebrew words based on the root כפל are: (i) the verb לכפול (to double, duplicate, repeat, multiply); and (ii) the noun כֶּפֶל (duplicate, multiplication).

It is also important to realize that the word כִּפְלַיִם (cif-lie-im) is in a dual form. In other words, there are two sides in this doubling. Furthermore, as recorded in Exodus, a specific curtain in the Tabernacle and the cloth of the breastplate are to be folded double.

Exodus 26:9 (NIV) *Join five of the curtains together into one set and the other six into another set. Fold the sixth curtain double [וְכָפַלְתָּ; v'cha-fal-tah] at the front of the tent.*

Exodus 28:16 (NIV) *It is to be square - a span long and a span wide - and folded double [כָּפוּל; kah-fool].*

The concept that God would exact double punishment for Israel's sin is certainly unpalatable to many theologians. For example, Meredith Kline, the late Professor of Old Testament at Westminster Theological Seminary in California has argued that the doubling that is implicit in the folds of the temple curtain and the priestly breastplate never speaks of **twice the quantity** of material.[13]

Accordingly, he suggests that a better interpretation of כִּפְלַיִם is the *"equivalent"* or even *"duplication"*. In other words, the punishment matches the sin. There are, however, other verses that might indicate that the Lord has given double punishment. For example:

Jeremiah 16:18 (NIV) *I will repay them **double** for their wickedness and their sin, because they have defiled my land with the lifeless forms of their vile images and have filled my inheritance with their detestable idols.*

The word rendered *"double"* here is the Hebrew מִשְׁנֶה (mish-neh). Professor Kline also addresses this word in his article.[13] However; he is rather selective in the study of this word because, even if it might occasionally be interpreted as *"equivalent"*, there are several instances where the word has to be interpreted as *"double"*. For example,

Exodus 16:5 (NIV) *On the sixth day they are to prepare what they bring in, and that is twice as much [מִשְׁנֶה; mish-neh] as they gather on other days.*

But in what way might the nation of Israel have received double for all her sins? I will give you some tentative suggestions. But let us, first of all, return to the verse in Isaiah chapter 51 which we have already considered.

---

[13] Meredith G. Kline (1989) *Double Trouble* Journal of the Evangelical Theological Society 32:171-9.

Isaiah 51:19 (YLT) *These two are meeting thee, who is moved for thee? Spoiling and destruction - famine and sword, who - I comfort thee?*

Isaiah 51:19 (NIV) *These double calamities have come upon you, who can comfort you? Ruin and destruction, famine and sword. Who can console you?*

Isaiah 51:19 (KJV) *These two things are come unto thee; who shall be sorry for thee? Desolation and destruction, and the famine and the sword: by whom shall I comfort thee?*

From this verse, we can see that drinking from the cup of God's wrath (Isaiah 51:17) is expressed in two ways. The NIV translates this as *"double calamities"*. There seems little justification for this as the Hebrew word translated as *"double"* is not, for example, כִּפְלַיִם [cif-lie-im], as in Isaiah 40:2, but שְׁתַּיִם [shti-im] which simply means *"two"*.[14]

The interesting thing, however, about the numbering in this verse is the fact that four things are listed, not two. These are:

1. Desolation (Ruin or Spoiling)
2. Destruction
3. Famine
4. Sword

How are we to explain this anomaly? Actually it is not that difficult as there are clearly two categories of affliction.

The first category involved the **fabric** of the city. The desolation of Jerusalem took place when the Temple was destroyed in 70 CE.[15] The destruction of Jerusalem took place at the end of the final Jewish-Roman war in 135 CE.

The second category involved the **people** of the city. The famine of Jerusalem began with the Roman siege which began in February 70 CE. Josephus writes about this period.

---

[14] It is interesting to note, however that both Hebrew words, namely כִּפְלַיִם [cif-lie-im] and שְׁתַּיִם [shti-im] are in a dual form. Anything effectively doubled such as legs; hands; eyes; ears etc. are all expressed in Hebrew in a dual form.
[15] **Matthew 23:38 (NIV)** Look, your house is left to you desolate.

Throughout the city people were dying of hunger in large numbers, and enduring unspeakable sufferings. In every house the merest hint of food sparked violence, and close relatives fell to blows, snatching from one another the pitiful supports of life. No respect was paid even to the dying; the ruffians [anti-Roman zealots] searched them, in case they were concealing food somewhere in their clothes, or just pretending to be near death. Gaping with hunger, like mad dogs, lawless gangs went staggering and reeling through the streets, battering upon the doors like drunkards, and so bewildered that they broke into the same house two or three times in an hour. Need drove the starving to gnaw at anything. Refuse which even animals would reject was collected and turned into food. In the end they were eating belts and shoes, and the leather stripped off their shields. Tufts of withered grass were devoured, and sold in little bundles for four drachmas.[16]

After the city walls were breached, the people were put to the sword. Josephus writes that 1,100,000 Jewish people perished at the hands of the Romans at that time.[17] Milman has also written about this period:

The slaughter within was even more dreadful than the spectacle from without. Men and women, old and young, insurgents and priests, those who fought and those who entreated mercy, were hewn down in indiscriminate carnage. The number of the slain exceeded that of the slayers. The legionaries had to clamber over heaps of dead to carry on the work of extermination. [18]

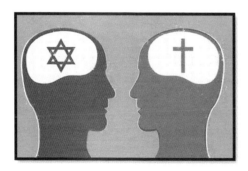

---

[16] http://www.rjgeib.com/thoughts/desolation/josephus.html
[17] http://en.wikipedia.org/wiki/Siege_of_Jerusalem_(70)
[18] Milman HH The History of the Jews, book 16

Thus, the two categories of affliction each have a dual aspect or even two sides. Here are some other suggestions as to why the Jewish people may have received double for all their sins.

1. The dreadful cry made by Jerusalem resulted in their taking and drinking the cup of God's wrath but they also passed it on to their children.
2. There have been two exiles. The first was to Babylon which is the immediate historical context of the passage in Isaiah chapter 40. The second and much greater exile followed the Jewish-Roman wars in the first and second centuries CE.
3. This second exile began and ended in Holocaust. It is sobering to note that, on two occasions, 1.1 million people have been slaughtered in one place. The first was in Jerusalem in 70 CE, the second was in Auschwitz.
4. Throughout the last two millennia, it is possible that two-thirds of the people have perished in accordance with the verse in Zechariah 13.

Zechariah 13:8 (NIV*) In the whole land," declares the LORD, "two-thirds will be struck down and perish; yet one-third will be left in it.*

In other words, double the number of those that survived - actually perished.

An Alternative Interpretation

The word כִּפְלַיִם [cif-lie-im] and the concept of folding double have encouraged another writer to suggest a rather different interpretation of *"double for all her sins".*

> *A person in Isaiah's time would declare bankruptcy by making visible their "certificate of debt "at the gate of the city for all to see. Also the elders sat at the gate to transact such business. Someone would see the "certificate of debt" and agree to pay the person's debt. The elders would receive the amount owed, fold the "certificate of debt" and nail it to the announcement board at the gate. When the bankrupt person returned and saw the paper folded and nailed to the board, they knew their debt was cancelled. Someone had paid it in full. The word DOUBLE is the word for FOLD (the same word in Exodus 26:9 when reference is made to the double or fold in the curtain in the Tabernacle). In our Isaiah passage, the word fold refers to the certificate of debt which was folded and a nail driven through it to signify it was paid in full.*[19]

---

[19] http://www.representationalresearch.com/the-double-isaiah-401-2/

This is an interesting interpretation. However, I have yet to discover any historic or archeologic evidence in support of this. I shall continue to search. This concept, however, may have been in the mind of Paul:

Colossians 2:13-14 (NIV) *When you were dead in your sins and in the uncircumcision of your sinful nature, God made you alive with Christ. He forgave us all our sins, having canceled the written code, with its regulations, that was against us and that stood opposed to us; he took it away, nailing it to the cross.*

The NASV translates these verses as follows:

Colossians 2:13-14 (NASV) *When you were dead in your transgressions and the uncircumcision of your flesh, He made you alive together with Him, having forgiven us all our transgressions, having canceled out **the certificate of debt** consisting of decrees against us, which was hostile to us; and He has taken it out of the way, having nailed it to the cross.*

The word *"certificate of debt"* is the Greek word χειρόγραφον [cheirographon] and literally means *"handwriting"*. The word does not appear anywhere else in Scripture including the Septuagint, the Greek translation of the Hebrew Scriptures.

The word, however, is found in other ancient Greek manuscripts as a legal term. It was used of a document, presented in a courtroom that listed evidence of a person's guilt.[19] This website continues:

In ancient times the accuser would present the cheirographon from the middle of the courtroom, called [τοῦ μέσου] tou mesou, "the middle" the exact same term Paul uses [in Colossians 2:14] when he says the cheirographon is taken "out of the way" [tou mesou]... The cheirographon lists the dates, the times, the locations, the testimony of witnesses, and all the other details of law-breaking. The information on this written document is not based on hearsay or unfounded suspicions. It is recognized by the Court as a legal and legitimate document. The Adversary holds in his hands the indisputable proof of guilt, along with the penalties that the Court prescribes for such crimes, and he presents the cheirographon to the Judge.

---

[19] See for example http://church-of-yehovah.org/nailedtotree.html

Conclusion

We have carefully considered all the elements of Isaiah chapter 40 verses 1 and 2. Accordingly, I think my translation of this passage would be as follows:

Isaiah 40:1-2 (GB) *"Comfort, comfort my people" says your God. "Speak [tenderly] to the heart of Jerusalem and cry out to her that her appointed time [of warfare] is [now] fulfilled; that her punishment has been accepted favorably [by God]; because she took from the Lord's hand double for all her sins.*

Having said that, I believe the passage is written fairly enigmatically, like so much in Scripture. No doubt it has many layers of meaning. The words are both tender and loving, days of hard service have been completed, and we await the fulfillment of this promise which is also recorded in the book of Isaiah.

Isaiah 61:7 (NIV) *Instead of their shame my people will receive a double [מִשְׁנֶה; mish-neh] portion and instead of disgrace they will rejoice in their inheritance; and so they will inherit a double [מִשְׁנֶה; mish-neh] portion in their land, and everlasting joy will be theirs.*

If there has been double punishment, then there will also be double blessing. This is justice as God sees it. And if there has been double punishment, all the more reason that the Lord would now say:

נַחֲמוּ נַחֲמוּ עַמִּי יֹאמַר אֱלֹהֵיכֶם

Nachamoo, Nachamoo ami yomar elo-haychem

Comfort, comfort my people, says your God.

APPENDIX

Other Resources Available

This DVD is in three parts:

1. The Commentary of the Fountain of Tears which is shown in Arad.

2. Rick's Testimony about how he came to Israel and discovered his gift of Sculpture.

3. Details of the Fountain in Birkenau

Available via the website: www.castingseeds.com

This booklet is a study guide to be used in association with DVD shown above.

The booklet is intended for small groups. Each section of the DVD is watched leading to discussion and prayer.

Available via the website: www.castingseeds.com

Rick Wienecke

"Seeds in the Wind" is Rick's autobiography. It tells of his journey to the Land of Israel as a young man searching for God. This search came to an end when he gave his life to Jesus. The book tells of his life on the kibbutz when he found his gift of sculpture. He gives a detailed account of the way God directed his steps that would lead to the creation of the Fountain of Tears in Arad and then Birkenau.

Available via the website:
www.castingseeds.com

This DVD is in two parts:

1. In *"Suddenly"* Rick describes many of the momentous events in that ultimately brought him to create the Fountain of Tears.

2. In the second part of the DVD, Rick takes us on a guided tour of the Fountain.

Available via the website:
www.castingseeds.com

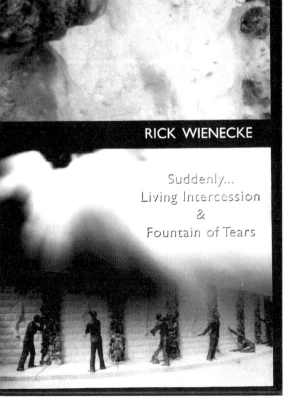

RICK WIENECKE

Suddenly...
Living Intercession
&
Fountain of Tears

Is it Safe?

An Issue that Divides the Evangelical World

Geoff Barnard

In this detailed Bible study, the author argues that the *"time of Jacob's Trouble"* was fulfilled in the Shoah during World War 2 and out of the ashes, Israel has been re-gathered never to be uprooted again (Amos 9:15). Israel is now the only safe place for Jewish people and it behoves the Christian community to help the Jewish people return to the Land with every resource at their disposal.

Available from the author:

Email : gjrb2@aol.com

As the title suggests, this book is a very detailed exposition of the teaching that Jesus gave to his disciples on the Mount of Olives. The author presents a view that is intermediate between the various schools of eschatological interpretation. He is convinced that many of the words spoken to Israel have already been fulfilled. However, it is vital that the Christian world is prepared for the days that lie ahead.

Available from the author:

Email : gjrb2@aol.com

When will These Things be?

An In-Depth Study of the Olivet Discourse

Geoff Barnard